Agile Contracts

Praise for *Agile Contracts*

"Agile development is starting to become popular in Japan, though Japanese companies have used 'all in one contracts' for the last three decades. In this movement, the new type of contract is a critical issue in achieving success in agile development. The concept and solution in this book is a step in the right direction. It will help Japanese companies and vendors transform development. The management change described in this book and in general in IT projects needs to advance toward the unique market in Japan."

—Naoyuki Miyahara, IT Manager, ABeam Consulting Ltd.

"It is a challenge to fully establish the positive aspects of the agile software development project within customer–supplier relationships. This applies especially to highly structured business organizations. . . . This book closes all the remaining gaps and presents a methodologically sophisticated and comprehensive approach, as well as valuable practical experience and templates. At the same time it is technically sound and pleasant to read. All readers will benefit from the described methodology, especially the suppliers and the clients of such projects. A higher success rate of projects, partnerships, and sustainable ways of working are ultimately a benefit to all concerned."

—Steffen Kießling, Manager, Product Lifecycle Management, Bearing Point

"Agile software development methods have become the de facto standard in recent years. . . . This book should be required reading, primarily for buyers and sellers of software projects, in order to truly handle continuous 'end to end' projects for agile. This book describes the appropriate interfaces and templates for the contract work, based on a cooperation model. The application of these approaches provides both parties with a decisive competitive edge over the (still) de facto standard form of contract."

—Dr. Stefan Klein, Head of Development, Infonova

WILEY SERIES IN SYSTEMS ENGINEERING AND MANAGEMENT

Andrew P. Sage, Editor

A complete list of the titles in this series appears at the end of this volume.

AGILE CONTRACTS

Creating and Managing Successful Projects with Scrum

Andreas Opelt
Boris Gloger
Wolfgang Pfarl
Ralf Mittermayr

WILEY

Published by John Wiley & Sons, Inc., Hoboken, New Jersey
Published simultaneously in Canada

For general information on our other products and services or for technical support, please contact our Customer Care Department within the United States at (800) 762-2974, outside the United States at (317) 572-3993 or fax (317) 572-4002.

Wiley also publishes its books in a variety of electronic formats. Some content that appears in print may not be available in electronic formats. For more information about Wiley products, visit our web site at www.wiley.com.

Library of Congress Cataloging-in-Publication Data:

Opelt, Andreas, 1978–
   Agile contracts: creating and managing successful projects with Scrum / Andreas Opelt, Boris Gloger, Wolfgang Pfarl, Ralf Mittermayr.
      pages cm
   Includes bibliographical references.
   ISBN 978-1-118-63094-5 (cloth)
   1. Agile software development. 2. Scrum (Computer software development)
3. Computer contracts. I. Gloger, Boris, 1968– II. Pfarl, Wolfgang, 1979–
III. Mittermayr, Ralf. IV. Title.
   QA76.76.D47O64 2013
   005.1–dc23
                                 2012050396

10 9 8 7 6 5 4 3 2 1

Contents

Preface

How can you create a contractual framework for agile projects that provides the necessary security for buyers, sellers, and project managers?

Agile methods for software development—in particular Scrum—are already in place. However, for both suppliers and buyers of information technology (IT) projects, one issue arises repeatedly: how to get out of the trap of fixed pricing without the disadvantages of time and materials contracts. How can you buy or sell agile software development? The answer is provided in this book: **The agile fixed price explains the contractual relationships between clients and suppliers for agile-delivered IT projects.**

We bring to this work several years of experience in IT projects, working with teams and designing contracts, and have experienced the challenges of our customers from different perspectives. We have discussed, frequently and intensively, the approach to preparing the specifications, the contractual framework as such, and the invitation to tender. These discussions were based on the perspective of the project manager, key account manager, negotiator, and top management of the contractor, as well as on the perspective of the client's procurement and top management, or from the perspective of a coach for the project implementation. We know most of the pitfalls of traditional IT projects delivered according to the waterfall method, and we know how agile management frameworks reveal these pitfalls while simultaneously demonstrating new and successful approaches.

Being able to define the scope or subject matter of a contract in detail, especially at the start of a project, is one of the biggest challenges for conventional fixed-price contracts. Alternatively, many people use time and materials contracts to maximize the benefits of Scrum for project implementation, which is quite suitable from a development perspective. In IT projects, it is unfortunately not just about a development department feeling comfortable with the way work is done; there are other requirements to consider. Thus, to get an internal go-ahead, it is usually necessary for the client to fix the costs during the business case analysis. If an IT project were ordered based on time and materials, a firm would need to assume a lot of the project's risk.

Jochen Rosen, IT director of A1 Telekom Austria AG, highlighted another aspect in an interview with us in April 2012 on the topic of conventional contract types in projects delivered with agile methodology:

> Companies have learned in recent years the value of the positive aspects of the agile development and project approach, and they are actively using the implicit benefits for end users, departmental organizations, and the IT organization. Traditional implementations using Scrum are mostly based on time and materials–related contracts. The IT procurement, accounting, and IT organization were thus often facing the challenge to present the iterative procedure and the stepwise enhancements that were achieved, in a form to fulfill capital expenditure criteria. The agile fixed price, which sets a fixed price for a large project while not yet even describing the exact amount of detailed scope, can be the solution here, so that Scrum can also play its part in large IT projects!

With the agile fixed price, we are introducing a new concept in the world of IT contracts. The agile fixed price solves the alleged contradiction between fixed-price and agile development on the basis of a suitable commercial and legal framework. The evolution of traditional fixed-price contracts is discussed in detail in the following chapters and explained by means of practical examples.

We wish to move a step beyond what has occurred previously in the literature related to the preparation of contracts for Scrum or fixed-price contracts: for example, using function points. In this book we describe the entire framework and most of the problems—it would be presumptuous to say "all"—that exist in large IT projects. Different groups of readers will bring their own focus. IT procurement representatives will realize in the course of the book what role they play in the success of an IT project. We also show top management why the price of an agile project can be fixed while the scope of the project is not out of control. Since all IT projects are different, and IT project managers want to get practical hints, we present some brief examples as well as two very large sample project descriptions in the final chapters, to demonstrate the use in practice of this new type of contract.

We wrote this book because we want to make the work of software development teams, buyers, and suppliers easier, so that IT projects can reach their full potential for success in the future. With agile fixed-price concepts, we offer

offer a tool that allows you to create the conditions necessary for success in your organization.

ANDREAS OPELT
BORIS GLOGER
WOLFGANG PFARL
RALF MITTERMAYR

Vienna and Graz
March 2013

Acknowledgments

To write a book in such a short time, in addition to busy workdays, house construction, children, partners, business trips, and presentations, is quite a challenge. The fact that we still managed to finish on time is due to the support of many people who could not take over all the work but did greatly facilitate reducing the workload.

We would like especially to thank the following colleagues, clients, managers, and experts: Dr. Walter J. Jaburek, DI Jochen Rosen, Mag. Birgit Gruber, Dr. Stefan Klein, Stefan Friedl, Steffen Kiesling, and Alexander Krzepinski, who through their reviews of the original manuscript, critically questioned and thus sharpened our consideration of individual points. Their comments and suggestions have increased the quality of the book. In addition, they convinced us, each time in new ways, that a book on this subject was urgently needed. Their encouragement and positive words have helped us through all the stages, when sometimes it was not always easy to stay motivated.

The graphics were created with the usual efficiency of our favorite graphic artist, Max Lacher. Thank you!

Dolores Omann supported us in structuring and formulating the German blueprint of this book, and Carolyn Bompard displayed her good soul in spending a summer inside doing translation work instead of enjoying the nice Austrian summer! Thanks!

Kari Capone displayed a lot of patience and creativity in unraveling our "fascinating" sentence structure and formulating it clearly. Without this help, the book would not have been so concise.

We would also like to thank Horst Mooshandl, Elmar Grasser, Gerald Haidl, Matthias Schranner, and Markus Hajszan-Meister for valuable discussions on agile software development and agile fixed-price contracts. They have been working on this subject for years in different areas, and with their opinions and statements they have provided us with valuable input.

A big thank you, of course, goes to John Wiley & Sons. You have enabled us to pursue creation of this book.

The principle of agile teamwork is: One head alone cannot work out solutions as well as a team (trust us: never)! In this sense, we want to thank the team of Infonova and Boris Gloger, who have conveyed, and participated in, the subject of Scrum and agile for years. The success of their work is one of the reasons why a book on agile fixed-price contracts has become necessary.

Without the support and patience of our partners, families, and friends we would never have found the strength and time to sit still numerous weekends and nights preparing this book. Thank you!

A.O.
B.G.
W.P.
R.M.

1

Agility: What Is That?

Ideas that began to form a decade ago among a handful of enthusiasts are today fundamental, one of them being agile product development using Scrum. Companies such as Immobilienscout24.de at least doubled their productivity due to the introduction of Scrum (Zeitler, 2011). These impressive results led large automobile and telecommunication enterprises to adopt the same product development method. Despite the success of the agile approach, there is one drawback: the realization that company processes that may have seemed to have in fact nothing to do with a project will now also need to undergo change. This may include strategic purchasing, key account management, demand management, and development departments. These processes need to be adapted to form a framework that will benefit significantly from the agile development process. Only when this is achieved can enterprises recognize the full extent of the enormous potential which results from their information technology (IT) teams adopting the agile approach.

Commercial-legal agreements with suppliers and partners are a substantial part of these basic conditions. They set the requirements that drive service providers to produce products faster and more effectively.

Agile Contracts: Creating and Managing Successful Projects with Scrum, First Edition.
Andreas Opelt, Boris Gloger, Wolfgang Pfarl, and Ralf Mittermayr.
© 2013 John Wiley & Sons, Inc. Published 2013 by John Wiley & Sons, Inc.

Cannot Be Stopped

The U.S. software vendor VersionOne conducted a survey on the extent of agile method implementations over the past six years. Participants from the worldwide software development industry took part between July and November 2011 (VersionOne, 2011). Of the 6042 responses, the following can be concluded:

1. More than half of the participants questioned have already worked with agile methods for over two years.
2. Approximately one in five of those surveyed (17%) expressed the fact that they were aware that their company was planning a shift toward agile in the near future.
3. Almost two-thirds of those interviewed indicated that their companies complete almost half of all projects by using agile methods, and that three or more teams already work in this way.
4. For almost one-fourth of the participants (22%), time to market is the main motivation for applying agile methodology.
5. Those questioned rate higher productivity as one of the most significant advantages (75%). An even greater advantage is the ability to handle changing customer requirements (84%). Project progress also becomes more visible (77%).

It is not only the teams' employees who are losing their apprehension of agility. Management—despite a certain fear of scaling, legal regulations, and a lack of documentation—is more open to the agile approach. In two-thirds of the cases (64%), the initiative came from management. Interesting to note is that despite rising support by management, the largest hurdle in the conversion to agile methods is not knowledge of the methodology but of the internal organizational culture.

Let's us emphasize this again: **An understanding of the methodology is not the largest hurdle in a conversion to the agile model. Rather, the challenge is the internal organizational culture and the potential changes to the internal processes.**

Clearly, the organizational structure will not change from one day to the next. The following situation is characteristic: In one of our projects, the top management of a worldwide company decided to implement agile methodologies. So far, so good. Often enough it is management that is toughest to convince that the majority of self-organized and responsible work functions that have their own clear goals experience enormous leaps in productivity. However, the employees, who should fulfill the order of priority set by top management, were forced to infringe on the rules given by the purchase department. By no means did the purchase department want to permit contracts with providers to be closed according to an agile model. Such a reaction immediately poses a question among employees as to whether an agile approach toward tenders has a future in the company and whether it can be sustained. How successfully the agile model is received by a supplier does not depend only on the supplier but also on necessary changes within your own company. Meanwhile, the company has found a new way of aligning successfully the set up and handling of agile projects together with procurement.

Traditional processes block the way for new requirements. Currently, most purchasing and sales processes are based on the traditional *waterfall* methodology (synonymous with predictive processes) for project management and product development. However, the waterfall process model has plenty of shortcomings, and IT services often attempt to exploit these in their business models. It is only natural that the purchasing departments of large organizations are against new processes, as such processes create defensive strategies and demand tougher contracts. Nevertheless, a project may fail to succeed.

A number of disadvantageous facts have been known for decades:

1. New products are not developed using the waterfall method, and effective projects are not organized based on that method. This was shown by Nonaka and Takeuchi (1986).
2. Even Winston Royce, creator of the waterfall model, said that this process does not work entirely and that it has to be carried out at least twice (Royce, 1970).
3. Studies carried out by the National Aeronautics and Space Administration in 1996 confirm the testimony of Barry Boehm, a software engineer from the 1980s, who calculated that estimates given at the beginning of a project life cycle (before the requirements phase) carry on average an uncertainty factor of 4 (Boehm, 1981). Thus, the actual time needed for a project could be either four times as long or only a fourth of what had originally been predicted, which seems very close to being unpredictable.

Especially in large organizations, we can find yet another prerequisite for setting up contracts with IT service providers that would have a negative effect on the productivity of software development projects: Every project has a budget. As a rule, these budgets have to be allocated very early—often even a year before the project is scheduled to begin. This means that departments define how much money should be spent before knowing the actual project goals of the company. Since no one knows exactly what the requirements will look like in 12 months, they are broadly defined. These requirements are requested from the service providers and judged as well as priced by the service providers.

Buyers, sellers, departments—all of them are doing their best to ensure that project costs do not get out of control and that schedules are met. Despite this, more than 60% of all IT projects fail. Many large IT projects extend their budgets by up to 400% and deliver only 25% of the desired functionality. Such "black swans" can destroy entire companies, as Bent Flyvbjerg and Alexander Budzier wrote in the *Harvard Business Review* of September 2011 (Flyvbjerg and Budzier, 2011). This also results in a tremendous loss for the economy.

[***Note:*** *The term* black swan *was coined by the financial mathematician Nassim Nicholas Taleb. He describes those events (both positive and negative) that are not only rare and unpredictable but also have major consequences that in retrospect were not actually so unlikely. Flyvbjerg and Budzier use the term only in its negative form.*]

There is as much discussion about the details of the analysis and facts of IT projects as about the actual success of IT projects themselves. And rightly so, because if we study the details of statistics or the background of an analysis, we will find a wealth of information that may shed a different light on various numbers. The bottom line, however, is that all studies agree.

Let's take a little tour d'horizon of some of the unpleasant facts:

- The *Standish Group* collects information on IT projects and their associated problems, and regularly publishes the Chaos Report. A project is defined as successful if time and budget constraints are met and if it complies with the required features and functions. However, some critical parameters are missing in this analysis, such as quality, risk and customer satisfaction. More important, and without focusing on the background details of the statistics as such, is how the measured success of projects has developed in recent years.

Findings of the Chaos Reports, 1994–2009

	2009	2006	2004	2002	2000	1998	1996	1994
Success	32%	35%	29%	34%	28%	26%	27%	16%
Partial success	44%	19%	53%	15%	23%	28%	40%	31%
Failure	24%	46%	18%	51%	49%	46%	33%	53%

Although the situation has improved significantly over the last 17 years, the percentage of successful projects is still well below 50%. According to the study, let's have a look at the most common causes for the failure of IT projects (Standish Group, 2009):

1. A lack of reliable input from users (2009: 12.8%)
2. Incomplete requirements and specifications (2009: 12.3%)
3. Changes in the requirements and specifications (2009: 11.8%)

To phrase it differently: The hit list for these stumbling blocks would be as follows:

1. Lack of cooperation
2. Missing knowledge of the requirements (the customer does not know what he or she really wants)
3. The fact that what is partially unknown is usually also described incorrectly or incompletely

- Unpleasant findings on the project's success can also be found in a study by the *Technical University of Munich* (Wildemann, 2006): Only about half of all IT projects of the period examined were successful. Either the projects took longer than planned, cost more than expected, or emerged with different results. Other projects actually had to be canceled and the costs had to be written off. The renowned Viennese IT expert Walter Jaburek (a court-certified expert on information technology and telecommunications) said in an interview that we conducted with him:

  Here is my experience congruent with the study by the Standish Group: Most projects take three times as long as planned, thereby costing approximately 2.8 times more and bringing 70 to 80% of the planned functionality. The contract and the negotiating skills decide who carries the additional 180% of the costs.

- In 2007 *Assure Consulting* reported that most IT projects fail due to unclear goals, unrealistic time constraints, and lack of coordination of the project participants (Assure Consulting, 2007).
- The consultants at *Roland Berger* reported that 20% of all IT projects are canceled. Every second project exceeds the agreed-upon time frame or is more expensive than planned. Vital is the indication that the probability of failure increases with the duration and complexity of projects (Roland Berger Strategy Consultants, 2008).
- A fall 2004 Forrester survey indicated that nearly one-third of customers are dissatisfied with the time it takes to deliver the custom applications requested (Forrester, 2005).
- Various studies and the experience of experts give reason to believe that requirements of IT projects change by up to 3% per month. As is referenced in the literature over and over again: The requirements for a software solution cannot be described deterministically. This can be summarized with the observation that, typically, 35% of all requirements change during a software project (Schwaber and Sutherland, 2012).

In your own daily practice you may also experience the fact that IT projects often take one step forward and two steps back. This could be for one or more of the following reasons:

- There is not enough user input.
- There is no simple, clear vision that describes a project's purpose.
- There is very little teamwork.
- Projects are becoming increasingly complex.
- The technologies used in projects have become more versatile.
- Systems have increasingly become more widely distributed.
- Functional and transparent monitoring of progress is often not possible.
- Experts on all sides (supplier, consultants, and customers) find it increasingly difficult to predict potential problems.
- The planning of projects is often very complex, sometimes almost impossible.
- Knowledge is poorly distributed.

We need to put a stop to this immense waste of resources, time, money, and creativity. This was first noted by some software developers in the 1990s—without trials or lengthy discussions. It was simply due to their own suffering that they discussed ideas for new project management and the development of new methods to allow teams, together with their project managers, to deliver continuously.

1.1 THE AGILE MANIFESTO OF 2001

To indicate at what points there is a rethinking of the purchase and sales processes and how this affects the setup of a contract, we follow the popular agile management framework: Scrum (in the State of Agile Survey by VersionOne (2011), Scrum was named as the method of use by 52% of respondents). Scrum is a perfect example of agility as we understand it. It is not merely just a method. It is based on very specific values and principles of cooperation that are aimed primarily at self-understanding of development teams. Of course, due to its strengths, it also affects the relationship between customers and service providers. Let's start our journey through the agile methodology at the origin, the *agile manifesto*. In the winter of 2001, a few representatives of the agile movement got together to discuss how they should promote the emerging trend in software development to reach as many people as possible. They also wanted to clarify what agile software development methods could actually achieve. It turned out that there are deep beliefs or even values that define agile's capabilities.

Agile Manifesto

We are uncovering better ways of developing software by doing it and helping others to do it.
Through this work we have come to value:

- *Individuals and interactions* over processes and tools
- *Working software* over comprehensive documentation
- *Customer collaboration* over contract negotiation
- *Responding to change* over following a plan

That is, although there is value in the items on the right, we value the items on the left more (http://www.agilemanifesto.org).

What do these values mean in more detail?

Individuals and interactions over processes and tools

Once again, look at your own project practice: How often do you realize that just talking to others can create shortcuts and solve a problem? That working together more effectively helps reach goals in a shorter time? How often do you experience that the available rigid processes are actually more of a hindrance than a help?

All agile development processes assume that to deliver a product it is essential that the team members and all other stakeholders talk to each other and exchange ideas constantly. For self-organization, it is essential to respect and recognize that individuals differ from each other. Obviously, teams with clearly defined processes and good development tools are productive. However, processes and tools are by no means more important than the individuals and their interactions.

This statement is often misunderstood and is interpreted as if team members are suddenly allowed to do everything. It is understood, mistakenly, as if all the walls are broken and, for example, no external influence or requirements should be provided to Scrum teams. Management feels especially strongly about hierarchical organizational cultures and is threatened by this aspect of the agile manifesto. But this is obviously not the case. Many developers have this attitude when they first come into contact with Scrum, but Scrum does not tell them how they should work. In Scrum, it is assumed that developers use their common sense and do everything necessary professionally to deliver the product. The principle of this thought is the essence of self-organization. **The nature of self-organization is that within a clearly defined framework,**

creative freedom is allowed and that this is actually the only way in which creative freedom can happen.

There are, of course, requirements and guidelines that must be followed. You can certainly not build a car and say: "Let the team get on with it and we'll see what comes out at the end." In the present day, no one would do that. Of course, cars must be built in a way that takes all legal guidelines and physical circumstances into account.

The next misconception: The customer is no longer able to define what he wants in a Scrum project. This, too, is nonsense. All of these misinterpretations have, contributed to the history of Scrum failures, as people who wanted to use Scrum were faced with these misinterpretations. Tragically, for this reason, Scrum projects often did not show the success that was possible. Rather than looking closer, the simple conclusion often was that the method was bad.

Tip: Accept the statement of the manifesto as it stands. It states the belief that people are successful only if they communicate with one another, and that this is especially effective when using tools that allow them to achieve their results faster.

Working software over comprehensive documentation

No statement from the agile world has been and will probably continue to be misunderstood more frequently than the one regarding the value of software. That it is gladly and consciously depicted incorrectly makes development teams open to attack. We hear again and again from customers and partners that teams do not document anything, due to the fact that they are using Scrum. Let us consider again the underlying problem: Do you enjoy documenting? Do you enjoy writing reports, and are you passionate about writing notes on the course of events? How many documents are not relevant because they were written solely for the filing cabinet? And let's face it, particularly in the software development environment, an excessive number of pages of documentation are produced.

However, this is not the reason that good or improved software is written. Most people see documentation as a useless by-product that is inevitably not going to help to make their work more meaningful and of higher quality. We're not talking about cases where people are sloppy at work. That obviously does exist. No, it's about making it clear. Documentation is only useful when it enables a person to handle a task or understand a topic faster and more efficiently.

Obviously, there are documents that we consider meaningful and that are necessary. For example, a doctor's note is necessary in order for hospital personnel to know how to help a patient. The plans of an architect, which support work at a construction site, are useful, meaningful and above all, necessary. In software development, this could be documentation that allows the customer to pass the work on the current software increment to another software provider (e.g., an incrementally growing document on the high-level architecture of the software). This may be necessary if the relations have weakened for the initial service provider or the service provider decides to discontinue product development. This documentation is also useful and helps to make sure that we can continue from where others have left off.

In conclusion: *Necessary documentation must be produced, either by the Scrum team itself or by the Scrum support teams from within a large development department.*

What does the agile manifesto statement say? At the end, a project's success should not be based solely on whether the plan was provided or whether a doctor's diagnosis is present on paper. The document is not the product. Thus, the measure of product success is not about whether the documents were written correctly according to a process. Very often we have seen projects which were in trouble even though the first steps in the waterfall process, which delivered hundreds of pages of requirements and detailed design were present. However, we know of hardly any customers who stopped projects that delivered high-quality software even if the number of "documentation pages" was minimal!

Customer collaboration over contract negotiation

The next argument: No, the third principle does not mean that no contracts should be concluded or negotiated. Why would we write a book like that if this were the case? We even present in Chapter 7 many details on how to negotiate a treaty framework for the agile approach. This is, instead, how we interpret this basic principle: Of course, you need contracts. Clearly defining *together* how you want to collaborate is useful: to regulate how payment is to proceed and how much is to be paid; to think about what happens if one of the parties no longer cooperates as originally agreed—all that is necessary and must be done.

It appears, however, that the best contracts do not always lead to the fact that they also shared the success of the project. Especially in the software industry, IT and software development departments like to be regarded as service providers. The software suppliers are typically pushed into a corner when it comes to service, and here they remain with too little information to perform their task purposefully and successfully. However, it appears that software development projects are successful only when those who write the software and those who require the product work closely together. It is clear that customers get the products they really need only if they involve themselves actively. They must make themselves available as partners during a project. The functionalities, which facilitate productivity, are obtained when the software development teams are assisted. From our own experience we can say that if the parties work together and want to succeed, the probability is extremely high that the product delivered will be satisfactory.

Thus, it is important to express the duty to cooperate fully and to emphasize the cooperative approach without placing the responsibility for quality on the contractor. If you read the agile manifesto carefully, you'll see that it does not say that the item on the right is not useful. It says that item is valid and useful; however, the item on the left is even more important from an agile perspective!

Keyword respect: *The former indicates what this principle wishes to express. We are respectful of each other. The customer should not pressurize the service provider, and the service provider should not attempt to mislead the customer.*

On the Agile Tour 2011 in Vienna, Mitch Lacey, an agile practitioner and consultant, told the following story about a conversation between customers and suppliers. A client came to him and explained his project in half an hour. He then proceeded to ask what such a project would cost. Mitch replied:

> This is a question I cannot answer because you should expect a professional response from me. I do not have enough information after 30 minutes to be able to make a meaningful statement. That would be totally unprofessional. I'll make another suggestion: You work for two weeks with us and if you like what you get, then you pay for these two weeks. If not, then you don't pay. And so we continue. You pay when you are satisfied with the work we deliver. You could of course abuse this principle, since we obviously cannot exclude the functionality, which you are not satisfied with and for which you have not paid, from the product. New functionality is developed on top of the supplied functionality of the last iteration. In this case you would pay for the development in the first two weeks, then you would not pay for the next two weeks, and then you would pay again and so on. This would cut your costs and at the end you would have the finished product with all the functionality at half the cost. However, we would note in this case that you had not dealt with us fairly and we would have to stop working.

This way of dealing with a customer who we may not yet know minimizes the risk. It is also a successful practice to be able to start from a basis of trust and to respond if the trust is broken (this is called the *tit for tat strategy*). The beauty of agile projects is that at the end all that counts is what is actually delivered.

Incidentally, this is a first indication of how contracts should be designed. It is expected that the result desired would be that software is delivered and not a question of whether intermediate steps were generated successfully.

Responding to change over following a plan
Reading this head, our attention jumps immediately to the last word: plan. This wording is interpreted by many to mean that in agile projects and agile product development, there are no plans. As if there would only be chaos: No one knows what he or she will get and no one can say how expensive a project or product will be.

This interpretation is obviously wrong. With agile projects, you plan more frequently and more concretely than with traditional methods—on a total of five levels:

- On the level of the vision
- On the level of the road map
- On the level of release
- On the level of the sprints and iterations
- On the level of daily work

Agile methodologists have developed countless planning procedures and tools, beginning with clear conceptions about how you produce a vision and how you subsequently produce release plans. There are concrete procedural instructions on how to arrange sprint planning and much more. At all levels, the participants are aware that each of these planning activities will be repeated iteratively and that the plan must be adjusted continuously. The development team plans every day to collaborate to achieve the sprint goal. During the sprint, the development team and product owner discuss (or to phrase it differently, they plan in cooperation) how the next sprint will be executed. At the beginning of a release, the Scrum team and customers discuss what they would like to see produced in the forthcoming release.

During the current release, the product owner and the customers talk about how the product is to be developed further in the long run. The product road map and the vision of the product are tested in the market, and if necessary, a more sustainable vision for the product is generated. Ideally, the entire planning process is therefore completely transparent. Recently, Pries and Quigley (2011) have compared Scrum to standard project management techniques, with the result that there are comparable planning mechanisms in this agile methodology.

Each of these planning processes has its own visualization techniques and presentation methods. For the plans to proceed as effectively and as rapidly as possible, the communicative process among the various parties must be coordinated. In agile development, not having a plan is not an option.

1.2 AGILE DEVELOPMENT BASED ON SCRUM

Scrum is now the de facto standard in agile software development. In recent years it has evolved from a project management methodology to a new understanding about how to manage dysfunctional working teams, departments, entire organizational units, and companies [in software development and even in industries such as education (Pries and Quigley, 2011)]. Typically, companies use Scrum initially at the team or project level as a project management method. Some companies continue to use it that way. Others evolve even further and shape the life cycle of their entire organization with Scrum. Basically, it is not a method of software development but a management framework within which software development, in whatever way and by whatever means, is taking place (Table 1.1).

TABLE 1.1   Agile Development Methods Within an Agile Framework

Agile Development Method	Agile (Management/Process) Frameworks
Adaptive software development	S
Agile data warehousing	
Crystal	c
Dynamic system development method	
Extreme programming	
Feature-driven development	r
Software expedition	
Universal application	u
Usability-driven development	
Kanban	m

With Scrum, there are a few principles and just a few rules. However, these rules and principles are adhered to strictly. Completely in accordance with the agile manifesto, Scrum is based on another conception regarding people: Scrum respects each person involved and the subject is perceived of as a literate member of the team. Scrum is designed to give teams freedom so that the talents of its members are exposed and so that an enjoyable and productive working environment can exist. In our interpretation, Scrum enables each team member to regain the skills and competence they need to take over responsibility.

The opinion that Scrum is a development method is a common misunderstanding. That Scrum leaves unrestricted freedom to team members is another misunderstanding. Agile approaches such as Scrum are based on a meaningful interaction of rules, discipline, personal responsibility, thinking together, assisting each other, and not using your knowledge simply to shine personally.

- **Product development vs. project management.** Scrum is not about producing a predefined end result but, rather, a steady stream of product parts, resulting in an overall end product. Using Scrum, the developers create a product that approximates the future by the constant inclusion of current changes. By default with Scrum, the applicable software is developed at the end of each sprint. In addition, this results in *continuous intermediate products*. These products make it possible to start risk-free and to measure the progress of a project based on the product parts already supplied. This is the real reason that agile software development projects do not conform to traditional contractual concepts. Something is always delivered, which is not the case with traditional project management methods.
- **Management framework vs. development methods.** Scrum has no regulations on how to work, but sets out roles and responsibilities very clearly. It also defines very clear limits for the development part. The principle of the time box produces not only creative pressure but also the security that is necessary for the development of self-organization.

- **Product owner vs. project manager.** The term *project manager* does not exist in Scrum. A *product owner* is a product visionary who can deliver the product idea to the team, thereby encouraging the team members to productivity. The product owner is responsible for the financial success of the product but, in contrast to a standard project manager, also, has a deep understanding of the client's domain and requirements.

Before we take a closer look at Scrum, we need to resolve the three greatest misconceptions.

1. **Scrum is based on temporary thoughts and hence involves no planning.** Planning in Scrum is carried out consistently and strictly on three levels: at the daily level (daily Scrum), at the sprint level (sprint planning), and at the release level (release planning). Scrum follows the Deming cycle, the basic idea of continuous improvement and permanent planning following the motto plan–do–check–act (Deming, 1982).
2. **Scrum promotes unprofessional work.** This view has its foundation in a world where freedom is perceived as a threat to problem solving and where inches-thick documents are considered quality criteria for good software. Scrum allows freedom of creativity for the team and prescribes in no way *how* a problem should to be solved. In sprint planning, you dog however, specify *what* needs to be present at the end of a sprint. If documentation is deemed to be necessary, it will be included at the end of the sprint. Scrum reveals unprofessional work relentlessly. Due to the daily Scrum, unprofessional work by individual developers is visible to all team members.
3. **Agile methods and Scrum are not disciplined.** Agile processes are extremely consequential in their implementation, as each person's actions become permanently visible and obvious. Discipline in Scrum is, in fact, so extreme that every meeting starts on time and to the minute and whoever is not present must remain outside.

The values of Scrum

It is quite clear that people's perception of the agile manifesto and consequently of Scrum is different from that of the command receiver and the executing aides, who work according to a strict plan. **In Scrum, we assume that intelligent people have a fundamental interest in contributing their ideas to improving things or even to developing new things** (see, in addition, the X and Y theory of Douglas McGregor). Those who promote Scrum are of the opinion that we are all adults and are therefore basically responsible for our own actions. In Scrum we believe (and know) that people give their all if they are fascinated by a vision. *Commitment, focus, openness, courage*, and *respect* are therefore the values of Scrum on which the thinking of those who work with Scrum should be based.

1.2.1 The Principles of Organization

The concepts on which Scrum is based, require a different form of organization. In principle, the procedural principles of the Toyota production system are transferred to software development.

- **Small, self-organized, and cross-functional teams.** Ideally, a Scrum team is made up of seven people: the scrum master, the product owner, and the five members of the development team. The members of the development team do not rely solely on their own specializations but are able to perform various tasks in the work process (according to the concept of the *T-shaped person*; see, e.g., Reinertsen, 2009). This means that they can share their knowledge with each other, applied in various combinations, and they have no fear of tasks that do not correspond directly to their core competencies. They organize their tasks entirely by themselves.
- **Working according to the pull principle.** The team has sole authority to decide how much labor and how many product parts can be delivered during a sprint. The team has control over how much work it receives. (For a description of the pull principle in production, go to http://de. wikipedia.org/wiki/Pull-System.)
- **Intervals with a clear time limit: the time box.** The team gets challenging targets, which are specified at intervals with specific time frames. All actions are limited in time and require a result. This creates a clear framework.
- **Useful business functions: potential shippable code.** At the end of each time interval, the team must deliver a product that meets the standards, guidelines, and requirements of the project.

1.2.2 The Process Model

The Scrum process model defines the framework for running all the activities of product development (Figure 1.1). Besides the six roles outlined above, the Scrum process consists of six meetings and 12 artifacts, shown in Table 1.2.

A weakness of traditional development methods is that they separate customers and developers. This causes a separation between the strategic and the tactical-operational levels. As a result, the team knows that it should do something, but not why. Knowing why is background information essential to developing innovative approaches to problem solving. This fact has long been known. For example, Richard Feynman observed during the Manhattan atomic bomb project that his team's productivity increased extremely as soon as they were given more information about the "why" (Feynman, 1985).

Software developers in traditional processes are usually focused strongly on their work and ignore existing medium- to long-term business issues. With Scrum, however, the software developers are included in the strategic

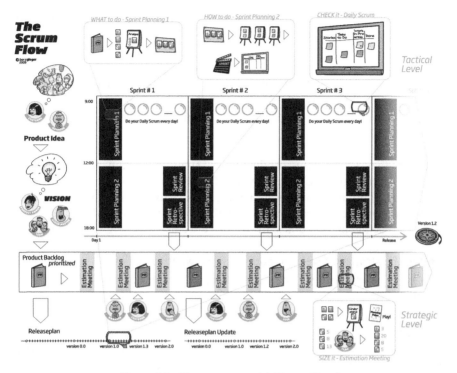

Figure 1.1   *The process model:* "Scrum Flow."

TABLE 1.2

Roles	Meetings	Artifacts
Team	Estimation meeting	Product vision
Product owner	Sprint planning 1	Product backlog item (story)
Scrum master	Sprint planning 2	Product backlog (list of stories)
Manager	Daily scrum	Sprint goal
Customer	Estimation meeting	Selected product backlog
End user	Sprint review	Tasks
	Sprint retrospective	Sprint backlog
		Release plan
		Impediment backlog
		Product increment: usable software
		Definition of done
		Burndown chart

considerations in the following two ways, and developers begin to understand the context in which the success or failure of their work affects their firm and its customers.

- On the one hand, the product owner develops a product vision for the product, either alone or together with the team.
- On the other hand, the team always becomes involved in later strategic planning.

In these two substrategies, product line strategy and organizational strategy higher-level strategies are obviously also factored in.

Strategic planning provides us with a perspective from which, to assess whether a project can succeed, and with the ability to decide which approach will lead to achieving the goals. In summary, we are planning the following:

- On the strategic level, the goals that we want to achieve
- On the tactical level, the actions that are necessary to achieve these objectives

The roles

The strength of Scrum lies in the clear allocation of responsibilities and the separation of responsibilities of Scrum master, product owner, and team. In practice, to strengthen the situation intellectually within the teams or in an organization, we add the roles of customers, end users, and managers.

- **The development team: the suppliers.** The development team delivers the product. It manages its own affairs and is authorized to do anything goal-oriented that is necessary to achieve the desired result. This is done while complying with the standards and procedures of the organization. The team itself controls the amount of work that it can handle and therefore accepts responsibility for the quality of the delivery.
- **The product owner: the visionary.** The product owner steers the product development and is responsible for ensuring that the team develops the desired functionalities in the correct order. He or she ensures that the project results justify the financial investment for the project. The product owner works on a daily basis with the team and takes all necessary decisions in a timely manner. He or she is working continuously on the product backlog and the release plan.
- **The Scrum master: the change agent.** The Scrum master helps the team achieve its goals. He or she works to ensure that all the difficulties, obstacles, and problems that are present are solved. Although not authorized to give instructions, this person ensures that the Scrum process is followed. One of the main tasks of the Scrum master is to educate all persons involved in the project so that they can understand and carry out their roles.

- **The manager: the provider.** Management provides resources and guidelines within the organization. It creates the framework within which the team, the product owner, and the Scrum master may move. Management often solves the problems identified by the Scrum master.
- **The customer: the financer.** The customer is the requester of the project; he or she buys it or has been ordering the project. Typically, executive managers in organizations buy products from external companies. In an internal project development team, the person responsible for the budget often has the role of customer.
- **The end user: the user.** The user of the product is an essential source of information for the Scrum team. He or she is the one who will eventually use the "usable software." Therefore, the Scrum team includes the user in the product development process. During the sprint planning, the user collaborates with the product owner to define the requirements. Later, he or she will work together with the team to ensure that the application is deliverable.

Scrum on a strategic level

- **Develop a product vision.** Initially, a team member is faced with a product idea that is often introduced by the customer: the product owner. He or she handles this idea until there is a product vision. The product vision includes the basic idea for the project, including the necessary contraints, which are envisioned from the start.
- **Create a product backlog.** The product owner develops, either alone or with the help of team members, the product functionality (product backlog items). These items are listed in a very simple form: the user stories (or contextual groups of user stories, called epics). A *story* is a short sentence that represents a part of functionality in a special way. It is described by Mike Cohn (2004), who establishes the following structure for user stories:
- As a user with a role, I want a function, so that I can get benefits.
- **Example.** As a bank customer, I want the ability to identify myself, so that I can retrieve my customer data.
- All user stories (or epics) are included in a list, the product backlog.
- **Order the list by priorities.** The product owner places the items in the product backlog list in order of expected financial gain from the respective functions (http://www.scrum.org/scrumguides, last accessed on 6/3/12).
- **Hold an estimation meeting.** Next, each product backlog item must be valued as to its size. The estimation is performed by team members. A Scrum team includes all those people who are necessary to ensure that the backlog items are transformed into software that can be delivered. The team members estimate the extent of each product backlog item to be delivered and communicate the result to the product owner (Gloger, 2011).

- **Estimate and prioritize the product backlog.** The product backlog estimate is now completed. All team members have an idea of what the product should look like, and the product owner has a first impression of how much effort it will take to create the product.
- **Determine the velocity.** To determine when something can be delivered, we need to know the order and the size of the stories as well as the capacity (i.e., velocity) of the team.
- **Create the release plan.** With the capacity of the team we can calculate the duration of the project. Assuming that the team will remain as it is now, we can determine the number of sprints and, consequently, specify release dates for the various stories.

Scrum on a tactical level

The actual implementation phase in Scrum is carried out in clearly defined time intervals, the sprints. Until the end of each sprint, the team must do its best to deliver functional and quality software (*potential shippable code* or, as termed more recently, *usable software*). At the beginning of a sprint, the tactical implementation is discussed, based on the plan that was developed in the strategic planning phase. On the basis of rough ideas about what features (user stories) are to be delivered in the respective sprints, it is now decided how much can actually be delivered in this sprint. A sprint covers a maximum period of 30 days and is divided into a series of (planning) workshops: sprint planning 1, sprint planning 2, daily Scrum, estimation meeting, sprint review, and sprint retrospective.

- **Sprint planning 1: explaining the requirements for the sprint.** In this first sprint workshop, the product owner, the team, the management, the users, and the Scrum master are present. The product owner explains the stories and, together with the team members and management, defines the goals for the upcoming sprint. The stories are then selected suitably, according to the goals and abilities of the teams to deliver them. This is how sprint backlog develops (in accordance with the Scrum Guide, http://www.scrum.org/scrumguides, last accessed on 6/3/12).
- **Sprint planning 2: design and planning.** Here the team members plan, together with the Scrum master, how they will meet the target agreed to in sprint planning 1. They advise each other on how the application should be structured, what architecture should be selected, which interfaces should be written, and whether test cases should already have been created and written. In short, they discuss in detail what needs to be done.
- **Daily Scrum: coordination and feedback.** Every day the team members meet (the product owner may also participate) at the same time in the same place for 15 minutes for a daily planning meeting moderated by the Scrum master. Here, each team member selects the task that he or she will work on that day. The team members inform the Scrum master of

obstacles and problems so that he or she can solve them as quickly as possible.

- **Estimation meeting: advance planning and estimation.** The product owner and team members update the product backlog at least once during the sprint. Thus, stories containing new estimates are provided and new stories are included in the product backlog. At the same time, the order of the backlog items is adjusted, to take the new information into consideration. This meeting allows the product owner to update and complete the release plan of the project.
- **Sprint review: presenting the results.** At the end of the sprint, the Scrum team presents the stories that have been developed. The team shows only the stories that are really complete, that is, that could be put into production.
- **Sprint retrospective: constantly improving.** The sprint retrospective enables the team to learn systematically. In this stage the team analyzes which processes must be improved in order to work more effectively. The results of the retrospective are captured in the impediment backlog and contribute as suggestions for improvements in the sprint planning.

The key principle is: At the end of a sprint, the development team must provide potentially useful functionality. This means that no further work is needed to pass this functionality to the end user. This principle must be adapted to the respective conditions of development. Therefore, the level of completion is agreed between the development team and the product owner (the "definition of done"). The Scrum master is working continuously with the Scrum team to improve the efficiency of the teamwork. Ideally, the end user receives a tested delivery at the end of the sprint.

Scrum can help companies to compete in the global marketplace. It does so by designing the software product development to be more responsive and problem-oriented rather than just a work-through project. The principles of Scrum, the roles and the process framework, create structures and rules by which to guide the staff but at the same time to give them the freedom to develop their potential. In this way, they find new, innovative approaches and begin to think beyond their horizons. The fact that Scrum is much more than simply a single method is usually not recognized by companies until they are already working with it.

1.2.3 Estimation in Scrum

Estimating the complexity of the functionality to be delivered is an essential part of the cost negotiation and implementation of projects. This is not special for Scrum, but the way this is done within an agile framework agreement is different. To prepare you for later work as to how estimates in Scrum are analyzed and prepared, we provide here an explanation and basic overview.

In the real business world there are many reasons why the product owner must create a release plan. This plan should show at which point certain sets of specific functionality are available. To create this plan, the product owner needs three pieces of information:

1. The size (in terms of complexity) of the backlog items.
2. The prioritization: that is, the order of the backlog items in the list of functions.
3. The capacity of the Scrum team: that is, the number of backlog items (counted in complexity points or story points, which are discussed later) that the Scrum team can develop in one sprint.

If these factors are available, the product owner can very easily calculate at which point the functionality will be available. The problem is that this information is not known at the beginning of a project. Therefore, a way must be found to estimate the size of the backlog items and the capacity and/or velocity of the Scrum team.

Predictability and estimates

Why is estimating functionality so problematic? The answer is because estimating as we generally think of it estimates the wrong thing: namely, the effort. When estimating a project, we must distinguish between:

- Estimating the effort
- Estimating the size (i.e., the complexity)

Very often, the estimate of the size of the functionalities is confused with the estimate of the effort. It is understandable that a project manager would appreciate an estimate of the effort, because this gives the project sponsor information about the cost of the project. But if estimates are based on effort, this also means that the project plans must be based on an estimation of the activities.

In software development, where a more productive programmer is up to 25 times as effective as a weaker one, it is impossible to predict the time taken for a particular programming task. What is even more extreme is that there is no correlation between the time required for a particular task and the end result. Even if the project manager asked the developer for an estimate each time a task was performed, he or she would still have the problem that the same developer does not always complete the task. Estimating in Scrum means to estimate the size, not the effort.

In Scrum, the team performance is measured by its *velocity*, the amount of functionality that a team can provide in a time unit or sprint. In other words, the velocity is an expression of the throughput (measured in terms of the size of the functionality) of the team. The more a team gets done during a sprint, the higher its throughput (i.e., velocity). If the product owner knows the measured velocity of a team, he or she can accurately calculate when a specific product part is finished.

Estimates with story points

Before we can determine the size of the backlog items, we need to establish what size means. Size refers to the degree of understanding that a team has of the functionality of the backlog item. The more accurate the understanding, the smaller the associated size.

To estimate the size of a backlog item, we require only three things:

1. First, we need a *reference*. We obtain this by selecting an item from the list of backlog items, which at first glance appears to be small and manageable. While browsing, the team together determines which properties the backlog item has, thus establishing the reference. The reference represents the dimensions or aspects that the team needs to use to determine the size. If, for example, we want to determine the size of countries and we had a list of all the European countries, we might first look for the smallest country. For this we would first have to agree on the properties according to which we determine size. We could take into consideration the area as well as the size of the population. We could, of course, also use a combination of many properties. The factors incorporated in the determination of the size are set when estimating backlog items. Here you select the dimensions that best help you understand the backlog items. The responsibility for setting the dimensions of the unit lies completely with the team. The reference should express all relevant aspects.

2. If you have agreed to a reference, that is, a backlog item that appears suitable as a reference, the next step is to establish the *unit of measure*. The unit is simple in our case. We need something that expresses the size of a backlog item. The agile community has agreed to call this unit of measure *story points*. This is completely arbitrary; you might as well count gummy bears, as long as you are aware that we are dealing here with the designation of a unit.

3. Finally, we need a *scale*. Scaling is difficult because it leads easily to misinterpretations. We are dealing with estimates of relative size (i.e., the relative understanding of the functionality that will be generated). We therefore require a scale that takes into account the fact that estimates have larger fluctuations when big things, which are often associated with a greater lack of understanding, are estimated. In other words, an estimate will be more accurate if we are dealing with a small, manageable package than if it is a very large package.

The agile community has, not least thanks to the work of Mike Cohn (2005), selected Cohn's impure fibonacci series as the agreed-upon scale (Table 1.3).

TABLE 1.3 The Impure Fibonacci Series According to Cohn

Step	1	2	3	4	5	6	7	8	9
Value	1	2	3	5	8	13	20	40	100
Standard deviation at 50% accuracy	0.5	1	1.5	2.5	4	6.5	10	20	50

This scale already indicates to us, simply through its values, how "accurate" the estimate is. A high value means automatically that the standard deviation is higher. The estimate is therefore not inaccurate, but the range in which our backlog item is located is much larger. We will see that we use this property to schedule the release plan.

Now we have everything that necessary to estimate the backlog items: a reference, a unit, and a scale. At this point we invite the team to an estimation meeting. As this can sometimes be a rather large meeting, we have to perform as efficiently as possible.

Planning poker

Planning poker generates estimates in a relatively short time, based on expert opinion, and it also makes the proceedings entertaining. The use of Planning Poker in the estimation process is so effective because it uses the intuition of experts and helps to avoid the communication problems that every group of experts experiences. Planning poker is "played" by all the Scrum team members. It is, in fact, important that all team members (i.e., software developers, database engineers, testers, business analysts, and designers) estimate the backlog together. In an agile software development project, that usually involves no more than 10 team members. If the team is any larger, you should split it up and carry out the estimation in two teams. It is crucial that the product owner be present, but he or she has no right to estimate.

Planning poker is played with planning poker cards. To prepare in advance, each team member is given a set of "playing cards" with the values of the impure Fibonacci series according to Cohn (i.e., 0, 1, 2, 3, 5, 8, 13, 20, 40, 100). When all team members have their card set, in the next step they agree on the reference backlog item or call to mind once again what the reference backlog item was in the last round of estimations and which features were relevant in the assessment.

Once the reference backlog item has been found, the actual estimation process begins. The moderator of the meeting then reads out loud the description of the backlog items that are to be estimated. Any questions about the understanding of issues for this backlog item are answered at this meeting (where relevant, these answers are used to extend the description of the backlog item). When all questions have been answered, each team member selects a card which represents the value that this team member believes to be correct. While poker is being played, nobody announces his or her selection. Only when all team members have decided are the cards revealed (simultaneously).

Almost always, the estimates of individual team members differ. This is good, as it gives each person the opportunity to learn something. The two team members with the highest and lowest estimates now explain how they got to their respective numbers. This explanation is only for the exchange of information, not about who is right. At this stage, the moderator of the meeting should ensure that no conflicts arise. Perhaps things can be clarified once again through the exchange of information or via additional information supplied by the product owner. The moderator may, if deeming it necessary, retain this information in the form of notes.

Once both team members have explained how they arrived at their values, the estimation is repeated. Once again all the parties involved select a number and show it simultaneously. Generally, the figures have now aligned themselves: for example, the values 8, 8, 5, and 8. The moderator then asks whether we can agree on a value of 8. If the team members are in disagreement, a third round is played. This time, the values should be almost identical. If not, the "most sensible" value is considered. This estimation procedure is not about accuracy but, rather, about selecting a value that makes sense.

In this way we are able very quickly to obtain a valued product backlog in which all team members were involved. This factor is crucial because only when all team members have together completed the estimate of the backlog items can they get involved in these estimates. More important is the fact that during the poker, all team members manage to gain an idea of what is to be developed. For larger teams and projects, Boris Gloger has developed another method of estimation: magic estimation, which is described in Chapter 3.

1.3 AGILITY FROM THE PERSPECTIVE OF PROCUREMENT

It is already quite common in modern procurement of custom software to insist that after no later than four weeks, the first fully functional increment of the product be shipped. (Custom software is designed specifically for the client. As part of the custom software or product concept we also understand software development that happens during customer-specific software integration projects.) The "elevator pitch" of Scrum inventor Ken Schwaber has always been: "I help companies deliver software in 30 days" (Schwaber and Sutherland, 2012). That's what the agile software development is: fast, iterative, one increment at a time. The buyer is able to learn from mistakes on both sides and does not have to make a big decision without the possibility of handling the risks properly in the course of the project.

The contractor should deliver product features consecutively. Feedback from the customer should be incorporated as soon as possible, and despite possible changes to the scope of the project, the overall result desired should be delivered. It is, however, very unlikely that for large orders a contractor will be able to deliver an entire product within 30 days, but there is a high probability that after 30 days a first increment will be delivered with which the customer will be able to start working.

The traditional development processes of Winston Royce are not able to meet the foregoing expectations placed on software development services. The traditional model, developed in the 1970s, is still in frequent use. It is, somewhat, a contradiction to Scrum, as the capturing of requirements, the creation of the entire design, and all the contractual duties and a subsequent tender often take much longer than four weeks. Thus, first units are typically delivered much later than with the agile model.

The problem inherent in all software development projects and all services is the variability as to what should be delivered: *the inability to know what you actually need.* We know that this is difficult to digest for those in procurement (and perhaps for many others, too). However, the understanding that this inability is a systematic, even a necessary principle is essential. The simple fact that you agree to purchase and develop a project for which you cannot describe all the details in advance is actually the first important step toward project success (Reinertsen, 2009).

An example: A mechanical engineer wanted to implement a new method of materials testing. Part of the work of the project team consisted of operating the essential innovation and inventing the vital approaches and components. In this example it is obvious that you cannot know whether the team will manage to deliver the desired outcome on a given time line and at a specified cost. The value of the product lies in the new product ideas, or the invention. If you know what you want to invent but still do not know how to get there in detail, the value of the new product is to eliminate the lack of knowledge as to how to get there.

And here lies the paradox. To plan would mean to know what to do and to know how the result can be achieved. This is not so because you want to explore new territory. The waterfall project cannot help here and it is understandable that it would be a waste of money to invest in detailed specifications as to what should be done. A project based on traditional practices simply cannot consider all the uncertainties associated with the problems that exist.

Despite the weaknesses of traditional tendering processes and classical implementation approaches, it is interesting to hear the following from some procurement representatives and even key account managers. These statements are often linked to the rejection of an agile contracting model and show the tendency toward fixed-price contracts:

- "I want to know what I get for my money!"
- "We need to know exactly what the client wants; otherwise, we cannot estimate our costs."
- "The customer always wants more than he or she asked for initially!"

- "How can I be sure that the contractor will not inflate the price? They can simply work more slowly."
- "I need a work contract, not time and materials development, because I can capitalize the investment accordingly."

We hear such statements in almost any discussion of agile software development and agile project management approaches. They suggest a deep-seated conflict among the parties—development, seller, and buyer—as to trust and, of course, the fact that on the one hand you want to buy something as inexpensively as possible and, on the other hand, sell something at the highest possible price with manageable risk in the development process.

Wait a moment. Can we not do anything about this? Is it not true that the nature of the business follows this exact principle? We buy things as cheaply as possible so that we can make as much profit as possible. We cover this point in subsequent chapters. It is, however, important at this point to understand that it is clear that this principle concerns business, and that we need new approaches for complex IT projects and custom software. Traditional contracts with fixed-price agreements or, at the other extreme, contracts based on time and materials often lead to lose–lose situations with just the illusion of solving the concerns listed above. In Chapter 5 in particular we show that modern procurement is capable of conducting tenders for agile fixed-price contracts jointly with the business departments, thereby awarding a contract to the supplier who reveals the best quality and price with the lowest associated risk.

1.4 AGILITY FROM THE PERSPECTIVE OF THE SOFTWARE PROVIDER

A seller of software services should be able to make customers pay adequately for the value and quality of the product and service provided. The sellers' (also called key account managers throughout the book) job is to offer a product that the customer wants at a higher price than a product that the customer does not want. The actual underlying problem is described brilliantly in an article about the agency David and Goliath:

> "We cannot complain about too little work, quite the opposite," says Matthias Czech, owner and creative director [of the agency David and Goliath]. There is however a catch. More and more frequently, says Czech, the agency is invited to pitches where the customer evaluates which agency best suits the company, based on the offer. This as opposed to evaluating based on creativity, efficiency and performance (http://bit.ly/rNiNAC, last accessed on 5/1/12).

Customers want the cheapest provider. They want to buy software integration services and software development services as if such services were a standard consumer product. They want to know at the beginning what it will cost, but as described above, they do not have a detailed idea of what they really want. Sellers or service providers cannot offer a product when they do not yet have one. They have no idea at what price they can offer a product, because they do not know the market for a new product. This can only be established in the course of a project. At the same time, a seller knows that there will always be someone who claims to be able to offer the same thing more cheaply.

The variability and illusions surrounding expenses play a trick on sellers. If there is a really creative, highly effective team in the background which provides excellent quality quickly, a seller can potentially make a favorable offer. Even if he or she knows that the team requires little time (low cost), a seller cannot be sure that competitors will not offer lower price and provide lower quality. Indeed, the customer and even the seller cannot define exactly what is to be delivered, but both believe in the illusion that this can be described perfectly.

And then there is the fact that the seller should in no case offer a project at a discounted cost. He or she puts a team to work that is very good, works fast, and offers high quality. As a result, the seller should offer the project at a fairly high price because, after all, the customer is being provided with a product of high value. In both cases, whether a fixed-price project or a time and materials project, the situation is not advantageous for the seller. This is different, of course, if the seller follows a philosophy of offering at lowest cost and then generating additional revenue based on tons of change requests.

1.5 THE 12 PRINCIPLES OF AGILE SOFTWARE DEVELOPMENT

In addition to the four pairs of values, the authors of the agile manifesto have named 12 additional principles that apply to the agile management framework. Next we show how the parties involved—customer, supplier, and development or Scrum team—can shape these principles and achieve project success through shared support.

The practices listed below are just a few of the possibilities for collaboration. They symbolize a different way of dealing with customers, suppliers, and teams. Implementing Scrum or other agile management framework always influences the entire organization. Often, not all parts of an organization are able to implement all aspects at once. Therefore, consider the statements below only as references of where relationships should evolve.

1. Emphasis is on delivery
"Our top priority is to satisfy our customers through early and continuous delivery of valuable software content."

How do we behave as a customer?

- We participate in sprint reviews.
- Our department takes on finished software at the end of a sprint if possible, otherwise as early in the process as feasible.

- We integrate the software into our existing systems as soon as possible after delivery, as this often deters the risks inherent in the fact that the software operations department has a very specific view of the software delivered.
- We give critical but respectful feedback.

How do we behave as a service provider?

- Our software development processes allow us to show the customer fully functional software after each sprint.
- We make appropriate environments accessible to the customer.

How do we behave on the Scrum team?

- We optimize our development practices in the team so that we are able to present completed software at the end of a sprint.
- We talk extensively with users and customize applications according to the user's requirements.
- We deliver the most effective solution that fulfills the user's requirements.

2. Free exchange
"Accept changes in requirements even late in development. Agile processes use changes to the competitive advantage of customers."

How do we behave as a customer?

- We distinguish between functional requirements and the conditions of the project.
- We are personally involved in the project vision and understand the technological implications.
- We are aware that we are permitted to make changes.
- We understand that there is a profound change when we alter the environment.

How do we behave as a service provider?

- We welcome changes.
- We develop in such a way that we are able to respond rapidly to changes.
- We make this possible with good documentation, refactoring, and continuous and open communication about what has actually occurred.
- We invite customers to daily Scrums, sprint plannings, and reviews.

How do we behave on the Scrum team?

- We communicate with customers to fulfill their needs. We try to think like customers and users.

- We are open to criticism when our applications are under review.
- We acknowledge our errors and correct them immediately.

3. Deliver in iterations
"Deliver functional software regularly within a few weeks or months and favor these shorter time periods."

How do we behave as a customer?

- We are present at sprint reviews and give feedback.
- As quickly as possible, we integrate into our existing infrastructure the partial functionality delivered.

How do we behave as a service provider?

- We invite customers to sprint reviews and openly discuss the current status.

How do we behave on the Scrum team?

- We deliver complete functionality at the end of each sprint.

4. End user and developer sit together
"Experts and developers must work together daily throughout the project."

How do we behave as a customer?

- We make experts from various departments available to the development team.
- We are available when the development team has questions.
- We take time for the project and respect the fact that nobody can guess our wishes without us giving feedback and helping to understand the details.

How do we behave as a service provider?

- We welcome the experts when they are present in the Scrum team.
- We call them when we have questions.
- We make a point of inviting them to sprint planning.

How do we behave on the Scrum team?

- We work with the experts daily.
- We make an effort to understand the experts.
- We observe how the expecrts work. However, we do not ask them what they want; instead, we work with them until we know what they need.

5. Trust the individual

"Build projects around motivated individuals. Give them the environment and support they needs and trust that they will get the job done."

How do we behave as a customer?

- We search for an agile development partner.
- We provide motivated experts.
- We trust the delivery team for at least the first three sprints.
- We also check whether they deliver what we expect.

How do we behave as a service provider?

- We select project team members who really want to work on the project.
- We give them the tools they need for their work and remove unnecessary bureaucratic hurdles.

How do we behave on the Scrum team?

- We state openly when we need something or when we are obstructed by something.
- We have a Scrum master who clears obstacles out of our way.
- We behave respectfully toward customers and management.

6. Face-to-face communication is more effective

"The most efficient and effective method of delivering information to a development team is face to face."

How do we behave as a customer?

- We understand that good documents are always only a result of successful face-to-face communication.

How do we behave as a service provider?

- We communicate openly with the client. All information, including problems and areas where we are lagging behind, is visible to the customer.
- We do not hide anything.

How do we behave on the Scrum team?

- We talk to users.
- We understand their needs.
- We observe users while they are working.

7. All that matters is completed functionality

"Functioning software is the primary measure of success."

How do we behave as a customer?

- We call on our service provider to deliver the first part of completed software within 30 days.
- We are not satisfied with documents as representing of progress.

How do we behave as a service provider?

- We deliver software in short intervals.
- All obstacles on the customer's side are discussed openly, and all obstacles on our side are also addressed and resolved openly.

How do we behave on the Scrum team?

- We constantly deliver software that is potentially usable.

8. Sustainable pace
"Agile processes promote sustainable development. Clients, developers, and users should be able to maintain a steady pace indefinitely."

How do we behave as a customer?

- We will not push the team for functionality and deadlines, and we will not demand overtime or changes at the last minute.

How do we behave as a service provider?

- We constantly work professionally and to a high standard.
- We deliver only tested, documented, and representative software.
- We do not commit to functionality over long periods.

How do we behave on the Scrum team?

- We honor our commitments in the sprint.
- We work as a team, striving continually to deliver consistently on a high level.

9. Quality is an attitude
"Continuous attention to technical excellence and good design promotes agility."

How do we behave as a customer?

- We expect high technical quality from our contractors, and we know that this is not something that we can buy for a bargain price.
- We do not, therefore, select our service providers according to price, alone.

How do we behave as a service provider?

- We deliver to the customer an excellent design with extensible architecture, and we invest in the training of our staff.

How do we behave on the Scrum team?

- We look constantly to the future and search for solutions that are extensible.
- We perform test-driven development, we automate, and we document.
- We educate ourselves continuously to correct weaknesses.

10. Keep it simple, stupid (KISS)
"Simplicity. The art of maximizing the amount of work not done is essential."

How do we behave as a customer?

- We check constantly whether we still require what we requested.
- We cancel projects if we already have what we need.
- We accept contracts that allow us these things.

How do we behave as a service provider?

- We deliver from the start the features that are most valuable to the customer.
- We favor short project lead times.
- We deliver fast, we deliver functionality, and therefore we do not bill in hours.

How do we behave on the Scrum team?

- We are always looking for the simplest solution that can be produced professionally.

11. Complexity can only be answered with self-organization
"The best architectures, requirements, and designs emerge from self-organized teams."

How do we behave as a customer?

- We make how our systems work completely transparent.
- We do not yet define solutions.
- We allow the teams to do their work.

How do we behave as a service provider?
- We educate the staff in such a way that all the necessary skills are present in the team.

How do we behave on the Scrum team?
- We reveal when there is something that we cannot achieve due to a lack of skills.
- We actively ask questions.
- We work proactively with customers.

12. Learn from postmortems

"At regular intervals, the team reflects how it can be more effective and adjusts its behavior accordingly."

How do we behave as a customer?

- We expect to hear of errors made by the teams that have led to improvements.
- We participate by invitation in the project retrospective.
- We respond to requests for change and respect them as having the potential to increase productivity.

How do we behave as a service provider?

- We work with customers continually to improve our relationships and inform them as to where we see potential for improvement.

How do we behave on the Scrum team?

- We perform our retrospectives rigorously.

1.6   SUMMARY

Companies that want to meet the requirements of dynamic markets are relying more and more on agile methods of software development. The management framework Scrum is the method most commonly used. While development teams using agile methods are already presenting impressive results, the benefits of agile development are still not obvious to many buyers. Therefore, agile-developed products and projects are often grouped into inappropriate "traditional" contract constructs.

The main drawback: Valuable principles of cooperation between customers and suppliers, as they are to be implemented in the agile way of thinking, based on the agile manifesto, continue to be disregarded in these rigid contract constructs. Customers as well as suppliers do not have a successful project in sight as a goal but, rather, each entity to its own advantage. Both sides struggle with the same problem: the inability to know what is actually needed and how the details of the scope will change during the project for various reasons. The basic problem for all software development projects and all service providers is therefore the variability of what is to be delivered.

2

The Missing Piece of the Puzzle

As discussed in Chapter 1, whether as a development method or as a management framework, the use of agile methods is on the rise, yet there are very few approaches where suitable contractual frameworks are established. Slowly, the challenges and new requirements behind this topic have become more obvious to leaders in the IT industry. For most IT projects the traditional fixed-price contract (also called FFF for *firm fixed fee*) is currently employed. The second common alternative is the contractual framework for time and materials (also called a cost plus firm-fixed-fee contract).

None of these contractual frameworks considers the new form of cooperation in agile projects optimally; neither do they define clear rules as to how to treat the obvious changing subject matter (scope). For agile IT projects it is necessary to find an agreement that supports the balance between a fixed budget (maximum price range) and agile development (scope not yet defined in detail) in the context of Scrum. Such a contract is not necessarily a new invention but is primarily the natural evolution of the traditional fixed-price contract. This means that its major parts and legal formulations continue to exist. Alan Kelley (2008) wrote that tools and techniques exist and are well documented and that the challenge is to learn to perform in a more agile way; it is a similar situation for the agile sourcing and contracts. We have to use existing techniques and ideas and learn how to manage this contractual part in a more agile way.

Agile Contracts: Creating and Managing Successful Projects with Scrum, First Edition.
Andreas Opelt, Boris Gloger, Wolfgang Pfarl, and Ralf Mittermayr.
© 2013 John Wiley & Sons, Inc. Published 2013 by John Wiley & Sons, Inc.

We refer to this form of contract as an agile fixed-price contract (an agile contract with a fixed price). We need to make a very clear distinction for situations where the term *agile contract* is used in time and materials contracts for projects that are developed using an agile framework. We see these currently available agile contracts based on time and material as suiting the development method and perhaps rather small projects quite well, but we see a lack of its applicability for large projects.

Definition of an Agile Fixed-Price Contract

The agile fixed-price concept balances the interests of suppliers and customers. It creates a new contract in the form of a cooperative model for implementation that does not set aside clear goals and a framework for achieving these goals. This is achieved by combining principles of cooperation and flexibility in designing the best possible requirements. In terms of budget security and cost awareness in the implementation, it incorporates a price ceiling. This agreement provides a clear method as to how parts of the subject matter (scope split in sprints), based on the overall concept (backlog representing the scope) are defined and implemented jointly, but the agreement contains no final detailed specifications.

For easier understanding, we subsequently always speak of an *Agile fixed-price contract*, to avoid confusion with the commercial element of this type of contract. The key commercial element is the "real fixed price" or "maximum price." It is the agreed-upon maximum amount of money within which an IT project is to be implemented.

Figure 2.1 illustrates the fundamental problem. Project types listed at the left side of the figure exemplify a coordinated system of price variability and scope variability. The first quadrant (top right) shows cases of projects with a fixed price and a fixed scope, such as machines built using the same design and based on the same plan (which perhaps the supplier used often before). The complete opposite of this is found in the fourth quadrant (bottom right). Here we find projects where the scope is fixed but the price is variable. Looking at an example of a mechanical engineering project, one may know the initial plans of a new machine (fixed scope). However, this is only the first prototype to be built. Certain techniques to achieve the aim might not yet be known. So the price cannot be fixed precisely, as numerous changes can occur during the construction which result in necessary adjustments to the plan and to the execution.

In the third quadrant (bottom left) we find projects with variable prices and variable scope. These include, for example, temporary service work or consulting tasks, where the scope is not known precisely and the price varies accordingly. Some IT projects may also be placed in this quadrant, but in practice we

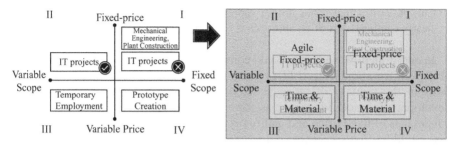

Figure 2.1 *Contract-type applications.*

usually find IT projects as a combination of variable scope with a fixed price. We certainly should not (as often wrongly assumed) place IT projects in the quadrant fixed scope and fixed price (we discuss the details around this "should not" later in this chapter). Realistically, IT projects are characterized by a fixed price or budget requirement (this is the realistic situation in company business), but a variable scope at least over the lifetime of the project.

Why software projects are special compared to other sorts of projects has been nicely summarized by George Stepanek. He notes a list of major points that are affecting unsuccessful trials to manage these IT projects by means of traditional contracts, such as "Requirements are incomplete" or "Change is inevitable" (Stepanek, 2005). Looking at available well-known contractual frameworks, quadrants I, III, and IV are covered by traditional types of contracts (as shown on the right in Figure 2.1). The second quadrant (IT projects, top left) lacks a proper contract, however. The agile contract in the form of the agile fixed-price contract closes this gap.

Which IT projects are we talking about?
An important distinction at the start concerns the nature of IT projects, for which we see the agile fixed-price contract having a clear advantage. This sort of contract is suitable either for projects where software is integrated in a complex IT environment or for projects in which new functionality is created. Basically, these are projects that through honest examination can be defined in detail clearly only on the path to the goal. This new form of contract is only slightly relevant for highly standardized IT projects. If the same ERP system is introduced for the hundredth time in a similar environment, surprises and changes in the course of the project's progress, through the standardization, would be strictly limited (although still not eliminated).

For the projects that we want to focus on here, Elmar Grasser, CTO of Orange Austria, provided a suitable statement (from an interview with Andreas Opelt in March 2012):

> Only when you begin to work with these sorts of IT projects, that is, when you perform the first steps in the implementation and see the results or detect what problems occurred, can customers and suppliers learn to ask the right questions.

Current contractual forms do not support this, and any type of contract that clearly administers such an approach is certainly of great interest.

In addition, however, one should consider whether it is feasible and reasonable even for standardized IT projects to include existing detailed specifications in the context of an agile fixed-price contract when the underlying developmental method is agile, as, for example, Scrum. This allows use of the advantages of fixed price and agility even in those types of projects, where the case could be that something does not run in quite as standardized a manner as expected. To give an illustrative example here: We have just recently had a workshop with a big insurance company which had started to integrate and harmonize to a standardized software solution. Everything seemed very clear in the beginning, but now, many years later, no output was produced, as the methodology selected was not agile and a suitable contract did not give clear transparancy and minimization of the risk of stranded investments. Currently, this company is changing its delivery model and contractual processes to agile, to be aligned with the ideas reported in this book.

We have been asked by the CEO of a small software company whether this contract framework is also relevant for small IT projects. By "small" he meant projects around 100 person-days. The answer is that the effort to set up a traditional contract is just as high as the effort to set up an agile fixed-price contract (if we exclude the work to be performed to generate the detailed description of the scope). Still the advantages are present even if there are just two or three sprints of work to be performed. We admit that it might be an initial investment to guide the customer on the right way to be open to this new sort of contract. However, the usual case is that such small software companies do 80% of their business with a handful of customers, so it might be worth the effort to try once to switch to a cooperative model (and then instead work on an agile frame contract where the procedure described in this book is fixed and the scope is then added for each small project).

A Few Definitions from the Contract World

- **IT projects.** When we cite IT projects in this book, we are referring to large-scale projects with a scope of more than 200 and quite often up to thousands of person-days. The smaller the IT project, the less relevant are the factors that speak urgently for an agile fixed-price contract (which does not mean that this contract form isn't still beneficial). The opposite is true for large projects. We mention this so explicitly because in practice we often meet exactly the opposite opinion. In our consideration we generally exclude IT projects that can be developed according to strong standardizations and for which a final specification is (almost) possible. We embark on these IT projects selectively at a suitable stage.

- **Successful IT project.** Whether a project succeeds or fails often depends on how the project will be marketed internally and externally. This depends strongly on what commercial and political leverage is used to set the different sides in motion, to enforce a particular point of view. Parts of this approach are necessary. However, the dramatically poor performance of IT projects seems to inspire endless creativity in these presentations. In this book we describe success as follows: An IT project is considered successful if neither budget nor time is exceeded by more than 90% and customer value achieved is not below 90%.
    - Budget represents the maximum price range fixed at the start of the project.
    - Time represents the time frame for completion of a certain project vision.
    - The achievement of customer value is fixed at the start of the project and is based mostly on the business case values of the individual functions in the high-level backlog.

Of course, these are by no means the only factors that make an IT project successful. In the present context and in many other reports and publications, these are, however, important indications.

- **Traditional fixed-price contract.** This contract is governed on the basis of subject matter (scope) that is complete and specified in complete detail according to compensation and acceptance and delivery dates. The contract is based on the assumption that customers know, or assumes to know, what he or she wants to have delivered. We use the common expression *fixed-price contract*, which is, of course, a work contract with the main commercial "fixed-price" item as a basis.
- **Time and materials contract.** This contract is usually governed on the basis of experience levels (e.g., junior, senior) and roles (e.g., analysis, testers, developers, project managers, or even an entire Scrum team) and the subsequent cost for one day (or hour) of delivery within the framework of an IT project (design, management, testing, etc.).

2.1 THE PROBLEMS WITH TRADITIONAL FIXED-PRICE CONTRACTS

Who benefits from a traditional fixed-price contract, the customer or the supplier? Usually, the broad common belief is that from the perspective of the customer, the fixed-price contract has the lowest risk and thus is benefical for

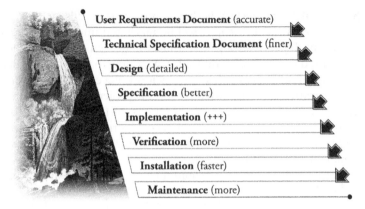

User Requirements Document (accurate)

Technical Specification Document (finer)

Design (detailed)

Specification (better)

Implementation (+++)

Verification (more)

Installation (faster)

Maintenance (more)

Figure 2.2   *Software development according to the waterfall model.*

the customer. The motivation to change the contractual agreement is therefore lowest on the side that has a choice and seems to benefit most. Therefore, the customer is the initiator of the project tender, which is asking primarily for fixed-price proposals. But let us view whether the supplier is perhaps not the one who enjoys the major advantage of a fixed-price assignment.

A fixed-price project is based mostly on a clearly specified waterfall project cycle (a predictive process). For a better understanding, one should understand the details of what happens in this model, as the model itself is one of the basic reasons that the traditional fixed-price contract was employed for IT projects. As shown in Figure 2.2, this approach means that delivery of the subject matter of the contract is managed on the basis of a detailed user requirement document in a major iteration (or sometimes in two or three major iterations, i.e., releases). The steps shown in the figure follow accordingly.

If problems arise on projects that follow this model (which happens regularly), the first reaction is usually the following: In the context of the tender and the contract, the specifications in the user requirement document should be described more precisely. Increasing effort should flow into the technical specification document and into the design to allow for finer and more detailed work. The specifications should improve continuously and become clearer, and the quality of the implementation should be of the highest level. Quality is ensured at the end of the project through thousands of tests. However, the errors that prevail are corrected at a very late stage and at a very high cost.

The waterfall model was originally intended only to show important steps in large IT projects. However, it has now been used in the software industry for about 40 years, even though it has the following serious drawbacks:

- **Wrong assumptions.** The waterfall model assumes that it is possible to describe the subject matter of a contract (the scope) at the start of a project, and that the description does not change, or sees only marginal changes, during the project period. In the meantime, we know that a full description of the development of custom software or software integration projects is rarely possible, if at all. We operate with only partial knowledge of what the contract subject matter will actually look like—and this is exactly the foundation for changes, additional costs, and discussions.

- **Wrong expectations.** Due to the weakness of incomplete and unpredictable information from insignificant descriptions, the project lead time is often extended to months, sometimes even years. Between the experts and management and between IT and the departments, the fact remains unspoken that requirements cannot even come close to being captured in 100% detail. Completely counterproductive expectations are created by these enlarged lead times, so that this (pointless) description is also assumed to create budget security. In the course of the project, the opposite is often presented and the project team has great difficulty in getting rid of the existing expectations.

- **Wrong timing of detailed requirements.** Naturally, requirements are declining such that their value depreciates more and more over time. In waterfall projects it often goes like this: First, a few (hundreds of) pages of requirements are written, a year later the project begins, and perhaps 20 months later the requirements are tested. Many people are not sufficiently aware that the decline of knowledge in such a period of time is enormous. To return to the original value of the requirements is a very costly operation. No automobile manufacturer would consider preparing and stocking all conceivable car doors one year before the start of production. This is, however, exactly what happens in software development for large waterfall-driven fixed-price projects.

- **Wrong requirements.** If we recall the results of various studies from Chapter 1, the requirements in software projects vary by up to 3% per month. Therefore, in one and a half years, half of the requirements will change (and you can be certain they will). In contrast to the decline of knowledge, it actually involves changing the starting point in the requirements. This is probably the most serious drawback of the waterfall model and/or traditional contracts that cannot handle this nature of IT projects.

Incidentally, Winston Royce, the creator of the waterfall model, wrote in his article "Managing the Development of Large Software Systems" that the waterfall model is risky in its purest form. Royce even said that only the iterations between the process steps can reduce the risk (Royce, 1970).

Mark Hajszan-Meister, the former CFO of Austria-based telco provider Silver Server (a subsidiary of Tele2), has witnessed many IT projects from the perspective of business management but also from the perspective of former roles in controlling. In an interview in February 2012, he gave us his assessment of the main reasons that according to the traditional fixed-price model, IT projects were not successful:

> Often, a lack in the translation of business requirements into detailed technical specifications has repeatedly led to unnecessary and costly iterations under fixed-price contracts. Of course, these are usually based on change requests between the client and the supplier. Also, and perhaps more serious, a lack of knowledge of the appropriate personnel of the providers can lead to problems, especially in the scope and formulation of the request. This very quickly leads to a creeping descoping during the course of a project. In every large company, the CIO should monitor the progress of the project and implement countermeasures early, in case of disagreements.

We consider this a suitable example of a reduction in customer value (remember that this already makes the project "officially" unsuccessful) and a lack of communication between the right people and the inability (for different reasons) to describe the requirements at the start of the contract. It is also interesting that the first discussions on the quality and completeness of the requirements are already being held internally by the client at the interface between IT and the business department. The parties involved do not have the possibility to continually improve their knowledge and communication.

Figure 2.3 summarizes the practical situation. You begin the long planning phase on the basis of a definition of the scope, which, although made with the best knowledge and intentions, will change significantly during the course of the project. During this time, costs are incurred but there is no value for the customer (business value) because no usable product is produced. Planning is followed by a comprehensive development cycle. All changes to the scope are handled with massive change requests. As the product is not usable until the end of the project, there is no possibility of canceling a project at a specific point without massive losses. The excesses of this deviation (unfortunately, of course, also handled by a traditional fixed-price contract) can cause unpleasant additional costs and shift delivery dates, escalating to the point of resulting in "black swans"(see Chapter 1).

We have had discussions with a customer who said quite frankly that it is difficult to decide to stop an $8 million project after $7 million have already been invested, almost no business value was created, and the supplier argues that for a variety of reasons (e.g., many change requests) an additional $4 million needs to be invested.

What legal and commercial framework is needed for these issues to assure continued successful running of an IT project? How is a traditional fixed-price contract viewed from the point of view of the parties involved?

The traditional fixed-price contract from the perspective of the customer

The traditional fixed-price contract results partly from the traditional tender process that is already well established in the average company. Purchasing

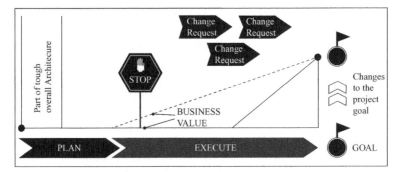

Figure 2.3   *Classic failure of the waterfall model.*

department staff members often still view it as an attractive alternative because they are familiar with the associated purchase and negotiation process, and the ex ante price is considered to result in the lowest risk for the customer. The existing target achievement models (employee bonus) for the purchasing department are aimed primarily at fixed-price contracting. By holding on to the waterfall principle, the procurement people also escape conversion to project-oriented behavior (see Chapter 7). It is exactly the target achievement model seen from the perspective of the customer ("how much can the original fixed-price offer be negotiated down?"), which is often a point for discussion, as the company's goal ("the company requires a specific value or a specific function and can allocate a certain budget for this") may not fit with personal goals. From the perspective of the overall advantages in achieving a successful IT project, for many years it has been debated whether it is time to abandon fixed-bid projects in view of their disadvantages to customers (Ambler, 2005). In fact, the numbers of those who have already witnessed massive failures on the customer side are increasing, and they are therefore willing to try new ways to minimize risk and ensure success. Or, as expressed by Markus Hajszan-Meister: "Yes. New approaches are desirable."

The traditional fixed-price contract from the perspective of the supplier

Viewed from a supplier's perspective, you can very calmly face the disadvantages of the traditional fixed-price contract with a good project manager and the appropriate expertise in place. In the traditional fixed-price contract, the supplier must ultimately deliver what is specified in the contract requirements. If parts are missing, there is a change request, which, since the project has already been awarded to the supplier, can be priced without pressure from the competition. Such change requests are, of course, produced only when requirements change. However, as noted earlier, in a project lasting one and a half years, this could easily be up to 50% of the total project scope! All this is additional revenue for the supplier while leaving the doors wide open for the supplier's attempts to conceal its own failures (e.g., a time delay) during discussions about additional expenses and revised schedules.

Normally, the expertise on a project is higher on the supplier side than on the customer side. In this respect, the fixed-price contract usually contains a comprehensive catalog of assumptions added by the supplier. These assumptions allow a supplier to clearly differentiate its offering despite incomplete or poorly detailed specifications (of course within the legal obligations of being the expert). Perhaps you have built or renovated your own house or know someone who has done so. We guess that the construction company did not assume great risks in their offer regarding the construction work. With their expertise, the construction company could clearly differentiate between the original offer and often overpriced, services/changes requested later and thus create a very acceptable outcome. If you are a not a practicing structural engineer yourself, the supplier is at a clear advantage, and so it is with the supplier of IT projects.

The average customer's opinion that he or she is at least on the "safe side" in selecting a large supplier when it comes to a fixed-price contract is not shared by the present authors. Due to their political weight, large suppliers can enforce additional revenue on the basis of change requests without customer resistance, and this makes the situation even worse for a customer executing a project based on a traditional fixed-price contract. For example, Vodde and Larman (2010) reported that a large software supplier in India made very good business from such a setup and did not complain at all that too many change requests were being generated.

We have witnessed a discussion between key account managers regarding a project with a volume of $2 million with an estimated additional $5 million in change requests! And we were not, in fact, too surprised by this incredible handling of the revenue stream.

The traditional fixed-price contract from the perspective of the consultant

Consultants are often brought in as external experts to assist in the selection process or for key roles in a project. The biggest drawback is that most consultants have no experience with the agile form of contracting, which is not surprising, as this is not yet a widely discussed area. Or they may unfortunately be of the opinion that customers feel more comfortable with the current traditional fixed-price contract, with which they as consultants also have more experience. The traditional fixed-price contract is therefore an opportunity for them to hone their expertise.

In particular, for contracts that are not supported by cooperative spirit and mutual trust, customers like to use external expertise and experience to increase the probability of a successful project. Success is never guaranteed, however, and this is a risk for a consultant who is not content with being associated with failing projects. Basically, the number of customers who need assistance in the scoping and implementation of an agile fixed-price contract is likely to be large. Because projects based on an agile fixed-price contract are accompanied by a much better atmosphere, they should become more interesting to consultants. This would improve the customers' view of consultants thus increasing their reputation after such a project.

2.2   THE PROBLEMS WITH TIME AND MATERIALS CONTRACTS

Many IT projects cannot be described fully and clearly in advance. Such a description is not even useful, because you often cannot guess what could still change during the project. This raises the legitimate question of whether IT projects should not be carried out based on time and materials contracts. The customer buys the resources with appropriate knowledge and experience and uses it to achieve the project goals. Project managers can compensate for changes in project scope simply by shifting the focus of the delivery performance of these resources. But let's look at what in practice constitutes a time and materials contract from the perspectives of the parties involved.

The time and materials contract from the perspective of the customer
Micromanagement and constant supervision are necessary to get the maximum value out of the resources available to a project. The entire responsibility for what and how something is done is up to the project manager and thus the customer. This is not an easy task, because a project manager is usually confronted with a large number of employees of the service provider. Experience has taught us that the constant risk should be averted, making the resources indispensable ("knowledge hiding"). The customer is required to work with transparency and constantly monitor the level of documentation delivery performance. This produces questionable efficiency and means paying at the end for time rather than for performance.

Have you ever tried to link a time and materials contract with specific performance commitments? This is usually possible only with difficulty or, if you think it through, means ending with a contract construct very similar to that of an agile fixed-price contract.

The time and materials contract from the perspective of the supplier
In the sales process, the supplier always places the best horses in the race. They work under the premise that the maximum performance, transparency and documentation must be delivered to the customer. However, the staff of the provider often performs inadequate documentation, thus promoting client dependency. More purchase orders from the customer inevitably follow, and the skilled employees responsible for the missing documentation make a career move on the supplier's side. Additionally, the supplier's management wants to maximize profits and will try, within a framework of acceptable quality, to replace the expensive resources and skills with cheaper ones. And let's face it: A project that takes much longer but is still acceptable under the

political term "successful project" (not "successful" as defined above) is definitely commercially successful from the perspective of the supplier if it is delivered based on time and materials contracts.

The time and materials contract from the perspective of the consultant

A time and materials type of agreement is often in the best interest of the consultant as well as of the supplier. The consultant is also usually a supplier on the basis of time and materials. Apart from this, the consultant can be very experienced in this part of the overall picture in counteracting disadvantages that arise for customers during these contracts. He or she can judge whether the service provided was of adequate quality and whether it has been documented sufficiently. However, the effort and detail inherent in this work are rarely sufficient to secure the performance of such a time and materials–based project over a longer period.

In an interview in February 2012, Walter Jaburek, a court-certified expert on information technology and telecommunications, described an appropriate framework for time and materials contracts:

> In rural areas a small supplier can successfully work for years for a company in the small and medium enterprise sector on the basis of time and materials. The interdependence ensures quality and honesty, which is the foundation for a functioning time and materials project and which is still taken seriously.

What is lacking in this type of contract is the clear position to pay, not for time, but for performance (value or business value) which is necessary to achieve the common project goals. This is precisely one of the core aspects of an agile fixed-price contract.

2.3 SOMETHING NEW: THE AGILE FIXED-PRICE CONTRACT

We have seen the disadvantages and problems brought on by traditional forms of contracts. We also know the inevitable trend toward Agile replacing traditional development methodologies more and more. There are therefore clear signals from both sides that a new form of contract is advisable for IT projects. This fact is also a major topic of recent discussions of "Agile experts," who are thinking in similar directions (Kelly, 2012). An optional form of such a contract must offer, at a minimum, the possibility to:

- Deal with changing requirements
- Avoid costly detailed requirements before the start of a project as much as possible, while keeping the subject matter, principles of cooperation, and the price within limits
- Comply with the quality and budget limits specified

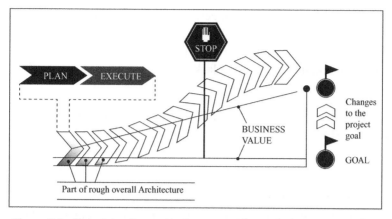

Figure 2.4 *Project development in the context of an agile fixed-price contract.*

- Ensure transparency and timely communication
- Evaluate performance in short intervals
- Deliver an early return on investment through a sprint's results, which may already be used after successful acceptance
- Establish a permanent feedback cycle to include the learning curve in further detailed planning
- Work with a project vision that supports the target focus as a basis
- Make agile development projects clearly capitalizable

What all this means exactly we look at in later chapters. Corresponding to the representation of fixed-price and waterfall contracts, Figure 2.4 summarizes the idea of agile delivery, for which the agile fixed-price contract has been created. After the first sprint, which might still be influenced by overall architectural issues, the direction (detailed scope) is adjusted accordingly through small iterations during the course of the project so as to adapt to the changing requirements. From the beginning, software is created that has an ever-increasing customer value (business value). The option to terminate the project, for whatever reason, exists because the customer can use the product already delivered.

2.4 SUMMARY

For traditional fixed-price contracts, there is:

- Only one regulator, in the tendering stage
- A scope that must be clearly described in detail initially

- The possibility of scope changes, but only through expensive change requests
- Almost no transparency during the project
- Limited communication and a lack of cooperation and responsibility for success on the customer side

How often have we heard that until close to the end of a project, everything actually looked very good.

For time and materials contracts, there is:

- A permanent regulator in the optimal case.
- Dependence solely on price per job level, not on performance. Thus, there are no consequences for the supplier if the project should get out of control financially.

For this reason you can specify this method for a customer, but you carry the entire burden of project management and project risk.

3

What Is an Agile Fixed-Price Contract?

The main characteristic of a shift to the agile paradigm is that the scope of an IT project is in contrast to the classic waterfall model, no longer fixed in detail from the start (Figure 3.1). Instead, costs and time are defined on the basis of principles agreed over the course of the project, and the scope of services is developed and implemented step by step in short iteration cycles (see Chapter 1). This means that the assumption of a detailed prediction of the scope is omitted. For this model to be reflected in the contract, an agile fixed-price contract does not define an exact scope but, rather, supports an empirical process.

An agile fixed-price contract defines a contractual framework within which time and costs are agreed upon, as well as a structured approach to steer the scope within boundaries and by processes in a defined and controlled manner. Thus, the contractual structure of an agile fixed-price contract reacts to two uncertainties. On the one hand, you never know exactly what details will be needed at the start of a project. On the other hand, you do not always need everything that had originally been considered to be important. This may only become apparent during the project's progress or perhaps only after project completion. An agile fixed-price contract therefore includes scope control,

Agile Contracts: Creating and Managing Successful Projects with Scrum, First Edition.
Andreas Opelt, Boris Gloger, Wolfgang Pfarl, and Ralf Mittermayr.
© 2013 John Wiley & Sons, Inc. Published 2013 by John Wiley & Sons, Inc.

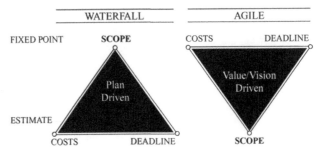

Figure 3.1   *Value-driven projects.*

which makes a decision possible as to whether a specific feature should be more or less complex or whether it needs to be produced at all during the actual development process.

This does not mean, however, that customers have no idea what they are getting for their money at the start of a project. It means that customers know right from the beginning what they will have to spend to meet the business requirements, which have been defined at a moderate level of detail at the start of a project.

3.1   EXISTING APPROACHES

The literature on agile methodologies often includes evidence that points in the direction of a contractual framework similar to the one described here (see, e.g., Poppendiek, 2011). However, up until now, nobody has dealt with it in much detail from the overall process perspective (how to tender such a contract and how to negotiate and manage it). Rather, the focus has been on the agile methodology in the project (with various books on Scrum and agile project management, such as Pichler, 2012) with some brief comments on contracting. This is a definite deficit, and experts such as Walter Jaburek address it in the following way: "If agile methods are used, this should of course be reflected in the contract" (interview in February 2012). Our research has shown that lawyers are also starting to deal with this subject. For example, the Munich-based lawyer Marcus Antonius Hofmann has devised a template for projects that are being developed using agile methods: http://www.ra-hofmann.net/en/kompetenz/itrecht. Another sample contract can be obtained from the DSDM consortium (www.dsdm.com; accessible by members only). These can at least act as starting points on this subject. However, you may need to supplement various practical approaches to how to steer an IT project in the direction of a genuine fixed-price contract according to the agile method.

Approaches that closely resemble the agile fixed-price model can be found in the literature on IT contracts for fixed-price projects. Also, the reduction in risk for cost estimates on the basis of reference values has already been mentioned in the literature. For example, Overly et al. (2004) and Landy and Mastrobattista (2008) have tackled this topic. The most suitable reference is that of Larman and Vodde (2010; also cited at www.agilecontracts.org), who have presented various contract types that come close to what we present here. In their work they have a strong focus on changing the mindset on the legal side, whereas this book focuses on the setup, the tender phase, and the practical aspects of project management as such.

One useful page is maintained by Alistar Cockburn (2012), who lists various possible approaches to agile contracting. Beyond this, the available literature on the details (e.g., how to tender such a project) is still limited, and this book sets out to help fill this gap.

One approach we also use in situations where one or two projects are based on the agile fixed-price method has generated a "feeling" for the scope on both sides, and an environment of trust is to sell scope in small junks: namely, in sprints. How this can be calculated has been described comprehensively by Jesse Fewell (2012). Based on a "bulletproof" traditional fixed-price contract, on the one hand, and the initial idea of contracts for Scrum-based projects, on the other, we have developed the agile fixed-price contract. It combines the need for a fixed budget with the basics of agile development and project management methods. Let's look at how this balancing act is possible.

3.2 THE AGILE FIXED-PRICE CONTRACT

We first describe, in practical terms, what steps are necessary to set up an agile fixed-price contract. An appropriate contract template with detailed formulation proposals for the individual topics is provided in Chapter 4. The agile contract is characterized by the fact that the initial work toward detailed specifications is distributed over the project phases. Thus, the requirements are refined just in time. This approach:

- Reduces the knowledge decay.
- Simplifies adaptation to changes of scope.
- Allows a quick project start.
- Offers the advantage that the new parts of the detailed requirements have already been created, on the basis of cooperation and knowledge of the previous deliveries within the framework of the project's accumulated experience. This allows communication between the parties to improve iteratively. This is an extension of the Deming cycle (see Chapter 1) in the detailed specification phase. This means that the quality of the detailed specifications from customers and suppliers is improved iteratively before each sprint. This is a huge advantage for understanding between departments, IT, and suppliers.

In addition:

- Changes in project scope (the "exchange for free") are possible and are provided at no extra cost.
- A common approach to cost estimation and deliberate governance is agreed to contractually.
- It is a cooperative agreement that keeps motivation high for all sides involved, and, hopefully, leads to project success.

In Chapter 8 we establish more precisely the advantages and disadvantages of the agile fixed-price contract compared to traditional contract models. Let us look at the fundamental process of how to get the key parameters and agreements in an agile fixed-price contract and how the approach is understood and lived over the course of a project. An example scenario for this process in a project practice example may be found in Chapter 10.

3.2.1   How Is an Agile Fixed-Price Contract Set Up?

Following are the steps you should consider when developing an agile fixed-price contract.

1. Define the **contract at the level of product or project vision, topics, and epics** from the perspective of the user (i.e., to a level at which the contract is complete but not yet described in detail). Subsequently, develop an appropriate and final legal and commercial framework for the respective agile-delivered project. Negotiate and agree on this framework with your partner to ensure a solid foundation for the negotiation and partnership from the beginning.

2. Specify the **details of an epic, down to the level of the user stories**. The result is a representative set of user stories of varying degrees of complexity if the epic has been selected carefully. A user story at this level has to be described in a sentence or short paragraph describing the feature without specifying all the details required to complete a user story to enter the development cycle.

3. In a joint workshop, an overall estimate is made of the effort required starting from a set of reference user stories from step 2, including the risks of implementation and business value for these user stories. With analogy estimation, the complexity of the entire scope is estimated. Breaking down experiences as to velocity and team costs, this result is an **indicative fixed-price range**—indicative because the price is really fixed only at a later stage.

4. Another step is the fixing of the **riskshare**, exit points, and the checkpoint phase (also with riskshare for exactly this phase). Neither side is obliged to buy a pig in a poke. This agreement also states that after the checkpoint phase, the indicative fixed-price range is converted into a real (i.e.,

"real" instead of the illusionary value of a random fixed price in the traditional contract form) fixed-price range.

5. Agree on the **scope and expense management process** and, of course, the governance of the decision-making process.

6. Agree on a **motivational model and a cooperative model**; consider a bonus system.

Figure 3.2 illustrates this process as divided into a scoping phase (i.e., scope description and cost calculation) and a process definition phase.

In an invitation to tender, these steps may possibly present themselves somewhat differently. In such a case, customers must, of course, specify the requirements according to a process by which they can compare all suppliers at the end. We explore this particular situation in more detail in Chapter 5. The sample of an agile fixed-price contract in Chapter 4 comprises various appendices for different subject matter. This ensures that different work and/ or negotiation streams can work in parallel.

Definitions

- **Indicative fixed-price range.** Before the start of the checkpoint phase, a provisional price is estimated, based on an unformulated rough scope of the subject matter (vision, themes, and epics). This indicative fixed-price range is not yet contractually binding.

- **Riskshare.** The riskshare describes to what extent (percentage) the costs incurred by the supplier will be charged to the customer on failure of the checkpoint phase or when the maximum price range is exceeded. This percentage may, however, vary for the checkpoint phase and the overall project.

- **Checkpoint phase.** A period of x sprints or a performance scope of y storypoints is agreed upon as the test phase of cooperation. The final milestone is a checkpoint whereby the customer and supplier can enter into implementation of the overall project (or maybe not).

- **Exit points.** These are clearly defined points in time where the parties may terminate the project in a controlled manner.

In the following sections we describe each step toward an agile fixed-price contract in more detail.

3.2.1.1 Step 1: Definition of the subject matter of the contract

The basis for the definition of the subject matter of a contract is the contract itself, which includes the fundamental legal, commercial, and sometimes

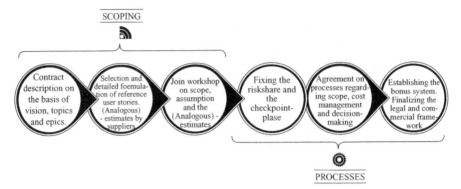

Figure 3.2 *Scoping and process definition for an agile fixed-price contract.*

technical principles and guidelines. Hence, the contract body (e.g., the body of the contract sample in Chapter 4) should exist before step 1 (Section 3.2.1).

The fundamental characteristic of this contract is that the details of the subject matter do not have to be defined and specified in advance (i.e., at the time of contract signing). However, at the beginning, a good overview of the project and its required resulting outcome should exist. Thus, a description of the subject matter should exist at a certain level of detail. The customer needs this, on the one hand, to argue the appropriate business case internally and to select a suitable supplier. On the other hand, it is necessary for the supplier to have a complete picture of the overall requirements at the start of the project and for the overall fixed-price estimation in general.

The agile approach inherently defines a project based on a product or project vision. For example, Roman Pichler (2012) notes that it is essential that the entire team, from the product owner to the individual team member, shares this vision. Therefore, as a first milestone, the vision is established as a central element in the contract. A vision should contain the topics that are the minimal outcomes of the project to maximize the business value. In addition, the vision should contain the major framework conditions for a project. One such condition could be, for example, that the software integration project does generally solve requirements with available out-of-the-box functionality of the software to be integrated.

As shown in Figure 3.3, this vision is then divided into more detailed levels.

1. We begin with the topics, a list of the major areas that should be covered by the project.
2. The topics are further refined into epics, which represent substantively related groups of user stories.
3. On the granualized level of detail, the user stories exhibit properties corresponding to the acronym INVEST: independent, negotiable, valuable,

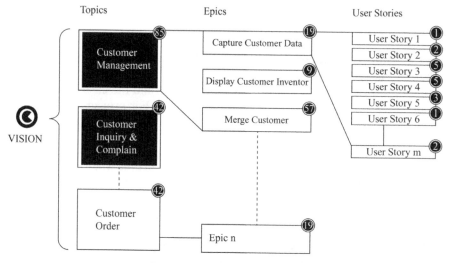

Figure 3.3 *Detailing the vision.*

estimable, small, testable. These requirements can be implemented and are also individual elements that represent an added value for customers. It includes clear functions that can pass quality assurance (and are definable and deliverable separately).

In the first step the contract is defined, at most, only up to the level of the epics. It is agreed upon that this list of all topics and epics (the backlog; see Chapter 1) is complete. The essential advantage of this approach is that the product vision can usually be broken down very efficiently to the level of the epics. Requirements and customer value are comprehensible here without additional definition requirements.

How extensive the description of the topics and epics should be lies at the discretion of the customer, who describes the subject matter of the contract. However, in practice it proves extremely useful that customers, service providers, and even the entire development team or parts of it perform this step together. In this way, one gets the greatest possible consensus and the greatest possible understanding or both. In the third step, this joint work allows us to extend these descriptions mutually in order to fill certain gaps in the possible different understanding of the parties (by clarification or assumptions). As a result, even if the scope has not been described in detail, it can be prepared very clearly at the start of the project without conscious "complexity holes." (*Note:* Complexity holes involve understanding the requirements on a certain level of detail, behind which at a closer look we find plenty of effort that one has not recognized in the initial description.) The challenge in trying to master this step is to limit the scope on the basis of facts. These facts are not, as often assumed, detailed specifications but, rather, high-level information, complexity, and uncertainty (see, e.g., Goodpasture, 2010).

3.2.1.2 Step 2: Detailed specification of an exemplary amount of reference user stories

In the second step, a representative epic is selected, and the customer creates a complete list of required user stories for this epic. For projects of a certain size, it might also be appropriate to select up to three epics for this step.

Representative here means that you do not select an epic when it is a side issue. For example, the epic "system health check" should not be selected during the implementation of a Customer Relationship Management (CRM) system. It is important for the operation of the system, but not for the core subject of CRM and its specific complexity. You might ask the question: How can people from various departments with different levels of knowledge and interests—which are often one of the major reasons that IT projects can become so complex—simply define user stories? For one thing, these department members have to make themselves available as contact persons for the development team. On the other hand, a "scope governance" committee should be formed on the initiative of the customer's project manager and the product owner, to define and steer the requirements. All the key people should be present: those with the appropriate expertise and decision-making power, depending on the type of user story. The user stories should be written together and mutual decisions made regarding their accuracy. This committee should perhaps be constructed on two levels: the authors and the decision makers.

This list of user stories is not yet specified in detail (for this epic); instead, each user story is described in only a paragraph. Depending on the option (time, effort, risk minimization), as many user stories as possible are then specified in more detail. You should make sure that different types of user stories with a differing range of functionality are selected. These user stories serve as reference user stories. On the basis of these stories, and in preparation for the joint workshop with the customer (step 3), the remaining epics from the supplier are estimated based on rough descriptions by the customer. On this basis, on the one hand, efforts can be extrapolated, and on the other hand, the reference user stories help the customer to assess the expertise of suppliers. In migration projects, such user stories support an assessment as to how well the standard product used supports the functionality required.

The agile estimation methodology applied by the supplier is based on an analogy estimate (A is twice as complex as B; see Chapter 1). In addition, a triangulation is used intuitively (A is more complex than B but not as complex as C). This method improves the accuracy considerably. [***Note:*** *We understand an estimate to be exact when it is close to the actual value and when the value has identical or very similar results after repeated estimation trials. Details on agile estimation methods are described by Cohn (2005) and Gloger (2011), among others.*]

Why story points and not simply person-days?   The question is often asked: Why do we not use traditional person-days to estimate efforts and costs but go, instead, via a new term and entity?

The first reason is, in fact, quite simple. In an agile project, we want to express project progress by the amount of functionality delivered. We want to know how many pieces of the total functionality will be delivered during the project. We also need to know how much functionality the entire product will cover. Story points (see Chapter 1) represent the value for the amount of functionality and give a very good indication of the productivity of a team: what share of the total delivery of the project has already been provided, not how many hours were "burned away."

A second reason is an empirical value: Estimations based on story points can be performed much faster than traditional cost estimates and also avoid certain traps inherent in a person-day estimation. Coupled with an estimation method called magic estimation introduced by Boris Gloger, very large projects can be estimated in just a few hours.

Magic Estimation

The planning poker described in Chapter 1 fails for large teams and extensive backlogs. Boris Gloger has developed a guessing game based on an idea of Lowell Lindstrom. This game surpasses all previous methods in accuracy and speed and allows a team to make better estimates in a shorter time than when using planning poker. Magic estimation is not only faster, it can also be played in large groups with more than 100 backlog items. A backlog of approximately 70 entries can be estimated by a group of approximately 10 people in about 20 minutes with sufficient accuracy.

Magic Estimation: The Game

1. The product owner prepares all backlog items on cards or printouts.
2. He or she prepares a scale from 1 to 100, and in setting up these numbers, attempts to represent the associations through the gaps between the numbers (it does not have be precise), something like this:

(Continued)

1, 2, 3, . 5, . . 8, ... 13, ... 20, ... 40, ... 100

3. The product owner then distributes the backlog item cards within the team. Each team member receives approximately the same number of cards.

4. The game is played completely silently, and cards may not be shared.

5. Each team member reads through his or her backlog items and submits them to the number representing his or her opinion of the understanding of the backlog items. The following applies: The higher the number, the lower the understanding. Only values displayed on the scale are valid and not intermediate values.

6. When a team member has distributed his or her card, he or she reads the cards that were interpreted by other team members. He or she may change the position of a card if the opinion that this card belongs to a different position. All team members perform this reading and "fixing" in parallel and without consulting others.

7. The product owner observes the team when performing this action. When the owner sees that a card jumps, he or she marks this card. A card jumps if it is moved repeatedly to a new position by a team member. It can be seen clearly when a difference of opinion exists.

8. The last step in distributing the cards: When a team member does not know what a card means, that card is placed in the 100th position.

9. The game ends when no more cards are moving or when only "jumping" cards remain. The game is also over when more and more team members become bored or turn away.

10. Finally, the team members write the figures obtained on the backlog item cards.

11. As a result, the product owner receives all backlog items according to the understanding that rated = estimated.

What is striking about this approach is that there is no reference value. It becomes unnecessary because each card automatically becomes a reference for every other card. For the procedure to work in larger groups, all backlog items should be written legibly. The larger the team, the more space is needed. The cards should be written so that they can be read from 4 meters away.

This game is about an "intuitive" estimate of the scope of functionality. Our experience shows that this estimate is significantly more accurate than other methods. The process belongs in the category "You have to have tried it once." Most teams that try it continue to use it.

3.2.1.3 *Step 3: Workshop on the overall scope*

After the second step, all the user stories from the epics selected are estimated based on their complexity in story points (do this for up to three epics, but not more). This serves as a basis for the joint workshop on the overall scope which is the goal of this third step. In Figure 3.3 you can see how these estimates are recorded in the form of story points as numbers in the circles in the user stories. The sum of these story points represents the scope for the first epic.

However, at this point it is recommended that you do an overall magic estimation on the epic level as well as for your user stories in a joint workshop with the customer. A joint workshop offers the following advantages:

- The customer understands at which point the supplier recognizes the complexity.
- Both parties understand how the other interprets the written requests.
- In the course of the workshop, the descriptions of the epics and topics are jointly complemented and enhanced through clarifications or assumptions, to eliminate ambiguity. On the one hand, the customer can narrow down the complexity with a better understanding, and on the other hand, the supplier can minimize the uncertainty of the estimates.

During the workshop the list of epics is estimated. In the last cycle, the epics for the topics are summed up, it being assumed that all epics exist. As mentioned earlier, the way the estimation is set up is strongly dependent on the project and the people involved. However, the key message is that this should either be done jointly or at least verified and approved jointly.

It is normal that during the workshop's magic estimation, discussions follow on epics that were moved often. These epics will be discussed and the result will often lead to an update of the epic (to make it clear what's meant and what's not meant).

- It is possible that all the topics are defined but that not all epics exist. In this case the estimate can be completed at the topic level with an estimate analogy on the basis of story points.
- It is also possible that the topic level is not used and the backlog is just build up on the epic level.

We recommend an additional verification and validation based on the sums of the topics. This means that the sums on the topic level can be checked against each other once again at the end of the workshop. For example, a topic "Administration Interface," with 200 story points, compared with the topic "Customer Management," with 20 story points, would indicate a possible error in the bottom-up estimating (unless this complexity distribution is the feature of this project). The result is the total number of story points for the project.

In the joint discussion among the supplier, consultant, and customer, assumptions taken originally from only one side with the existing information (in step 2) can be massively influenced by additional definitions that are made together. Here, variations of up to +500% and −80% compared to the original estimate are not uncommon. This uncertainty would have to be carried by one of the parties in a traditional fixed-price project (i.e., this uncertainty would increase the likelihood of project failure). This workshop is an essential part of the process of agile fixed-price contracts and reduces this uncertainty precisely.

We highly recommend that after or even during the course of the estimate, the parties also estimate the following values for each element (i.e., topic, epic, user story):

- **Business value.** Here the customer discloses why a particular feature represents a certain value for him or her in a business. For example, a mapping feature that appears quite unimportant from a supplier's perspective can mean the possibility to manage a legacy system to reduce currently high operational costs. A practical structuring of business values is, for example, the MuScoW method (Gloger, 2011) or also through this feature, a tangible deposit with anticipated savings or revenue in the next x years. Alternatively, the business value could be a distribution of 100% for the entire backlog down to its elements: that is, how much a feature contributed to the business case calculation on the customers' side (based on the assumption that all features are built because they help to earn money or reduce costs).
- **Implementation risk.** Here it is indicated which requirements contain a risk in the implementation (i.e., small, medium, high, or very high values). The reasons may be different (e.g., a complex algorithm that is difficult to test or an implementation part with which the team has little experience). It is important that these risks be discussed clearly and openly.

Cindy Alvarez (2011) has stated that without this transparency the prioritization and control of a project very often go in the wrong direction. If you do not understand why a party wants to have a certain feature given a certain priority, there is a risk that everyone will insist that his or her perception is correct. This is also essential in supporting the later scope governance process because you already have at hand the first arguments as to why something needs to be done.

The customer is always interested in the cost of a project. In this respect there is still a last estimate missing. The supplier estimates in detail the user stories that have been specified as to the cost of that effort/complexity. (The approach from the perspective of the tender is slightly different, as discussed in Chapter 5). This is one of the sticking points in which the entire experience of the supplier comes into play. Together with the widest expertise on the subject, the knowledge of the team and the resources available, the perception of the customer is added to assign a value here. This value should be explained to the customer so that he or she can better understand it. The explanation, comments, and assumptions also allow customers to understand any differences between multiple suppliers and to minimize their own risk (see Section 3.2.1.4). This estimate is often performed by a highly experienced panel of senior developers, architects, and project managers. With the experience and a large number of estimators, one can achieve relatively good accuracy. This is a crucial point where others also highlight the fact that extreme care has to be taken if predictions are made on this level based on past knowledge (Schaber and Sutherland, 2012). We recently had a project wherein a feature "create new customer" within the integration of a standard product was estimated with relatively high complexity and thus costs. Before it was explained that this is because eight different checks on external systems are required to be integrated, the customer was upset. Afterward he understood and decided which checks do have a high business value and which he could eliminate from the scope to reduce complexity.

The value that you now get for a representative set of user stories is averaged. The result is a conversion value of story points to team costs (or the other way around). This is an initial value that is verified in the course of the later-described checkpoint phase, corrected if necessary to represent a more realistic velocity. (*Note: Velocity refers to the number of story points that a team has implemented in a sprint, which also reflects the costs of each story point for a given team*).

Of course, it would be better if the customer would get only story points and the time line and costs would be obtained gradually (see the quote from Mitch Lacey in Chapter 1). But we cannot ignore the reality of large companies. Each customer must have budget security and know the costs in advance so that a business case can lead to a project being started.

Finally, customer and supplier discuss the applicable margin of safety (if necessary), which can be higher or lower due to the severity of the following factors:

1. The complexity of the topic
2. Knowledge on the customer side
3. Expertise on the supplier side
4. The quality of the description of the feature

The most important thing, however, is that both parties help to shape the emergence of the cost estimate and understand it.

At the end of this third step, there is a maximum price, called the indicative fixed price, for an agile IT project. This price is co-created, understood, and supported by both parties.

In contrast to the traditional fixed-price contract, a first step in a contractual framework emerges:

- That is understood by all parties
- That is based on assumptions that both parties have together taken deliberately
- Wherein the supplier and all those involved on the customer's side are aware of the customer value of each function

3.2.1.4 *Step 4: Riskshare, checkpoint phase, and exit points*

Trust-based cooperation is the essential foundation of an agile fixed-price contract. Neither party attempts to shift the blame after contract completion. The following three basic attitudes of cooperation are agreed upon contractually:

1. **Riskshare.** If something does not work (concerning the complexity estimation) as planned, and cannot be compensated within the agreed-upon process, both parties carry the additional expense.
2. **Checkpoint phase.** No one is expected to keep working in the unknown. Foundation and partnership are checked in the first phase (the Checkpoint phase, generally with quite an attractive riskshare for the customer).
3. **Exit points.** Each party may leave the project with a reasonable lead time.

Now we look more closely at how the details of the riskshare, the checkpoint phase, and exit points can be handled. It is important that the parameters can be customized individually in each contract. However, each party must be aware that when parameters are changed too much in favor of one side, it forces to absurdity the basic idea of an agile framework contract, and this, in turn, provokes undesirable behavior on the other side. A common saying also applies here: Structure creates behavior, and the agile fixed-price contract needs to provide the structure for the collaborative behavior of the parties. (see Chapter 7 for more details on negotiation strategy.)

Riskshare. In step 3, the indicative fixed price is "fixed" (where "fixed" means fixed for the time being but possibly subject to change if the Checkpoint phase reveals new information). After the checkpoint phase, this price is converted into a true fixed price (also called the maximum price range, as the final costs might be below the agreed-upon maximum range and not fixed at it). Here, of course, customer's care that this is a realistic price. They want to avoid unrealistic fixed-price values being established where the difference over the course of the project is offset by change requests. The customer wants to pay as few as possible (if any), mostly realistic, security surcharges. The supplier wants first and foremost to deliver a commercially successful project as well as to achieve long-term customer satisfaction by earning a reasonable amount of money. These points cannot be achieved by increased security charges (since the customer might then select a supplier who does not add high security charges at the point of offering a fixed price but presents the bill later) nor by greatly exceeding the customer's project budget through claims of additional expenses through change requests, even when they are justified.

Both parties are aware of this situation, and there are basically two solutions:

1. To prevent change requests and to avoid paying high security charges, the supplier, as an expert, should be able to understand and estimate

exactly what is required according to what the customer has described in detail and completeness. If you prefer this solution, we recommend reviewing Chapter 2, as we see strong evidence that most of the time, this is just not possible.

2. Both parties recognize that there is a chicken-and-egg problem and are open to a riskshare model. This model is simple: If exceeding the maximum price cannot be avoided even through the actions agreed to by the project's governance, the additional supplier costs are charged at only x% of the agreed-upon team costs (or possibly in daily rates per employee level). The value x should lie between 30 and 70% and is one of the parameters that must be fixed during negotiation. But it is important to note that it is absurd to implement the complete model with a value of x below 30%, as the idea of all parties working toward the same global aim gets lost.

If the value of the riskshare is close to 0%, the customer bears all costs in excess, and this is comparable to a time and materials contract. In contrast, high values, which tend toward 100%, are similar those of a traditional fixed-price contract. The processes within an agile fixed-price contract remain different and helpful, but their general advantage in such a one-sided motivation does not exist on the same scale.

How the value of x is defined depends on the following factors:

• Knowledge of the customer and hence of the risk assessment.
• Experience with strict scope control according to the scope governance described in Section 3.2.1.5.
• Experienced suppliers for a cost-based implementation of features. Does the supplier have employees who are so creative as to find a technical solution to the estimated cost that satisfies the customer instead of implementing the solution described?
• Experience within the cooperation between customer and supplier, if available, is also useful. However, this is generally not assumed, and therefore the checkpoint phase is established.

Checkpoint phase.   In principle, every project is quite new territory for everyone involved. Therefore, the parties agree initially to work together up to a certain checkpoint. We recommend three to five sprints, because in the first two sprints, the startup effects can still obscure the actual performance. After five sprints the project should have settled. This first phase, up to the checkpoint, should be set up as if it were simply the first sprint of the project (different from so-called Proof of Concepts, which are often decoupled from the main project); however, either party may leave the project at the checkpoint. In this case, 100% of the performance is reimbursed to the supplier, and delivery (the software increment) is passed to the customer. This is possible with agile development since a possibly usable increment is created. Alternatively, the value of this delivery is not seen by the customer, and the software developed remains the property of the supplier, with only $x\%$ of the work performed (according to the agreed-upon riskshares for the checkpoint phase) being billed to the customer. If it is a system integration project, a software license is required before the start of the project. In this case, the parties agree that the license does not have to be paid until the end of the checkpoint phase or, accordingly, the license may be returned (with the license fee being reimbursed). When a system integration project is terminated at the checkpoint, the customer may either not accept the delivery or the acceptance is possible only if the customer pays for the software license at this point in time (as the software increment would not be usable without the standard software that builds the basis).

At the checkpoint the experiences of this phase are evaluated by both sides and compared with previous assumptions and estimates. In a joint meeting, the definitions and assumptions of the scope of the contract are verified and, if necessary, revised. This must be confirmed in writing by the executive steering group because the contract has already been signed. (*Note:* An executive steering group is a group of decision makers from all parties involved which meets to decide landmark decisions on a project; see Section 3.2.1.5.)

In the process proposed in Chapter 5, these phases (the checkpoint phase and the subsequent total project phase) can also be divided into separate contractual phases. If it is decided by both sides at the checkpoint that the project be continued on the basis of possible modified output conditions, charges at the checkpoint phase are seen as part of the maximum price range of the project and billed according to the contractual payment agreement.

When extended cooperation with a customer exists, we recommend slightly modifying the procedure described in this book. From the customer's perspective, packages of x sprints of functionality can be ordered. Thus, the maximum price will be applied to small packages. This is essentially different from the commission for time and materials, as performance (= functionality) is paid for and not time. We have experienced the fact that collaborations often start with a standard agile fixed-price contract and then get modified slightly toward small package contracting (based on an agile frame contract defining the rules and principles).

The checkpoint phase can somehow be compared with a paid proof-of-concept phase, which is quite common nowadays. However, the difference is that the checkpoint phase is already a part of the project and the customer can, for example, expect that the same people are working in the same mode in the checkpoint phase as they will in the remainder of the project. In proof of concepts, this is very often treated differently. We have too often seen suppliers who provide a small team of their best people during the proof of concept to ensure that the project is won. Then as soon as the project begins, these experts suddenly disappear and the customer is disappointed by a change in behavior, which shifts from delivering to claiming philosophy. In a recent article on agile sourcing, the U.S. consultant Emergyn (2012) stated that they recommend not entering any larger fixed-price contracts without performing a representative trial phase.

Exit points. The first exit point in the project is the checkpoint described above. At the time of the checkpoint the practical cooperation has been tested and both parties make a decision to undertake the entire project together (or not to do so). This is, of course, only the first day of a long journey through still largely unfamiliar territory in which, moreover, the environmental conditions change constantly. In an agile IT project developed within a cooperative approach, each partner should have the option of terminating cooperation (within a certain time frame).

A reasonable time frame should include at least two sprints. In this way, the customer can still prioritize much needed features in these sprints. On the other hand, the supplier may reschedule the resources (to other projects) within this period: accordingly, avoiding idle time and extra costs.

This sounds very insecure. How can you sign a contract from which one party can exit at any time? To answer this, let us first recap the prevailing context parameters:

1. The customer receives a piece of executable software after every sprint. At the end of each sprint, the customer has the current state of development as tested, documented, and executable software. In the case of a standard software license as a basis of a system integration project, the exit points for a possible declining license reimbursement should be agreed upon.

2. The supplier receives compensation for his or her work on a regular basis (e.g., after every sprint).

3. We want to act according to the agile values and do not want to bind the customer or supplier to us simply for the sake of the contract, even in a case where cooperation is not working.

This means that each investment is offset by a business value received. If the supplier terminates the project early, the customer may pass the development on to another supplier, as this is high-quality software, not merely design documents. If the customer terminates the contractual relationship, the supplier can devote his or her time to another project where the customer still "wants" his or her delivery services. It does not generally have a major financial impact on the supplier because the services have been paid for.

Why should the parties use an exit point? Here are a few statements from our experience, and you may have already experienced a similar situation:

- **Customer:** "The project is no longer as important, due to external circumstances." *Question to you as a supplier:* Do you necessarily want to continue with a project when the support from the customer is steadily declining due to the project no longer being needed? Remember that as a supplier, your performance is paid for at the end of each sprint and you cannot expect lucrative change requests at the end of a project.

- **Supplier:** "There is constantly more work within an estimated complexity level, as the customer continually delivers false or inadequate specifications in the user stories, continuing to argu that this is fine." *Question to you as a customer:* Do you want a project delivered from a dissatisfied supplier, or is it so that the preparation or willingness for the project is not really adequate on the customer side? Do you think the project will still be successful if you are not able to provide stable specification's for what you (believe you) need?

- **Customer:** "The features that I need have already been implemented. I really do not need more." *Question to you as a supplier:* Do you want to force the customer to spend money on things that he or she does not need, or do you want to prepare a press release reporting that you have reached full customer satisfaction in the project within (below) the budget agreed upon? Depending on the bonus clause, the remaining budget will be used for other purposes, or just a fraction may be paid to the supplier.

- **Customer:** "The supplier's performance diminishes from sprint to sprint." No response can restrict this trend and for exactly this reason there is a risk that the costs will run out of control. This is not good, in spite of riskshares! *Question to you as a supplier:* There is a reason that performance decreases steadily. From the perspective of reputation, agile methods have a clear advantage in that one must admit to the customer that he or she should look for alternatives, if necessary.

For the following reasons, the supplier should not deliberately force a termination of the contract (unless there is good evidence from his or her perspective that project success will not be reached):

- It will damage the supplier's reputation.
- It influences long-term customer satisfaction and creates a comparative reference effect for other customers.
- The presales effort that resulted in a project should also lead to a project of the planned magnitude.

For the following reasons, the customer should not deliberately force a termination of the contract (unless there is good evidence from the customer's perspective that the project will not be successful).

- The project was started for a good reason and there is a business case behind it.
- A terminated project represents an internal loss of reputation, a disadvantage for all parties involved, even if the damage caused by an agile fixed-price contract is normally kept to a minimum.
- Additional transfer costs and times are created if another supplier takes over the project.

One can therefore assume that exit points are a good thing for both sides. When necessary, they tend to protect both parties against disadvantages. In principle and under normal circumstances, neither party wishes to exit the contract. In terms of the cooperation agreement, this bilateral trust in the partnership, as well as the methodology, should be contractually binding. However, the exit points are a final option to reduce the risk of massive financial loss in certain cases.

3.2.1.5   Step 5: Agreement on scope governance

For a successful IT project employing an agile fixed-price contract, it is necessary to have contractually specified control over the project content (the scope), called *scope governance*, a process that is controlled by contractually specified roles (organizational structure). This process is generally beneficial for all types of contracts; however, in an agile fixed-price contract it is essential, as the project has the task of creating detailed specification's within a high-level scope by keeping the complexity within an agreed-upon range. The roles within scope governance are:

1. **Project manager and product owner.** The responsible contact person on the customer side is the project manager and on the supplier side is the product owner (see Chapter 1).

2. **Scope steering group and executive steering group.** These groups consist of both product owners and authorized decision makers from both parties (project managers should be present for information requests). The scope steering group meets every two to four weeks. In case of urgent additional questions, it is guaranteed that the steering representatives will come to a decision within five working days. In addition to the scope steering group there might be an executive steering group. This group meets every one to two months. What is more essential for the process is the scope steering group, which decouples scope decisions from project day-to-day work.

3. **Independent instance.** An IT expert is selected from both parties before a project begins. For IT projects, this is a new step. A simple pragmatic solution needs to be found for fundamental differences in terms of the scope. This can happen but should not prevent the success of the IT project. (*Note:* For example, validation engineers have been around for a long time in the construction industry.)

The starting point for the scope of governance is a defined contractual scope. The contractual scope, defined in steps 1 and 2 of the process, is based on a high-level backlog (i.e., themes, epics, and a few reference user stories). In addition, at the start of each sprint the highest-priority requirements must be formulated as detailed specified user stories. The number of respective user stories that are formulated in this manner should be about 50 to 100% higher than the expected velocity of the team, projected on the basis of the estimate of story points for the epics. (*Note:* Velocity is defined as the number of story points implemented, tested, and delivered by a team within a sprint.)

This additional preparatory work required for the purposes of specification preparation is contrary to popular opinion. Others highlight that you should specify in detail just enough user stories, just in time (Cohn, 2005). However, a slightly larger backlog makes the following processes easier in that, in deviations and disagreements, a user story can simply be placed on hold, thus avoiding compromising the velocity of a sprint. Also, in recent work on agile project management (e.g., Pichler, 2012) it is recommended that backlog budgets deviate somewhat from the Mike Cohn–influenced optimized variants.

In the course of sprint planning [see Chapter 1 and, e.g., Pichler (2012), Gloger (2011), Schwaber (2003), or Larman and Vodde, (2010)], the development team, together with the product owner, edit consecutive user stories according to the priority in the backlog. The user story continues to be discussed until the development team understands in detail what is expected. The requirements, the tests, the constraints (nonfunctional requirements), and the acceptance criteria are all clarified. Often, a mock-up is developed so that all persons involved have an idea of what the functionality should look like from the perspective of the user. If during discussions on the story it turns out that the functionality of the story is more complex than was estimated originally, three scenarios are now possible:

1. The customer has doubts that the complexity of the request is actually higher. This often happens, due to lack of experience on the supplier side.
2. The supplier has underestimated similar reference user stories, and thus comparability is now missing.
3. The customer has provided additional information or changed assumptions such that the additional complexity points claimed by the supplier can be understood by the customer.

In all cases the scope governance process starts now. If it does not lead to the desired results, the scope escalation process follows.

Scope governance process. To comply with the maximum price range agreed to contractually, the scope governance process is defined within the sprint plannings as follows:

1. If the functionality of the user story lies within the boundaries of the contract's security limits, this value is entered in the scope governance list. If there are no security limits, the parties are aware that the high-level estimates will still deviate on single backlog items. If such a deviation is in a range where the parties have set limits on what is acceptable or a buffer has been created within the scope governance list during the project, this value is entered in the scope of governance list (it is assumed that the deviations even out over all the backlog items).
2. For each user story whose scope of function is now increased and exceeds the security limits or general deviation limit for backlog items that has been agreed the next step in the process is initiated.
3. Both parties work together to try to simplify the already defined user stories on the fly. The customer value must be retained. The complexity values (in story points) for the old and newly defined user stories are recorded and labeled in a scope governance list by the project managers (or product owner). In this way, you can trace from the original user story that a new one with less (but essentially enough) functionality was generated. The process can be completed for this user story and the parties can progress with the next prioritized user story.
4. If no solution is found in step 3, the parties define some more user stories for the epics that are to be carried out subsequently in one of the next sprints and try to reduce their complexity to compensate. Here, too, the customers' business values must remain, but the implementation costs should be at a much lower value compared to the initial analogous

estimate, as it is too high for the currently located user stories in the process. The values for these user stories should be entered accordingly and labeled by the project managers in a scope governance list. The process can be completed for this user story, and the parties can progress with the next prioritized user story.

5. In the next step, a proposal is developed regarding which user stories or epics could be eliminated or adapted significantly (customers' business values changed) in order to continue to maximize the business value achieved within an investment at the maximum price range. Our experience indicates that this is possible to achieve, as a part of the requirements usually offer only a very limited business value. These requirements are not must-haves but, rather, should-haves. This action may only be incorporated into the next sprint after approval by the steering group. (*Note:* This is in contrast to the "creeping" de-scoping of traditional fixed-price projects described in Chapter 2.)

6. If neither of these options is acceptable to both parties, either party may call the scope steering group to make a decision (the scope escalation process; see below). The parties therefore agree that this complexity is higher than originally estimated. This cannot be attributed to an aggressive estimate of the reference user stories but simply to "hidden" complexity. The project manager and product owner are unable to demonstrate a way to control the problem within the budget framework.

Scope escalation process.   The most important point of each meeting of the scope steering group is that the scope governance list is presented and evaluated with regard to the actual plan and also for deviations resulting from the preceding process. The scope steering group must sign this list in the respective steering group protocol in accordance with set policies and decisions. If no agreement is possible within the framework of the scope governance process, the following scope escalation process will be initiated:

1. The scope steering group representatives are presented with the facts prepared by the project manager and product owner. Special attention is paid to the actions that have already been attempted unsuccessfully.

2. The scope steering group representatives try to agree on finding a compromise. This can look different depending on the situation. An example would be that the supplier charges for only some of the story points. The risk of the customer trying to force this too often is low. Furthermore, the riskshare is in place for the total exceedance of the maximum price range, and this could still mean a time delay, which in turn would place the success of the project in jeopardy.

3. If no agreement is found during the scope steering, this must be escalated to the executive steering group (if this additional level is available in the project organization). The executive steering group has an even more

distant view on the project and might be able to negotiate a compromise.

4. If no agreement is found during this steering, then within five working days, and if required by one of the parties, a predetermined expert (independent instance) is entrusted with the facts. The costs, outside the maximum price range, are shared equally between the two parties. The expert delivers his or her opinion, and both parties include this information in the decision to proceed further in the project.

During this process the project itself continues unhindered at the operational level. Both parties understand that the working process is concerned as the normal change process in a project, unlike in the traditional fixed-price contract, where calling a third-party expert would be the ultimate escalation level, associated with stopping and reversing the project. This highest level of escalation should still be included cautiously in the process. At the very least, it should be stated in the contract that after the third decision by an expert, each party has the right to terminate the project with a lead time of only one sprint (the conventional exit point can be after one or after several sprints).

3.2.1.6 Step 6: How the cooperation model becomes the motivation model

"This project is a success because every employee contributes to the product vision of the project." This attitude should be supported by the contract framework. In practice it is usually not so easy, and often, corporate policy influences the project both directly and indirectly. Therefore, the cooperation model should be strengthened additionally by further action, to be even a motivation model. The motivation model increases the effectiveness of both sides, based on a functioning cooperation. This is made possible by the following two attitudes:

- "Share the savings that may occur."
- "Be the most efficient supplier."

Sharing the savings. Next we look at the contractual regulations of the question of what would happen if a project could be delivered more cost-effectively: completed much lower than at the agreed-upon maximum price. By *completed* we mean that the customer accomplishes the stated business values through the delivery of adequate quality, not through the implementation of all the features that were planned initially.

The customer will select this option when he or she does not yet have to pay the entire fixed price. This would be in contradiction to traditional fixed-price contracts, where under normal circumstances the customer would always demand receiving what was originally agreed upon. However, the supplier will only be motivated to complete the project below the maximum price range when he or she receives some form of bonus for work that is not done. Two possible feasible approaches to such a bonus are:

- The supplier receives a percentage of the price of the residual volume.
- The customer assures the supplier of a new contract to reflect the value of the residual volume.

One of these elements can be put into the contract to ensure that both parties are focusing on the same aim.

Being an efficient supplier. In the cooperation model it is relatively uncomplicated for either party to leave the project. Since the deliverables constitute stand-alone executable software, the customer can naturally use this option, even if the suppliers performance declines. The left side of Figure 3.4 shows how the performance of the team remains constant over time. This means that, on average, a consistent amount of functionality is delivered per sprint (story points). In this case, the supplier is not positioned positively compared to competitors, because each of them could possibly provide the same functionality with the same effort (costs) or even lower (if this alternative supplier would, for example, have cheaper team costs). Therefore, the supplier will endeavor to increase the efficiency of the collective knowledge and experience gained by the team through the duration of the project. In this way the motivation is utilized to ensure that the amount of functionality delivered per sprint is constantly increasing, as shown on the right side of Figure 3.4. The increase in efficiency should not be measured on the first sprint, since startup effects are

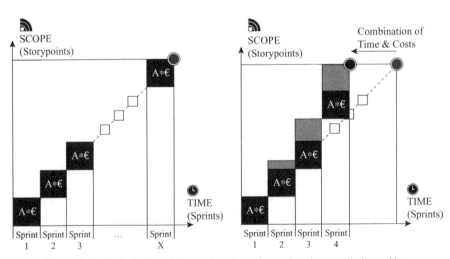

Figure 3.4 *Optimization of the part costs and securing the supplier's position.*

still operational at this stage. Note that the agile process here allows us for the first time to really measure "part costs" in the software industry, and the agile fixed-price contract also makes it possible to benefit from this effect from a contractual point of view. The efficiency will later grow and stabilize at an increased value, after which only slight changes will occur.

The scope steering report should make it clear that the customer also participates in the increased efficiency of the supplier. In the interests of cooperation and "open books," the customer should also be informed of its benefits (see Chapter 9). Any long-term customer relationship is the result of service and openness. Despite this "open" contract with possible exit points, the supplier may secure his or her position here. In addition, the cost per story point is relativized to the supplier over time. If the supplier does not manage to increase performance, there is something wrong with either the project or the supplier, and the scope steering committee should examine this case. Generally, the exit points do offer the opportunity to limit loss in projects that should be stopped or changed (for various reasons) and would perhaps not be stopped based on the wrong contract.

To prevent story points from inflating over time, the product owner and project manager on the customer side should at regular intervals verify new estimates against the original (reference) user stories. These inflationary estimates are quite easily recognizable and can be counteracted.

3.3 SUMMARY

An agile fixed-price contract provides a framework in which a project team can deliver a successful IT project within given budget constraints. The core elements of this agreement are:

- A definition of the scope of the contract in the form of a more detailed vision (epic)
- A definition of complexity for the epics and efforts on the basis of reference user stories
- A checkpoint phase to verify the hypothesis on which the cooperation and the project are based
- A cooperative model in which performance and cooperation are included, exit from the project is uncomplicated, and there is no fixed binding of the parties
- A scope governance process
- A scope escalation process
- Factors to further increase motivation

Naturally, this plan incorporates the setting of a fixed completion date (a milestone). With traditional methods, the impression is given that the plan presented in the contract or elaborated in detail at the start of the project is very realistic. The agile fixed-price contract does, however, just deal with a simple milestone for the start of the final acceptance. The rest of the project is simply divided into sprints (which could also be seen as milestones for every sprint). True to remarks by Helmuth Karl Bernhard Graf von Moltke, it is essentially agreed that "planning is everything, planning is nothing, and no plan survives contact with reality." No further details are poured into a plan that is constantly changing.

4

Sample of an Agile Fixed-Price Contract

In Chapter 3 we described the idea of the agile fixed-price contract and the general process for the preparation of an agile project. In this chapter we include a contractual template. This should not be applied indiscriminately but, rather, serve as a starting point for creating your own agile fixed-price contract. In Chapter 6 we go into more detail on the legal characteristics of the agile contract model.

We have recently worked with a customer who used the first version of this contract template, adapted it very quickly to its specific needs, and included it with the request for proposal (RFP) documents. This was another proof that this template is a good basis, saved time and effort on the customer side, and ensured that each contractor answering this RFP would be compliant with the general setup and methodology of an agile fixed-price contract.

The contract template includes some instructions and explanations (in italics type) that are used as an aid to understanding and are not part of the actual contract. Also, the distribution of contract parts in the main contract and attachments is merely a proposal. Such an arrangement has the advantage that during the tendering process, different teams can work in parallel during discussions on detail (e.g., the technicians within the technical context and the lawyers within the legal framework). This can save a lot of time. Nevertheless, it is necessary that at least the project manager (or product owner) and decision makers know all essential parameters of the agreement.

Agile Contracts: Creating and Managing Successful Projects with Scrum, First Edition.
Andreas Opelt, Boris Gloger, Wolfgang Pfarl, and Ralf Mittermayr.
© 2013 John Wiley & Sons, Inc. Published 2013 by John Wiley & Sons, Inc.

Agreement for the Software Project

[PROJECT NAME]

concluded between

[CONTRACTOR]

hereinafter contractor

and

[CLIENT]

hereinafter client

PREAMBLE

(***Note:*** *In this section it is particularly important to clearly highlight the essential basic principles as a backdrop for the project.*)

According to the defined scope (backlog in Appendix B) of this project and the current state of industry software development, the parties agree on an agile approach to the implementation of this project. In particular, the following principles apply:

(a) Maximum transparency of costs for both parties.

(b) Maximum price certainty for the client.

(c) After each sprint the contractor delivers a tested increment of the deliverables that fulfill the agreed quality criteria agreed upon (see Appendix D).

(d) Continuous monitoring of commercial and technical progress of the contract by both parties.

(e) Clear principles according to which the project is carried out and a clear project vision as a representation of the project objective.

(f) Cooperative partnerships within the project teams:

- Timely and practical specifications of requirements through user stories and sprints, whereby the client is actively responsible and involved in their definition.
- Instant communication in case of problems, even if the cooperation is at risk.

(g) Maximum flexibility in implementation of the project:

- One of the parties may find it necessary to change the scope during the course of the project, for whatever reason. In this case, the other party will consider whether this request can be met without the agreed-upon maximum price range being altered, perhaps through changes in the complexity of other—so far not implemented—requirements.

- If applicable, in the case of insurmountable problems of cooperation between the parties, the software project can be stopped without major expenses or transferred to a third contractor.

§1   DEFINITIONS AND CLARIFICATIONS OF TERMS

(***Note:*** *To avoid misunderstandings, definitions of key terms should be established and listed.*)

(a) **Definition of requirements.** All existing requirements are collected in the backlog. The nonfunctional requirements are listed as constraints to the project vision and are valid for each single backlog item.

The requirements of the overall project are specified in different levels of detail at the conclusion of this agreement: The overall project scope is defined by a project vision and the backlog defined in Appendix B. This backlog is divided into individual topics. These are further detailed in various subtopics: that is, as epics. For effective realization during the course of the project, an epic is divided into the required number of user stories.

- **Backlog.** The list of all topics with appropriate prioritization and complexity or effort rating. This list includes the epics and user stories contained therein where already defined. At least on the level of detail of the epics, the backlog is a complete description of the project scope. (*Note:* This means that the scope is flexible within its details but still defined.)

- **Topic.** A group of requirements, from a business perspective, whereby each topic is on a very high level of abstraction and is described concisely in a short paragraph. The description is sufficient for experts to assess the complexity and thus also the scope of work. For the avoidance of uncertainty, each topic can be extended by a list of delimiting assumptions.

- **Epic.** A topic is divided into functionally-related groups of user stories. These subtopics are called epics. An epic is described concisely in one paragraph with a list of delimiting assumptions.

- **User story.** The description, from a user's perspective, of a specific functionally independent requirement. It includes a sufficient number of test cases (at least three foreseeable and possibly also some bad cases) to check the correct functioning of this requirement.

(b) **Further definitions**

- **Client:** the customer consuming the services and deliverables provided under this agrement.
- **Contractor:** the contracting party providing the deliverables and services.
- **Agreement:** this contract.
- **Services:** the services that are delivered by the contractor in the course of a project to support the delivery process and create the deliverables; defined in Appendix B.
- **Deliverables:** the deliverables that are created and delivered by the contractor; defined in Appendix B.
- **Product owner:** a sort of project manager with deep knowledge of the content of the requirements.
- **Project manager:** the responsible person on the client's side who manages the project.
- **Project managers:** the project manager on the client's side and the product owner on the contractor's side.
- **Project vision:** describes the basic project objectives to be achieved, from the customer's perspective, to ensure the project benefits. The project vision also consider the nonfunctional requirements and constraints that govern the interpretation and realization of each single user story within the project.
- **Documentation:** includes software source code with inline documentation, user stories, and the design document. The documentation allows the client to continue developing the project without the contractor at any time and possibly lead it to completion given that the appropriate relevant expertise is available. However, it is agreed between the parties that this is sufficient documentation and the realization should focus on high-quality software instead of many pages of descriptions.
- **Free-exchange procedure:** a process by which requirements can be exchanged in the course of the project for requirements that are not contained in the project scope, provided that the scope for implementation is equivalent and the requirement exchanged is not yet being implemented.
- **Good case:** description of a desired outcome of a user story.
- **Bad case:** description of an undesired outcome of a user story.
- **Sprint:** the [x]-week iteration in which the client transfers the user stories, with the highest priority from the backlog, into development

by the contractor. The contractor develops and tests the functionality and hands it over to the client at the end of the sprint. The project managers of both parties sign user stories before handing them over to the development team and thus confirm their completeness and comprehensibility. The development teams select the content for the next sprint from this prioritized list of user stories. After delivery of the project increments at the end of each sprint, the project manager signs off on each sprint. Unless otherwise agreed upon, the requirements within a sprint can be developed and approved within two weeks.

(c) **Project managers**

[NAME FUNCTION] client

[NAME FUNCTION] contractor

The project managers of both parties are authorized to make all decisions for this project independently, as long as the steering board does not make certain decisions dependent on their consent.

(***Note:*** *This should be done if possible in the first session. It is advisable to impose as few restrictions as possible on the project managers, to avoid inhibiting the progress of the project by not enabling the project managers. This contract template gives a lot of power to project managers. Hence, such power to act and sign for the specific project as defined in the specific contract should be given formally to the project managers.*)

Decisions are documented at least in weekly protocols and, additionally, confirmed in writing.

(d) **Scope steering board:** the panel, which consists of the following individuals:

[NAME] decision-making representative of the client

(***Note:*** *For situations where more than one department on the client side has a decision mandate on the scope, you either have to decide on one decision maker or all decision makers have to be present on the steering board.*)

[NAME] decision-making representative of the contractor

[NAME] project manager of the client

[NAME] product owner of the contractor

Every meeting of the scope steering board results in a binding protocol signed by both parties. Every decision of the steering board requires approval of the authorized decision-making representative within the steering board.

(e) **Executive steering board:** the panel, which consists of the following individuals:

[NAME] executive representative of the client

[NAME] executive representative of the contractor

one or two people reporting from the scope steering board
Every meeting of the executive steering board results in a binding protocol signed by both executives.

(f) **Written form ("in writing"):** (given if an authorized person signed a document (delivery as PDF-format document possible). All declarations of intent (inspections, sprint specifications, etc.) must be in writing according to this contract.

(*Note: In written form the "signature" of a document has meaning, as masses of e-mails often weaken the importance of such decisions and reduce their accountability. In these times, when an inbox is flooded by masses of e-mails, it might be legally binding to send an email, but in reality many people cannot even read all the e-mails they receive each day!*)

§2   CONTRACT SCOPE AND HIERARCHY OF DOCUMENTS

(*Note: In case of a difference of opinion, the written agreement is used in the first step to find the solution. Therefore, it is important to define the hierarchy of the documents. This is the answer to the question: Which document stands out from the others? If this hierarchy is noted only in the purchase order of the IT project, this can lead to great uncertainty.*)

The project vision and the backlog in Appendix B define the contract scope [NAME] and contain, all the epics and user stories of the epics [NAME OF EPICS] at the time of contract signature.

At the time of order placement, the minimum standard of execution is the existing current state of the technology in terms of accepted industry standards, taking into account the contractual purpose.

The hierarchy of the documents is, in descending order of priority:

(a) Recommendation from a contracted independent expert signed by all authorized decision-making representatives of the scope steering board

(b) Signed protocol from all authorized decision-making representatives of the executive or scope steering board

(c) Signed requirements (user stories) or changes to epics or topics from both project managers, provided that these differ from the original reference user stories and epics in Appendix B

(d) This contract

(e) Appendix A, Commercial Provisions

(f) Appendix B, Technical Provisions: Backlog

(g) Appendix D, Definition of Done

(h) Appendix C, 12 Principles of Cooperation

The documents defined above represent the entire agreement between the parties. Verbal collateral agreements are not valid.

(*Note: We assume that Appendix B contains only the reference user stories for an epic; otherwise, this is the list to refer to. With regard to the analysis of the tender process, see also Chapter 5. The negotiation protocol or order should, if possible, not be included in this hierarchy of relevant documents. Although this is a standard practice, it always leads to legal uncertainties.*)

§3 USAGE RIGHTS

[*Note: License regulations for a usable software product should be in a separate license agreement. In such a case this contract should adopt the rules according to what happens to the license and when, under an agile fixed-price contract, on termination of the project (e.g., at the Checkpoint or any possible exit point).*]

The contractor must transfer to the client all foreground intellectual property rights (IPRs) that have been developed within the scope of this agreement. This includes the resulting software, copyright, and usage rights resulting from this project or acquired by the contractor within the scope of this agreement. In addition, the contractor commits to providing information on the extent of these rights at any time at the client's request, by submitting the appropriate documentation. The contractor keeps all rights on background IPRs (methods, tools, etc.) that existed at the start of the project or were adapted within the course of this project. The client is entitled to pass on to a third party the rights that were awarded to him or her, for free and unrestricted use. The moral rights of the contractor remain unaffected.

(*Note: Here it must be decided whether ownership is, in fact, transferred in the project. Moral rights can be transferred in some countries and not in others. If for example, the contractor is a legal person, it is possible that he may not have the rights. Background and foreground IPRs are generally defined terms but could also be included and listed in the definitions section of the contract. This must be agreed upon in accordance with the contract subject and environment.*)

§4 TRANSPARENCY AND "OPEN BOOKS"

(*Note: This paragraph states that a commitment to transparency exists. It is important to note this because the anticipated process of an agile fixed-price contract can function only in the event of transparency.*)

The contractor is obligated to document the project and the source code and maintain the agreed-upon documentation at all times during project implementation. This should be done such that the client can, at any time, use or further develop the project by sufficiently skilled third parties.

The contractor agrees to submit a detailed report to the client every two weeks. This report should include an accurate account of expenses already incurred, the project progress in comparison with the plan, and a forecast of the overall cost and duration of the project.

Furthermore, the client is entitled to participate at any time in the development process and in on-site meetings with the contractor. This allows the client to create a picture of the cost and of how the contractor operates. The client is actually encouraged within the framework of the procedure agreed upon to participate on-site in the development process.

The contractor agrees to hold daily standup meetings (daily meetings of the development team) that can (as can all other project meetings) be attended by the client.

The contractor agrees to maintain an impediment list (a list of things that impede the progress of development), which is freely accessible and is discussed between the contractor and the client at least every two weeks.

The contractor agrees to forward to the executive steering board all unsolved impediments older than 48 hours, to enforce the requitement for a speedy solution.

The client must assign a contact person on his or her side who is responsible for providing suitable and timely solutions to impediments.

The contractor must provide the client with full insight into development progress at any time, in addition to the two-week deliveries.

§5 ACCEPTANCE

(**Note:** *This paragraph is not formulated exhaustively; rather, it serves only to represent the fact that there should be an interim inspection and final approval. In Example 1 we provide a contract sample with a more extensive formulation. According to any standards, the formulation of the final inspection must still be completed.*)

The agile approach provides both parties with prompt quality assurance and inspections of the intermediate software deliveries (sprints). This is ensured by interim acceptance of the increment delivered from each sprint. The interim acceptances are completed and signed accordingly by both project managers and are binding with regard to the functionality accepted.

The scope of this partial acceptance includes the source code, documentation, and functionality of the software increment delivered. However, subsequent changes in the scope of any user story may lead to changes in the partially accepted functionality. These expenses are compensated for either by reducing the scope of the maximum price range or by additional scope outside the control of riskshares. Still the parties agree that the scope governance group will investigate each such case, as the user stories should generally be independent, although the parties are aware that this might not always be possible.

[***Note:*** *This finding is important because the possibility of changing the scope at a later stage also implies that for cases where the interaction between user stories could not be avoided, existing (partially accepted) parts might need to be reviewed later. The expenses of each change proposed are borne by the overall cost of the change and should not affect the costs of the scope of this agreement, which is guaranteed by both parties by taking over a respective riskshare.*]

A final inspection follows upon completion of the overall performance and concerns verification of the integrative components of the system (i.e., functions that can be verified only through complete integration and capability of the overall system). Functionality that has already undergone interim approval can no longer be withdrawn.

Both parties understand that for new ideas on functionality to emerge inspections are required in the sprint. These new ideas are welcomed, but it does not mean that they will automatically be included in the scope of the project. These ideas are discussed by both parties in the follow-up review (inspection) and it is decided whether these new functionalities should be added to the backlog as new entries. If a new functionality is added, it will be estimated by the development team. The steering board can then decide if this functionality should be included in the scope of the project and, alternatively, which functionality could be removed from the scope of the project.

(***Note:*** *Any additional requirement for the acceptance procedure, such as timlines that each party has to keep when performing acceptance or the resolution of defects that have been identified, must be added to the acceptance procedure.*)

§6 OBLIGATION OF BOTH PARTIES TO CO-OPERATE

(***Note:*** *This is one of the core sections where the cooperative process is already clearly regulated at contract completion, in contrast to other types of contracts. The formulation should not be changed drastically to preserve the essential benefits.*)

The client has the following cooperative duties in the iterative cycles (sprint cycles) described below. The project manager fixes these dates at the start of the project in parallel with the sprints (project managers can make other arrangements by mutual agreement):

(a) **Specification of the user stories.** The client specifies the user stories ***together with the contractor*** in advance, at least to the extent that the number of approved user stories within the contractually agreed format (see Appendix B) is always kept at twice the anticipated delivery of the next sprint performance.

(***Note:*** *It is important that the specifications be performed in collaboration, otherwise, you end up back in the classic specification procedures of the waterfall model, sending e-mails with questions back and forth.*)

The project managers discuss and finalize user stories and their prioritization in a workshop for [x] hours; these represent the proposal for the scope of the next sprint and prioritize the list of user stories accordingly. Before the start of a sprint, both project managers accept each user story specification jointly in writing. This delivery capacity is to be regarded as a likely delivery capacity, as the actual delivery capacity is agreed upon only after estimation and commitment by the team (in the sprint planning). If the actual delivery capacity in a sprint is, however, below the scope agreed upon between the project managers (the projected time frame regarding the scope necessary for a sprint to achieve the end milestone agreed upon), analysis is carried out as to whether the scope has been silently changed in the context of this sprint. Consequently, the scope governance process described in Appendix B is performed. If the scope has not changed, the contractor must expand the implementation team within [x] weeks, so that the corresponding necessary speed can be achieved in the implementation. This only affects the delivery performance, based on the scope agreed to, not on additional scope. In the case of additional scope, the process described in Appendix B is initiated.

(***Note:*** *The contractor is encouraged to take advantage of the escalation process accordingly if doubts are raised as to whether or not the scope is being extended through "scope creep." What must not happen is that the contractor has to provide more and more continuously in small increments, due to inconsistent governance and, nevertheless, the complexity of the backlog delivered is not reduced.*)

(b) **Availability for feedback.** Within a development cycle (sprint), the client's experts are available for further inquiries and are either reachable by phone or will reply to written requests within [ONE] workday. If changes to the scope of the requirements are reported by one of the parties during this discussion, the change is valid only after written approval by the project manager (and the product owner) for cases where the overall effort is not extended, and by the scope governance group otherwise.

(c) **Interim approval of project progress.** Within [x] days after every [x] sprint, the project manager performs a binding partial approval. In a joint meeting, the project manager verifies the approved functionalities regarding the good and bad cases for each user story. The set of acceptance tests agreed to are the tests that are defined and approved with each user story. For any defects resulting from partial acceptance, the rectifications are delivered at the latest two sprints later, or accordingly, by a mutually approved prioritization by the contractor, and these rectifications are verified again at this respective partial acceptance workshop. If functions are still being detected as faulty after being inspected [TWICE], it is escalated to the executive steering board.

Final acceptance

- Final acceptance is performed by the client and supported by the contractor with reasonable efforts. The scope of final acceptance is defined by the specifications under this agreement as set out in Appendix B and the respective user stories which have been approved within the course of the project. However, the partial accepted functionalities cannot essentially be reopened during this final acceptance procedure.
- Final acceptance has to be declared according to §7 of this agreement.
- The client must declare final acceptance when the following acceptance criteria are met:
  - There are no unresolved priority 1 defects.
  - There are no more than [x] unresoleved priority 2 defects.
  - There are no more than [x] unresoleved priority 3 defects.
  - The number of unresolved priority 4 defects is not unreasonably high.

  For all unresolved priority 2, 3, and 4 defects, a list must be provided by the contractor with a schedule of when the open defects will be fixed (within a reasonable time).
- If any part delivered within this project is used in a productive system, the client must declare final acceptance within 10 calendar days.
- The client shall notify the contractor in writing of any defects with the specifications in any of the deliverables.
- The contractor must correct the defects that prevent final acceptance pursuant to subparagraph (c) within 15 calendar days and notify the client when the corrections are complete. The contractor must test the corrected deliverable and/or resume the final acceptance test without undue delay.
- The contractor must remove remaining priority 2, 3, and 4 defects within a reasonable period, to be agreed upon with the client.
- The client must retest resolved defects within five calendar days.

(***Note:*** *This acceptance procedure is a suggestion that can be adapted accordingly.*)

The parties agree to communicate transparently, objectively, and openly even in the case of different opinions. Final acceptance can only be declared in writing by the client's project manager and a client's member of the steering board.

§7   CLIENT'S OBLIGATIONS

(**Note:** *From a legal perspective there might be a certain view on Appendix C. There is the option to include in an obligation paragraph some of the essential concepts as to how a client should behave in this project. We give some examples here. Additionally, these examples might be aligned with §6. However, in the spirit of cooperation, we would recommend retaining §6 and Appendix C and shortening §7 to a minimum.*)

(a) The client is obliged to approve the agreed-upon number of user stories within three calendar days after jointly defining these user stories.

(b) The client is obliged to participate in the joint preacceptance workshop after every [x] sprints and ensure that the defects are documented accordingly.

(c) The client is obliged to declare final acceptance within 10 calendar days after the contractor has fulfilled all final acceptance criteria.

(d) If the client fails to comply with his or her obligations of cooperation (from this paragraph and §6) the contractor shall grant a reasonable grace period in writing to the client to satisfy the client's obligation to cooperate. Furthermore, the contractor's project manager must pass the issue on to the executive steering group without undue delay.

(e) Insofar as the contractor is prevented from performing services due to the client's failure to comply with the obligations of cooperation and provision as agreed, the contractor will not be responsible for resulting delays or reduced quality of the deliverables arising from this specific failure of cooperation, provided that:

(f) The contractor has informed the client in writing without undue delay of the failure to duly cooperate and the impact of such failure if foreseeable.

§8   ESCALATION TO THE STEERING BOARD AND THE INDEPENDENT EXPERTS

(**Note:** *This clause is once again an agreement that, in the normal process of the project, one can serve in the event of a disagreement about costs for an additional instance. It is not often used, but the possibility alone creates positive motivation in previous levels and clarity where there is doubt.*)

Either party may summon a mutually recognized independent expert in the following situations:

- When there is no agreement by the scope steering board on the executive steering board in determining the efforts of a user story with respect to the assumptions drawn originally.

- When there is no agreement by the steering board for the approval of a sprint or for the partial acceptance or final accepance.

The parties agree that the following independent expert should, where appropriate, support the project by his or her decision:

[NAME—ADDRESS—E-MAIL—PHONE NUMBER]

The parties must share the costs of the expert equally for all circumstances. Although the parties are not bound by the decisions or the recommendations of independent experts, they should, however, consider their respective positions on the basis of the new information. If the expert should, for whatever reason, be indisposed, the Steering Board mutually determines another suitable expert. For the avoidance of doubt, it is stated that the decision of the expert is not legally binding and does not prohibit the parties from contacting the ordinary courts.

Both parties agree that this contract defines a cooperatire model. The nature of this cooperation is that no party will forcibly bind the other to itself. Therefore, either party may declare the project finished with a lead time of [2] sprints and free themselves from their obligation. On the one hand, after each sprint, the client receives usable software with the corresponding functionality implemented so far. On the other hand, the contractor is paid for the services of the sprints, for the most part, and has not done any massive scaling or spending for future functionality. For these reasons, the parties agree that this approach is beneficial for both parties and represents one of the foundations for the cooperation model. However, at the termination of a project, the contractor may no longer claim the remaining [x]% (withheld until final acceptance; see §6) of the already completed sprints.

(***Note:*** *This item is part of the negotiation. How applicable to the client is a change of contractor, and to what extent can the contractor be trusted to see the project through?*)

This is a convenient system for both parties, as this approach ensures the customer that the functionality already delivered is operationable and the contractor is compensated for the expenses already incurred in accordance with the agreed-upon intervals (see Appendix A).

§9 PROJECT PERIOD

The parties agree to finish the project scope by [xx.xx.xxxx], as stated in Appendix B. Handover of the last sprint is completed by [xx.xx.xxxx], and is followed by an inspection phase of [x] weeks, which then leads to approval at the above-mentioned completion date.

[***Note:*** *To avoid any doubts—of course there is a fixed end date! This rather rudimentary articulation should signal that there are no complicated milestone* *strategies. Instead, there is a set time period for each of the iterations and a completion date for the last sprint before the final acceptance starts, as well as the duration of this acceptance phase. This can be supported graphically and, if applicable, be introduced in the appendix. It is important, however, that no further plans made; for example, on April 3 the "user management module" is completed. This would undermine the agile process. There can, however, be an indicative release planning (with precisely the words:* indicative*).]*

§10   WARRANTY, COMPENSATION, AND INDEMNIFICATION

(***Note:*** *This definition is worded in a customer-friendly names. It is advisable to reconsider the definition for the case in question. The warranty is explored in more detail within the legal framework in Chapter 6.*)

The warranty period is to be [DURATION]. The warranty period starts at the date of final acceptance, or earlier in case a part of the software is used in production. The software is deemed to be used in production in case the project managers of the parties made such a remark at the writen acceptance of a respective user story.

(***Note:*** *It generally makes sense to stretch the warranty over at least a portion of the increments of software delivery, because later, when all the software has been delivered, it is difficult to differentiate the warranties for the individual components.*)

Within the warranty period, the client must prove any deficiencies to the contractor. The statutory damages provisions shall apply.

[***Note:*** *The last sentence is worded heavily from the perspective of the client and depends on the respective local law. During the negotiation you should find a middle ground in the limitation of liability, but this is not a specific topic in an agile fixed-price contract (e.g., limitation of liability with contract value and no liability for indirect damage).*]

The contractor abides and conforms to all applicable laws and maintains all applicable licenses. The contractor warrants that the software will not infringe any intellectual property rights, and indemnifies the client (holds the client) harmless from any third-party claim that software infringes an intellectual property right.

§11   LIMITATION OF LIABILITY

(***Note:*** *This paragraph is subject to discussion for each client, and any standard formulation can be used.*)

§12 CONTRACTOR'S COMPENSATION

(***Note:*** *This paragraph is subject to discussion for each client, and any standard formulation can be used.*)

The contractor's compensation and the processes to manage the efforts within an agreed-upon fixed price are defined in Appendix A.

§13 FORCE MAJEURE

Any delay or failure in the performance by either party hereunder will be excused if and to the extent caused by the occurrence of a force majeure. For purposes of this agreement, *force majeure* means a cause or event that is not reasonably foreseeable or otherwise caused by or under the control of the party claiming force majeure, including acts of God; fires; floods; explosions; riots; wars; hurricanes; sabotage terrorism; vandalism; accident; restraint of government; governmental acts; injunctions; labor strikes, other than those of contractor or its suppliers, that prevent the contractor from provision of services; and similar events that are beyond the reasonable anticipation and control of the party affected thereby, despite such party's reasonable efforts, to prevent, avoid, delay, or mitigate the effect of such acts, events or occurrences, and which events or the effects thereof are not attributable to a party's failure to perform its obligations under this agreement.

§14 SECRECY

Both parties agree to use the licensed data and documentation solely for the provision of services. Any other use requires prior written consent of the respective contract party, where it is expressly stated that the client has free access to the contract and the documentation. Both parties are obliged not to disclose anything associated with the provision of services that become known processes of the other party. The obligation to silence extends to all employees of the parties. The contractor must take appropriate measures to impose this obligation on its employees.

Both contracting parties must act in accordance with all relevant provisions of data protection:

[THE APPLICABLE LAWS AND REGULATIONS MAY BE ADDED AT THIS POINT]

After completion of the project, both parties commit themselves to destroying or handing ones all data disclosed to them unless the data are needed to manage a dispute with the other party.

§15 SEVERABILITY CLAUSE

The invalidity or unenforceability of any provisions of this agreement will not affect the validity or enforceability of any other provision of this agreement, which will remain in full force and effect.

§16 PLACE OF PERFORMANCE, JURISDICTION, AND APPLICABLE LAW

The place of performance and jurisdiction is [OFFICE OF THE CONTRAC-TOR OR CLIENT]. It is the law of the [FEDERAL REPUBLIC OF XXXXX] under exclusion of the international private law and the rules of the United Nations Convention on contracts for the international sale of goods.

(***Note:*** *In some cases it may make sense to agree on an arbitration clause, which requires the parties to resolve their disputes through an arbitration process.*)

[PLACE], on [DATE]

[CLIENT]   [CONTRACTOR]

APPENDIX A: COMMERCIAL AGREEMENTS

Prices

[***Note:*** *The prices are set in this paragraph, and the template offers various options. It is practical for pricing results but does not represent connections between people, experience levels, and days. The team cost is used in the background, or for the purpose of transparency. This is essentially only informative (as it is a fixed price for scope/performance and does not reflect personnel-related costs, such as time and materials). If the original planned team(s) do not perform to the level estimated for project completion, the contractor must change or expand the team at the expense of its profit margin. The initial phase to achieve the agile fixed price through an indicative maximum price may be established in a separate short contract, based on time and materials or agile fixed price, including the potential riskshare.*]

The indicative maximum price in the amount of

USD [AMOUNT]

results from an expert estimate by the contractor and is based on the following elements:

- Both parties understanding the maximum price defined in an agile fixed-price contract at the time of contract completion
- The project vision with the respective nonfunctional contraints

- Expenses for the reference user stories of epics, described fully in Appendix B
- A list of all epics from the backlog, as described in Appendix B
- The total expenses on the basis of an analogy estimate for all epics
- Uncertainty top-up in the amount of [**x**]%

(***Note:*** *There are two possibilities for setting the price for the work, such as Option A and Option B below. In the final contract, one should be selected.*)

- Option A

Prices based on the complexity of user stories (types might be, e.g., "interface," "user interface," "core functionality")

	Type 1	Type 2	Type 3
Complex	USD [AMOUNT]	USD [AMOUNT]	USD [AMOUNT]
Average	USD [AMOUNT]	USD [AMOUNT]	USD [AMOUNT]
Simple	USD [AMOUNT]	USD [AMOUNT]	USD [AMOUNT]

- Option B

Prices based on the complexity points of user stories

According to the complexity points (referred to as story points), which are associated with the reference user stories as specified in Appendix B, it is noted that the following costs will be incurred for all future additional user stories:

$$1 \text{ story point} = \text{USD [AMOUNT]}$$

(***Note:*** *The two versions are the same in terms of content. In one version we attempt to describe the complexity through classes, and in the other, through points. The most important aspect is to define the complexity of a representative set of reference user stories.*)

Optional: Hourly rate for a time and materials contract for additional (nonscopeable work, e.g., training)
Should the parties work together on the basis of time and materials, the following prices apply:

- Junior consultant: USD [AMOUNT]
- Senior consultant: USD [AMOUNT]

(***Note:*** *As the name suggests, this paragraph is optional and does not mean that the experience level is measured on the basis of daily rates within an agile fixed-price contract. Essentially, we simply calculate from the team. The team estimates from experience that it will provide [**x**] complexity points per sprint on average. The commercial offer and the responsibility for internal security surcharges are then the responsibility of the key account manager or engagement manager on* the contractor's side. The customer does not have to know who is working on the project, although he or she can know, as we are transparent. However, it's all about results. The daily rates are therefore in the contract, to achieve an agreed-upon appropriate guideline for actual additional expenses or follow-up tasks where it might not be appropriate to measure in complexity points. It is, however, also preferred that additional work continue on the basis of the complexity of user stories and their negotiated rates.)

Commercial Approach to the Project

[*Note: This chapter includes the process from the price indication (maximum indicative price range) to the actual fixed price (fixed and therefore maximum price range). During negotiations, both sides should make sure not to negotiate the commercial parameters too much to their own advantage. Why would one of the parties ever want to do this? It provokes unfair behavior which is not in the spirit of an agile fixed-price contract. See Chapter 7 for further details.*]

Initial (checkpoint) phase

To verify the estimation and quality of interaction, the parties agree on an initial phase in the scope of [y] person-days. The aim is to define and implement [2 to 5] sprints within this time frame. After completing the initial phase, either party may terminate the contract without giving any reason. For example, it could happen that the definition of user stories or the performance of a particular party does not meet the expectations of the other party. In this case, the contractor is (in terms of a riskshare model) compensated for only [50]% of his daily rates.

Agreement on a final maximum price

If, from the perspective of both parties, the initial (Checkpoint) phase runs successfully, the parties agree on a final maximum price, possibly with additional assumptions. This maximum price is a fixed price to the extent that the contractor agrees to provide additional expenses (within the scope frame agreed upon according to Appendix B) at a reduced rate of [50]% per story point. This does not include additional requirements that could not be compensated for by the free-exchange approach. Additional expenses will either be defined by mutual agreement or by point [7] of the escalation process of the contract. Again, it requires a written confirmation from the representatives of the scope steering board.

[*Note: As noted above, there is the possibility of regulating the indicative maximum price and the method for reaching the final maximum price in its own "small" contract ("true fixed price"; Section 4.1.2). In this respect, the checkpoint phase is still part of the tender with several contractors. Details are given in Chapter 5. In this case, Section 4.1.2 in this principal contract would be obsolete and Section 4.1.1 would be reworded in such a way that the indicative maximum price would read as the maximum price or real fixed price. Further-*

more, in Section 4.1.1, riskshare would be regulated for possibly exceeding the fixed price.]

Pricing in the context of maximum price for individual sprints during implementation

Both parties agree to ensure close cooperation and transparency in procedures regarding work according to certain principles. At the start of each sprint the expenses of the analogy estimate are verified and agreed upon in writing based on the final user stories presented so far. This is performed by an estimation of detailed knowledge of the fully formulated user story. If the work of an epic does not correspond to the initial analogy estimate, the parties will attempt to find a solution for the maximum price framework according to the following procedure:

- **Option 1.** The contractor's product owner finds that the deviation lies within the agile fixed price (possibly equipped with a security surcharge). In this case the client's project manager will be notified by e-mail and the changes recorded and accepted in writing by both parties in a centralized document.
- **Option 2.** The contractor's product owner informs the client's project manager in writing that the expenses for these user stories or epic are higher than those estimated originally. In this case a possible meeting will be agreed upon to reconcile, where possible, complexity reduction or elimination of requirements for the actual user stories or for specific user stories to be identified in the future. This agreement is also captured in writing.

Escalation process

If the project manager fails to reach an agreement on the specific cost of the specification (user story or epic), the scope steering board is convened to make a decision. The further escalation process of the experts is defined in point 7 of the contract. If it is not possible for the project managers to secure the final maximum price through a reasonable reduction of the complexity of user stories, the additional overhead on the final maximum price according to the riskshare agreed upon is split (of course only after appropriate approval by the scope steering board).

Efficiency bonus at the end of the project

Upon successful completion of a project within the planned scope and below the final maximum price, the parties may agree to the following:

- [50]% of the difference between the final maximum price and the actual price will be paid to the contractor as an efficiency bonus's or
- the remaining sum is assigned to the contractor for a follow-up project within [x] weeks.

Payment Milestones

[*Note: The payments should be made after each sprint (or possibly drops, i.e., after two or three sprints) on the basis of partially approved user stories. The principle that every sprint delivers functioning software also leads to a willingness by customers to pay for this service. This agreement also ensures that the partial acceptances are operated with great seriousness. The scope of the final acceptance is weighted according to its importance for the project. Values above 20 to 30% seem mostly exaggerated and can devalue the partial acceptance. On the other hand, they can artificially increase the final maximum price (i.e., the real fixed price) because the client must partially finance and assess risk until the final acceptance.*]

The delivery obligation of the contractor within this agile fixed-price contract, which is included in the final maximum price set forth herein, includes a total cost of [x] Story points. The delivery obligation consist of the deliverables defined in Appendix B, with a quality standard set forth in Appendix D of this agreement.

(*Note: Or for times when one is working on the basis of complexity classes of user stories.*)

In each case, after approval of two sprints with a performance scope of user stories with a complexity of at least [x] complexity points, the contractor is entitled to request an invoice in the amount of [80]% of the total compensation for the respective sprints. The last [20]% compensation for each sprint is linked to the final inspection and is invoiced only after the successful final approval. A net payment term of 30 days is agreed upon.

APPENDIX B: TECHNICAL SCOPE AND PROCESS

Requirements: Backlog and Vision

(*Note: The project vision is often forgotten. However, this is generally a no-go for IT contracts that deem to have a fixed scope. Every project that has its value ready to be started should be describable in half a page. Where the client defines a "Swiss army knife" sort of project vision, the project should not be started. The project vision forces the client to find the real value behind why this project is performed but also where intentional contraints are set.*)

The first item within the scope of this project is the project vision. The vision for this project is to [xx]. This project should allow the client's business to [xx]. The parties understand that the project vision respects the following constraints [xx].

(*Note: The format of the description of the requirements introduced here can be seen as a suggestion. Of course, other mechanisms may also be selected to*

TABLE 4.1

No.	Priority	Backlog Item	Type	Story Points
1	1000	Create user	User story	8
2	995	Search user	User story	5
3	990	Delete user	User story	3
4	985	Manage user requests	Epic	21
5	980	Manage user roles	Epic	13

TABLE 4.2

Epic number	5
Epic name	Manage user roles
Epic description	This epic contains the entire functionality required in the software for user administration. This includes displaying, searching, deleting, editing, and creating new users as well as assigning users to user groups.
Assumption	The assignment of authorizations based on user groups is stored in the software by default. The user groups are not recreated, but assignment of users to these groups is allowed.
	The search function is limited to pure search by last name.
	Dual system users will be secured only on the basis of avoiding duplicate user names.
	Notifications containing user credentials are sent via e-mail.

estimate costs, but we want to illustrate the operating process. In any case, the requirements described from the user's perspective.)

The entire contract is defined by the backlog shown in Table 4.1. It is important to note that user stories 1, 2, and 3 are considered reference user stories and represent the approved source for price determination and analogous estimation.

The details of a sample of an individual backlog item can be found in Table 4.2.

Process for Development and Approval

(***Note:*** *This process for the implementation is another essential point, and determines when to fix which part of the "flexible scope system." The most important thing at this point is that the speed of development is determined by the team, and the project manager is able to establish the appropriate actions with this information.*)

Before a sprint, the client's project manager and contractor's product owner agree in writing as to which user stories are, from both sides, sufficiently and fully described, approved, and how they are prioritized (an example of such a user story structure is shown in Figure 4.1). This represents the basis for the preferred (according to prioritization) functionality to be implemented in the

FEATURE/ USER STORY TITLE 2		TEAM:
SCHEDULED FOR SPRINT		

Team release:	⊗ **NO** ∗) Confirmation by team	
Architecture check:	⊗ **NO** ∗) Confirmation by solution architect	
Inspection successful:	⊗ **NO** ∗) Confirmation by product owner	

1. STORY DETAILS/ FEATURE DESCRIPTION

Achieved / Agreed

2. BASIC CONDITIONS

2.1
2.2
2.3

3. ACCEPTANCE CRITERIA

3.1 How/ where do i want to see the result?
3.1.1
3.1.2
3.2 GOOD CASES
3.2.1
3.2.2
3.2.3
3.2.4
3.2.5

3.3 BAD CASES (how to react in certain error situations)
3.3.1
3.3.2
3.3.3
3.3.4

Figure 4.1   *Structure of a user story.*

upcoming sprint. This agreement is made, at the latest, one week before the start of the sprint, in the form of sufficiently detailed user stories with corresponding good and bad cases.

If the client has not specified and approved enough requirements in the form of user stories a week before the start of a sprint, the cost of the already scheduled teams will be invoiced at an agreed-upon flat rate in the amount of [xxx] euros. The executive steering board will be informed immediately of this critical situation and the additional extra costs (not to be within the fixed price as the client has to bear these costs in the same manner as the supplier bears the additional costs if more developers are needed than originally estimated for the same complexity). The parties agree that they seek to have user stories with a number of story points of at least twice the estimated team throughput of a sprint finalized and approved on the backlog. This ensures the flexibility to use the available delivery capacity in an optimal manner.

If the client requests changes to a user story through a written agreement, additional costs may arise. To continue to achieve the total price agreed upon, paragraph [x] in this appendix refers to the process to control the scope. The client's team prioritizes the user stories in the backlog during sprint planning, and at the end of the first day a sprint feedback is delivered to the project manager and product owner. This feedback includes information on how many user stories the team commits to implementing in this sprint.

The product owner plans approximately how much of the complexity must be implemented in each sprint in order to keep the final project delivery date. On the grounds of this statement, precautionary actions can be taken in the event that the speed of implementation is too slow.

[***Note:*** *It is important to emphasize that it is at the expense of the contractor, if the speed is not sufficient, unless there is a cause on the client side (e.g., not fulfilling obligations or lack of access to test the interface, although noted in the user story). In both cases the steering board is informed.*]

The contractor carries out the development with extensive tests and provides the client with a piece of executable software, including documentation, at the end of each sprint according to the quality standards agreed upon as set forth in Appendix D. For the purposes of possible user stories, relating to the overall architecture, the product owner may, for the first [x] sprints, declare in writing that the pieces of software submitted are not yet fully executable.

The client agrees to review the sprint submitted, including documentation, within [x] working days. He or she will remove and report any defects to the contractor. Both parties commit themselves to prioritize the user stories according to the following criteria:

- Business value for the customer
- Technical complexity or risks
- Complexity of the functionality specified

It is understood that any other prioritization must be brought to the notice of the representatives of the scope steering board, as this constitutes a project risk.

(***Note:*** *There is a clear concern that an agile fixed-price contract should not be used to shift uncomfortable questions to a later stage in the project, only then to find out that you face a massive problem ahead. The formulation is designed to ensure transparency so that the scope steering board is informed and attention is given to complex requests that are still sufficiently unknown.*)

Changes to the Contract (Exchange for Free)

(***Note:*** *One of the key benefits of an agile fixed-price contract is the clear rule that one can alter or change requirements within the same high-level scope. However, this does not mean that you can simply add new things without removing anything!*)

Process for controlling the scope

The process to control the scope is initiated for each user story, where the cost predicted exceeds that which was originally estimated on the basis of an analogous estimate (as described in Appendix A). The process of scope substituation includes the following steps:

1. Both parties work together to simplify other user stories; or the parties define the user stories for epics that are not yet defined in user stories but where a potential to simplify and reduce complexity is recognized, and thereby try to reduce complexity; or the parties eliminate nonessential user stories or user stories with low business value from the product backlog.

2. If these options are not acceptable to both parties, either party may appeal to the steering board to make a decision. The parties then agree that this cost is higher than originally estimated. This cannot be put down to overly aggressive estimating of the reference user stories but rather to a simple case of "hidden" complexity.

In summary, this "scope substitution" means a reduction in the complexity of the system requirements or the elimination from the contractual scope of other system requirements—not as important and not yet begun to be implemented—such that the overall agreed-upon fixed-price compensation, effort, and time line stay the same (change is free).

If a detailed definition of a user story unveils a discrepancy in the initial scope and the scope that is now requested, or if a new requirement is requested to be added to the scope of the agreement, the parties agree on the following:

(i)   The project manager and product owner verify the scope change and try to avoid additional costs by scope substitution.

(ii) If the project manager and product owner can agree on such scope substitution, they proceed with subparagraph (viii) below.

(iii) If the project manager of the client and product owner of the contractor cannot agree on such scope substitution, they must prepare a joint statement with respect to this new or changed system requirement explaining why this is necessary to achieve the purpose of this agreement. In addition, the project managers must prepare a joint comprehensive report to illustrate why all other elements of the backlog in the scope are also essential ("must haves") in fulfilling the purpose of this agreement (VersionOne, 2012).

(iv) If the project manager of the client and product owner of the contractor are not able to agree on a joint proposal regarding a revised fixed-price compensation and/or time line with respect to this changed or new requirement, the project managers use the reference user stories to prepare a joint report for decision by the scope governance group.

(v) The project manager and product owner present this joint report at the next scheduled scope governance meeting, and the scope governance group decides how to handle that scope change (either by exchange, reduction of other complexity, or additional compensation to be paid to the contractor and/or time line change).

(vi) If the scope governance group makes a joint decision, the scope governance group shall proceed with subparagraph (viii) below.

(vii) If the scope governance group cannot make a joint decision, the issue is transferred to the executive steering group. The executive steering group makes a decision and proceeds with subparagraph (viii) below or agrees on alternative steps.

(viii) A change request form is filled in and duly signed by both parties, agreeing to this change of scope.

Free exchange

Before setting the sprint backlogs for the respective sprints, the client also has the possibility of exchanging new requirements for those already in the product backlog, without added overhead (as defined in Section 4.2.1). If the existing requirements are not eliminated from the product backlog, it is agreed that these additional requirements are not included in the maximum price, but rather, are incurred visibly as overhead (change request). To determine this, the process above is also employed in this case. It is essential that exactly these new requirements be compared to the known estimates (reference user stories) to ensure price certainty for the client.

Deliverables and Services

[*Note: The delivery performance of an agile fixed-price contract is usually not linked to the classic deliverables from traditional IT contracts (i.e., those normally requested in the waterfall process). In some cases, however, there is the possibility of iteratively generating some of these documents from the agile process (e.g., we are confident that a high-level architecture document is useful). This does not mean that agile fixed-price and agile methods are not appropriate if you absolutely need a detailed design or similar document for a specific template. However, you have to ensure that really valuable documents are created, in an agile interative manner.*]

The services provided by the contractor lead to the following deliverables:

- The backlog maintained for communication, reporting, and discussion of requirements with the client
- Biweekly status reports
- Maintenance of the impediment list
- Implementation of user stories

- Cost estimates for the budget framework for the implementation of the above (the sprint) includes:
  - Participation by the steering board
  - Weekly reports
  - Weekly project manager meetings

The following deliverables are provided by the contractor in the scope of this agreement:

- Software based on the specification of user stories that comply with the quality parameters listed in Appendix C.
- Tests and/or test protocols for:
  - Automated unit testing
  - End-to-end testing
  - Integration testing
- High-level architecture documents delivered as a pdf and MS Word file

Additionally required project management and project office support in the field of business analysis, rollout, and support for client-side testing is offered based on time and materials and invoiced according to expenditure.

Mechanism to Calculate Costs of Future User Stories

(**Note:** *It is important that the client not award the first project as a "door opener" and give the contractor the opportunity to make an initial offer that is too low and to make up for this loss in later assignments. This process is intuitive and should be included in the contract. Note that the contractor is also bound to these reference user stories for later assignments; thus, door opening would be very unattractive financially.*)

According to the agile approach, there is an agreement following a verifiable mechanism as to how future requirements or changes to the requirements will be jointly identified. The process is specified per user story as follows:

(a) The detailed specification (in the form of user stories) is transferred from the client to the contractor (based on a project vision with certain constraints).

(b) The contractor must review the user story, discuss it with the client, and add possible missing parts or assumptions in these detailed specifications.

(c) The final joint coordination and approval of the scope of the user story must be completed.

(d) The contractor creates the cost estimate and identifies the effective delivery date of the user story.

(e) The client reviews the cost estimate and delivery date. If both are found to be understandable and acceptable, point (h) of this process follows. If the cost is unjustifiable and therefore not acceptable, point (f) of this process follows. If the cost is acceptable but not the delivery date, point (g) of this process follows.

(f) The technical experts of both parties agree with regard to the work involved and try to create an understanding on the technical level. If successful, the resulting cost is discussed with the project manager of the client and the product owner of the contractor, and the value agreed upon is utilized. If not, the project manager, the product owner, and the technical experts will coordinate the expenditure with the inclusion of reference user stories (from the past). The next level of escalation is preparation for the decision and submission to the scope steering board.

(g) The scope steering board reviews the cost and the expected delivery date, which is discussed and defined in a mutual agreement between the parties. The next level of escalation is a preparation for decision and submission to the executive steering board, where a final decision should be reached. The final level of escalation is the third-party independent expert, who can be approached to seek a recommendation. If there is mutual agreement on one level, the next step in the process is followed.

(h) The cost and delivery date are confirmed and released by a designated contact person for the client. This is either requested from within an existing order (budget) or a corresponding order is triggered based on the contract framework.

The preliminary cost estimate in the story points (in order of abstraction and the resulting benefits) is the responsibility of each party.

Illustrative Example

Five additional functionalities are included in Release 1.1, which is planned after the main release of the project. The contractor will go through the following process (shown below as an example for such an additional delivery request) to determine the expenses:

- The client specifies the requirements, such as "the software should allow you to load a configuration table automatically over the interface." It is best if they are specified immediately in the corresponding user story format by the client with the required content, as this would allow the second step to be completed faster.
- The contractor aligns the corresponding user story for the request, which then reads as follows:

(Continued)

The user wants to navigate the interface, within the configuration area, with a separate menu item. A file selection menu is initiated by an "Import" button and when the user selects a file and clicks "OK," the configuration data are loaded in the XY table.

During the alignment procedure for this user story, the following assumptions are added in a discussion with the client:

- The file must be in CSV format:
    - Any other format brings the generic error message "Import failed."
    - Incorrect content in csv format generates the same error message.
    - The contents of this file will override any previous content in the XY table (i.e., it is first deleted and then the data are imported).
    In addition, three good and three bad cases related to the user story are added, as well as a mock-up presentation of where the interfaces are located.
- The user story is discussed at a joint meeting of the project manager and the scope governance board on the client side and the product owner of the contractor. The approval of the content and understanding thereof is confirmed in writing in the printed user story.
- The contractor estimates the costs in planning poker with the team at 13 story points. Due to the other three user stories which are prioritized before this, the delivery date is set at six weeks (this is an estimate, since the actual delivery of a sprint is not confirmed by the team until during sprint planning).
- The client reviews the cost estimation and delivery date and finds in this example case that the estimate is far too high. He refers to two (reference) user stories with similar scope (import of two other configuration tables on the interface), where the scope agreed to was eight story points.
- As a result, two experts from each respective side gather for a conference call to discuss the differences and to clarify why this user story means more cost. In this discussion they find no significant difference, and the experts then discuss it further internally with their team. It turns out that possibly too high a complexity was assumed, and the team now considers eight Story points to be realistic.
- The cost is fixed and the expected delivery date is discussed and defined in a mutual agreement between the project manager of the client and the product owner. If this agreement were not to have been reached, the next level of escalation would have to be entered, which is a preparation for the decision and submission to the scope steering board (however, we do not follow this way for the purpose of this example).

- Cost and delivery date are confirmed and released by a person designated by the client (the project manager or a representative of the scope steering group). This is either requested from within an existing order (budget) or a corresponding order is triggered based on the contract framework.
- The cost and delivery date are confirmed and released by a contact person designated by the client. Together with the other four user stories, a corresponding order is triggered based on the agile contract framework.

APPENDIX C: 12 PRINCIPLES OF COOPERATION

The contract parties undertake to apply the 12 principles described in the following *code of cooperation* for optimal collaboration in the project.

(***Note:*** *It is important that depending on where the parties are in the "transition of mindset toward the agile fixed-price contract," this appendix needs to be adapted as it represents an optimal case. Some clients' lawyers might see some points as strange: such as "We as a client do not push for delivery dates." So, depending on the client, the formulation should be cleaned up slightly. Additionally, it is another decision which of these points might even be moved to the client's obligations section of the contract. Still, this is an important appendix, as the parties agree that it is highly probable that the project cannot be delivered successfully without following the process of cooperation.*)

1. Emphasis is on delivery
"Our top priority is to satisfy our customers through early and continuous delivery of valuable software content."

How do we behave as a customer?

- We participate in sprint reviews.
- Our department takes on finished software at the end of a sprint if possible, otherwise as early in the process as feasible.
- We integrate the software delivered into our existing systems as soon as possible.
- We give critical but respectful feedback.

How do we behave as a contractor?

- Our software development processes allow us to show the customer fully functional software after each sprint.
- We make appropriate environments accessible to the customer.

How do we behave on the Scrum team?

- We optimize our development practices in the team so that we are able to present completed software at the end of a sprint.
- We talk extensively with users and customize the applications according to the user's requirements.

2. Exchange for free

"Accept changes in requirements even late in development. Agile processes use changes to the competitive advantage of customers."

How do we behave as a customer?

- We distinguish between functional requirements and the conditions of the project.
- We are personally involved in the project vision and understand the technological implications.
- We are aware that we are permitted to make changes.
- We understand that there is a profound change when we alter the environment.

How do we behave as a contractor?

- We welcome changes.
- We develop in such a way that we are able to respond rapidly to changes.
- We make this possible with good documentation, refactoring, and continuous and open communication about what has actually occurred.
- We invite the customers to daily Scrums, sprint plannings, and reviews.

How do we behave on the Scrum team?

- We communicate with customers to fulfill their wishes within the contractual scope. We try to think like customers and end users.
- We are open to criticism when our applications are under review.
- We acknowledge our errors and correct them immediately.

3. Deliver in iterations

"Deliver functional software regularly within a few weeks or months and favor the shorter time periods."

How do we behave as a customer?

- We are present at sprint reviews and give feedback.
- We integrate the partial functionality delivered into our existing infrastructure as soon as possible.

How do we behave as a contractor?

- We invite customers to sprint reviews and discuss the current status openly.

How do we behave on the Scrum team?

- We deliver complete functionality at the end of each sprint.

4. End user and developer sit together
"Experts and developers must work together daily throughout the project."

How do we behave as a customer?

- We make experts from various departments available to the development team.
- We are available when the development team has questions.
- We take time for the project.

How do we behave as a contractor?

- We welcome experts when they are present in the Scrum team.
- We call the experts when we have questions.
- We make a point of inviting the experts sprint planning.

How do we behave on the Scrum team?

- We work daily with the experts.
- We make an effort to understand the experts.
- We observe how the experts work. However, we do not ask them what they want; instead, we work with them until we know what they need.

5. Trust the individual
"Build projects around motivated individuals. Give them the environment and support they need and trust that they will get the job done."

How do we behave as a customer?

- We search for an agile development partner.
- We provide motivated experts to fulfill our obligations.
- We trust the delivery team for at least the first three sprints.
- We also check whether the delivery team delivers what we expect.

How do we behave as a contractor?

- We select project team members who really want to work on the project.
- We give them the tools they need for their work and remove them from unnecessary bureaucratic hurdles.

How do we behave on the Scrum team?

- We state openly when we need something or when we are obstructed by something.
- We have a Scrum master who clears obstacles out of our way.
- We behave respectfully toward customers and management.

6. Face-to-face communication is more effective

"The most efficient and most effective way to deliver information to a development team is face to face."

How do we behave as a customer?

- We understand that good documents only result from successful face-to-face communication.

How do we behave as a contractor?

- We communicate openly with the client. All information, including any problems due to limitations, is visible to the customer.
- We do not hide anything.

How do we behave on the Scrum team?

- We talk to the customer and/or end user.
- We understand their needs.
- We observe the user while he or she is working.

7. All that matters is completed functionality

"Functioning software is the primary measure of success."

How do we behave as a customer?

- We call on our service provider to deliver completed software after no later than 30 days.
- We are not satisfied with documents as a progress result.

How do we behave as a contractor?

- We deliver software in short intervals.
- All obstacles on the part of the customer are discussed openly and all obstacles on our side are addressed and resolved openly.

How do we behave on the Scrum team?

- We always deliver software that is potentially usable.

8. Sustainable pace

"Agile processes promote sustainable development. Clients, developers, and users should be able to maintain a steady pace indefinitely."

How do we behave as a customer?

- We do not push for functionality and deadlines in the team and do not demand overtime or changes at the last minute. We trust that the final delivery date agreed to will be respected by the contractor.

How do we behave as a contractor?

- We always work professionally and to a high standard.
- We deliver only tested, documented, and refactored software.
- We do not commit to functionality over long periods.
- We do early reviews and estimations to put more teams and people on a project, which allows everybody to work at a sustainable pace.

How do we behave on the Scrum team?

- We honor our commitments in the sprint.
- We work as a team, alwoays striving to deliver consistently on a high level.

9. Quality is an attitude

"Continuous attention to technical excellence and good design promotes agility."

How do we behave as a customer?

- We expect a high level of technical quality from our contractors and we know that this is not an effort to accomplish price dumping.
- We therefore select our service providers not only on the basis of price.

How do we behave as a contractor?

- We deliver to the customer an excellently designed software with extensible architecture and we invest in staff training.

How do we behave on the Scrum team?

- We look constantly to the future and search for solutions that enable us to develop.
- We do test runs, automate, and document.
- We educate ourselves continuously in order to correct weaknesses.

10. Keep it simple, stupid (KISS)
"Simplicity, the art of maximizing the amount of work not done, is essential."

How do we behave as a customer?

- We check constantly whether we still require what we requested.
- We cancel projects if we already have what we need.
- We accept contracts that allow us these things.
- We accept the fact that the contractor does deliver the most efficient realization of our requirements with respect to effort, as we do want to receive much functionality for a certain price and not unnecessary details with low additional value.

How do we behave as a contractor?

- We deliver from the start the features that are most valuable to the customer.
- We favor short project lead times.
- We deliver fast and thus do not bill in hours.
- We think how to deliver a requested functionality in the easiest manner.

How do we behave on the Scrum team?

- We are always looking for the simplest solution that can be produced professionally.

11. Complexity can only be answered with self-organization
"The best architectures, requirements, and designs emerge from self-organized teams."

How do we behave as a customer?

- We make the functioning of our own systems completely transparent.
- We do not define the solutions yet.
- We allow the teams to do their work.

How do we behave as a contractor?

- We educate the staff in such a way that all the necessary skills are present in the team.

How do we behave on the Scrum team?

- We reveal when there is something that we cannot achieve due to lack of skills.
- We ask questions actively.
- We work with customers proactively.

12. Learn from postmortems

"The team reflects at regular intervals how it can be more effective, and adjusts its behavior accordingly."

How do we behave as a customer?

- We expect to hear of errors in the teams that have led to improvements.
- We participate by invitation in the project retrospective.
- We respond to requests for change and respect them as a potential to increase productivity.

How do we behave as a contractor?

- We work with customers continually to improve our relationship and inform them when we see potential for improvement.

How do we behave on the Scrum team?

- We perform our retrospectives rigorously.

APPENDIX D: QUALITY STANDARDS—DEFINITION OF DONE

The contract parties undertake to apply the 12 principles as described in the following code of cooperation for optimal collaboration in the project.

1. Definition of done

(**Note:** *The definition of done is a general set of criteria; however, it can also be adapted to certain specific delivery quality criteria in a project.*)

Each increment of the software delivered in this project will be "done" according to the following criteria:

- Code is produced.
- The code passes the static code criteria (see the comments below).
- The code has been peer-reviewed.
- The test build has passed without errors.
- The configuration sheet for a release plan has been updated.
- Unit tests have been written and passed.
- System integration tests have been passed.
- An automated test build is carried out (if applicable).
- User acceptance tests have been performed, passed, and test protocol was created.
- Relevant documentation has been updated.

2. Code quality and code documentation

The contractor develops code following the "clean code developer" principles, which define best practices to develop readable and maintainable code. The fundamental concept of these principles is that professionally written code is easy to read and transports its functionality without the need for extensive additional inline documentation. To improve the readability of code the contractor defined other rules (e.g., sets of naming conventions for classes, methods, and variables) as well as structural patterns that are used in all parts of the system. These conventions are enforced by the use of static code analysis tools throughout the entire product development cycle.

The contractor uses the industry standard tools FindBugs and Checkstyle for static code analysis. Compliance with these rules is enforced by a suitable tool which is integrated into the build environment and shows a rules compliance index for the entire project source. This compliance index for the delivery of each increment will be above 90%, which indicates that 90% of the project source is implemented according to these rules.

3. Test coverage

Based on a high level of automated tests, the following indicators are contractually agreed to for sufficient test coverage:

- Unit tests; code coverage must be above 25%.
- An automated end-to-end test is carried out for each epic.
- Each good and bad case example agreed to jointly in the detailed formulation of the user stories is tested in the integration test and a corresponding test protocol is delivered with the code.

5

Tendering Based on an Agile Fixed-Price Contract

The tendering and selection of a supplier of a project based on an agile fixed-price contract is a new challenge for respective budget owners, the procurement department, and the key account manager (we presented the challenges for the sales team of a supplier in Chapter 2). All participants need to move away from the well-known waterfall and fixed-price principle. They should acknowledge that the agile fixed-price contract is a more successful variant of the fixed-price commission for many IT projects. It is, so to speak, a natural evolution of the traditional fixed-price contract.

Even in the agile world, you must proceed with caution: Agile models are indeed "en vogue" but are not the universal remedy for all sorts of problems in projects. However, in many cases, procurement experts have not properly analyzed or tested the agile model and are often very sceptical or even reject such a model entirely. Those who have tried it (e.g., based on time and materials contracts) often still evaluate the attempts as inexpedient, as no contract template was available (with a successful explanation of how to handle this from the IT procurement process perspective) or conflicts arose with existing internal processes, giving the impression of "uncontrolled work" and "lack of supplier control."

Agile Contracts: Creating and Managing Successful Projects with Scrum, First Edition.
Andreas Opelt, Boris Gloger, Wolfgang Pfarl, and Ralf Mittermayr.
© 2013 John Wiley & Sons, Inc. Published 2013 by John Wiley & Sons, Inc.

Testimonials from the Field

Horst Ulrich Mooshandl is the head of corporate and group procurement of Österreichische Post AG (Austrian Post Group). In an interview given in September 2012, Mooshandl pointed out that a differentiated approach is necessary and that it appears that there have been problems with agile contract models in the past:

> Let us put ourselves in the position of a procurement manager who must carry out a tender on the topic of migration or implementation of a complex IT system, for example an ERP system. Even with these complex subjects and still unclear terms of reference, the agile approach is not necessarily the only option for the whole tender. In the case of complex projects, it is probably tempting (especially for IT managers under extreme time pressure) to shift open questions that arise due to the complexity of the scope into the future.
>
> Unfortunately, the motto behind this is often, "We have no time now; we will eventually find a solution. . . ." In some IT projects, you can answer almost any question, or at least approach a decision, by simply taking the time and defining the basic rules for project implementation. For example, open questions on the principles of an ERP migration can be defined in advance (i.e., under what restrictive circumstances the software standard may be waived). For the tender and, most important, for the implementation, the principles of functional requirements need to be drawn up and examined together with the decision makers: whether or not they contradict the common principles *established*.
>
> If a request contradicts a principle, there should be a decision rule for whether the technical requirement is to be changed or not. This rule could be: A technical requirement (e.g., submission of a record in the ERP system) may contradict a principle (e.g., SW standard) only if the company's production would be forced to a standstill without the realization of this technical requirement: "The SW standard may be waived only if the production would otherwise stand still." This principle should be mutually defined in advance by the procurement expert and the budget owners.
>
> On deciding to handle a complex ERP migration project on the basis of an agile contract, you should not run the danger of postponing open questions related to any of the technical requirements.
>
> The main challenge for a typical migration project is often to reduce the complexity of the tender prior to implementation. This is done in order to reach the target price and ultimately make the project economically feasible.

This remains a challenge that also needs to be mastered within the agile framework agreement. However, complex migration projects also include many performance elements that can be better mapped within the agile approach.

An example of this is the evolution of a module. The features (business requirements) are roughly described and the interactions with other modules or systems are foreseeable. However, the client is not able to define the exact implementation and above all the project objectives in detail (yet). For this reason, the agile approach is ideally suited.

This statement indicates that the agile fixed-price contract must handle the following elements:

- The contract must prioritize defined project rules and set the technical framework conditions so that these major decisions are not postponed.
- If necessary, for certain parts of the project, the contractual terms of agile fixed-price contract should be designed to force, due to riskshare, the obligation of the contractor for highly standardized parts of the project.
- A methodology should be stipulated, in the contract or in technical notes, that commits both parties to work optimally (e.g., on a software standard, with a restrictive rule when a software standard can be given up).

We provide a brief answer to all of these concerns below but later discuss these topics in even more detail.

- The project vision consists precisely of general project rules and frame conditions.
- With riskshares each agile fixed-price contract can steer the obligation degree of the involved parties where certain highly standardized projects (or subparts of projects) might have more strict riskshares than others.
- Additionally, an agile fixed-price contract does contain specific contractually agreed-upon processes on how to manage the commitment for optimal work (i.e., create the maximum business value with the least effort).

Next, we consider the tender more precisely on the basis of an agile fixed-price contract and show that:

- It is in compliance with the principles of procurement presented in this chapter.
- It achieves the financial goals.
- It is better able to master the many substantive challenges in IT projects.

5.1 APPROPRIATE TENDER CONTENT FOR AN AGILE FIXED-PRICE CONTRACT

Initially, we must make clear what is put out to tender and what parts are negotiable in the context of an agile fixed-price contract (see Chapter 7 for details on negotiation). We often encounter the following sceptical question: Isn't the agile approach a very strong development-oriented system that eliminates the opportunity for the client to achieve the best possible price for the client, as with fixed price or daily rates for time and materials?

We think that this question can be answered "No." Quite the opposite is true. The agile fixed-price contract may, as shown in this chapter, be conducted just like a traditional fixed-price tender, that is, provided that the specific commercial parameters of the agile model are applied correctly. These commercial parameters are:

1. **Reference user stories.** The tender must at least be based on the user stories for an epic out of the backlog, which describes the scope of the contract. These user stories should be defined in every detail at the beginning of the tendering process. Only then and based on the costs of these reference user stories is the client able to optimize commercially the offers of suppliers through the appropriate tendering process, as in traditional fixed-price contracts.

2. **Overall scope/maximum price range.** Reference user stories do have an associated complexity value. This value results in a price. The supplier must submit a binding price (derived from the reference user stories) for each complexity point or for each complexity class of user stories. In addition, the supplier must estimate the overall scope based on complexity and deliver an initial indicative maximum price (fixed price, depending on the complexity points and the price per point). Depending on the type of project, this indicative maximum price is transformed into a final maximum price range (real fixed price) after a workshop or preferably a checkpoint phase. This corresponds essentially to a partially paid proof of concept, as is, in fact, standard in well-prepared traditional fixed-price contracts. However, the current proofs of concept have one major drawback: We have experienced the fact that the supplier brings the "heavy hitter" experts for the proof of concept, which will unfortunately not represent the later working project team. In comparison, the checkpoint phase is just the first phase of the project, with the same speed and the same team. This allows the client to have a much better prediction as to how the entire project could work.

3. **Riskshare.** The third parameter governs who absorbs what amount of risk, if the project exceeds the fixed price, or if during the checkpoint phase, implementation fails for other reasons. The riskshare factor shows clearly which supplier estimated the overall scope and reference user stories with a risk buffer so that he or she is able to feel confident and

takes over a high riskshare (e.g., 60%). It is also obvious which supplier offers an aggressive maximum price and thus assumes only, for example, a 10% riskshare, supposing the fixed price could not be maintained. The client can, of course, define the riskshare which "has to be absorbed," as a "minimum risk share" in the invitation to tender.

In addition to these commercial parameters, in an agile fixed-price contract it is also important that during the checkpoint phase, the client and the contractor verify the existence of expertise and a willingness to cooperate. The 12 principles of agile software development should be signed by both parties or integrated into the contract (see Chapters 1, 4, and 7). In the following sections we describe:

- How the tendering process for an agile fixed-price contract is set up optimally.
- How the main principles for a tender (competition and objectivity) can be met and why these are crucial for a successful tender.
- Which methods of procurement may be applied for IT tender procedures (i.e., auctions, request for indication, request for quotation, request for proposal, short list, long list, exclusive negotiation, etc.).

We also highlight how the tender for an agile fixed-price contract can be structured on a case-by-case basis. For example, it should be decided each time whether the agile project should be assigned as a complete tendering procedure or step by step: initially, the checkpoint phase with defined user stories, and then, for example, the indicative maximum price, and finally, the real fixed price.

Example of Tendering Possibilities

How might the commercial elements outlined above be represented in a Request for Proposal (RFP)? The backlog for IT project X includes the following commercial elements for the subject matter of the contract, which are prepared before the invitation to tender.

Epic 1: User administration

This includes a description of the epic (including the frame conditions if necessary) and all the user stories for this epic, namely:

User story 1: described precisely (= reference user story 1)
User story 2: described precisely (= reference user story 2)

User story 3: described precisely (= reference user story 3)
User story 4: described precisely (= reference user story 4)
User story 5: described precisely (= reference user story 5)
User story 6: described precisely (= reference user story 6)

Epic 2: Data analysis

This includes a description of the epic (including the frame conditions, if necessary). However, no user stories for this epic are defined at the time of tender.

Epic 3: Data migration

This includes a description of the epic (including the frame conditions, if necessary). However, no user stories for this epic are defined at the time of tender.

A complexity value and derived price for the reference user stories must be delivered (requested within the RFP) by the supplier. For this example, a supplier could deliver something like the following:

Reference user story 1 = 3 story points, $3000
Reference user story 2 = 5 story points, $5000
Reference user story 3 = 3 story points, $3000
Reference user story 4 = 8 story points, $8000
Reference user story 5 = 13 story points, $13,000
Reference user story 6 = 5 story points, $5000

The client is therefore informed that epic 1 corresponds to a complexity of 37 story points and that each story point from this supplier costs $1000. The important thing is that story points represent individual values for each vendor (we will see later on that there are even options to normalize this in the tendering process). By fixing the number of reference user stories at the beginning, you prevent the inflation of this value over the course of the project. Additionally, the set of more than one reference user stories ensures that the story points are evaluated in total for all these reference user stories, as the story point for one user story might have a different size or value for different suppliers. At the end, all that counts is the cost of the reference user story and the maximum price for the entire backlog.

The supplier estimates that epics 2 and 3, which are described on a high level with only one paragraph and a few assumptions, are two and three times as complex as epic 1. This means that epic 2 is estimated with a complexity of 74 story points and epic 3 with 111 story points. The supplier knows that he or she can include, for example, 5% security for the cost estimate with this type of project and, accordingly, submits an estimate of complexity of 233 story points (222 + 5%) at an indicative maximum price of $233,000.

(***Note:*** *In contrast to a traditional fixed-price contract, this cost of +5% is either paid or not paid, depending on the bonus system!*)

In view of their experience and with regard to the description and suitable assumptions of the epics, the supplier is willing to accept 60% of the riskshares for this amount. If the project costs exceed $233,000 due to a lack of measures being taken to prevent exceeding the complexity limit, additional story points, beyond the 233 story points, are invoiced at only $400!

This example shows that this type of tender is different and still allows for commercially objective decisions.

Based on the information (reference user stories and epics) from the business department, procurement is able to present a professional tender based on an agile fixed-price contract. Depending on the project, the procurement and business departments can decide together whether and with which methodology the already defined user stories are put out to tender (e.g., face to face, via e-mail, or via an online tool). There are two possibilities:

1. **Tendering for the entire scope of the project, including the checkpoint phase.** This means that the contractor delivers an indicative maximum price, which is converted into a final maximum price range during the checkpoint phase.

2. **Tendering for the checkpoint phase as a separate project.** First there is a tender for the checkpoint phase with a recommended scope of the reference user stories. After successful completion of the checkpoint phase, the entire project is negotiated with the suppliers that passed the checkpoint phase successfully or is even put out to another tender. Here, also, the business department has to change its mindset. If one supplier has positively completed the checkpoint phase from the point of view of the business department, this does not mean that the project automatically proceeds with this single supplier (as there might have been additional successful suppliers). If this is not conveyed to the business department, it is difficult for procurement personnel to enforce an objective tender based on fair competition for the entire project.

All these points must be analyzed accordingly and adjusted internally before an RFP is launched.

5.2 REQUIREMENTS FOR TENDERING AND SELECTION

Most companies award contracts through a specialized department, the procurement department. What principles should be included in the invitation for tender so that the ideal supplier—from a commercial and technical point of view—wins the tender? There are essentially two conditions that are necessary for a successful tender:

1. **Competition.** The potential contractor must make and negotiate a genuine (i.e., perceived competitive) offer.
2. **Comparability and transparency.** The offers of the suppliers must be comparable in all respects, so that the client can make an internally transparent and objective decision as to who is awarded a contract. Such comparability and transparency must be a part of all commercial, legal, and technical topics.

5.2.1 Competition

The client may award an agile fixed-price contract only under optimal market conditions and only if two or more companies participate in the tender. Neither of these may have a disproportionately large head start, as would be the case if exclusive workshops with only one provider are offered. In addition, at least two companies must be seriously interested in the job and be suitable for it. *Suitable* means that if you tender based on the agile fixed-price mode, experience in agile development methodology is taken into account. To meet the two basic conditions of competition and comparability, procurement personnel must confer regularly with the business department and perform internal negotiations before the actual tender. Finally, it is essential with this new process that despite conflicts of interest between the internal stakeholders involved, all share a common goal: a successful project delivered within an optimal commercial framework for implementation. An internally well-prepared tender ensures that the competition requirement is also fulfilled for the process based on the agile fixed-price contract.

Workshops and short lists
During the tendering phase, the customer offers the supplier workshops (at least one). Nevertheless, suppliers should communicate their prices exclusively on an online platform. This includes the reference user stories and the checkpoint phase as well as the indicative maximum price. This ensures that on the client side, only those people who should be influenced by commercial parameters know this information (in practice, procurement personnel and decision makers). The complexity values for each reference user story and epic and their descriptions and assumptions should be discussed by the supplier and the technical experts (ideally, without the price per story point).

As part of a workshop, clients discuss their interpretations of the technical description and whether they propose boundaries or assumptions for these descriptions. If not awarded in one project, the assignments in the checkpoint phase should also be based on an agile fixed-price contract defined by the client (basic principles, scope governance, riskshare, price matrix, or story points). In this way, potential contractors accept the approach of the agile fixed-price contract as early as possible, and the experience of collaboration can be evaluated within this trial phase.

After the workshops, the client can further reduce the number of potential suppliers to maintain acceptable costs for further steps in the tender (as we suggest that all the suppliers are—at least partially—paid for their efforts in the checkpoint phase as long as they succeed). Ideally, at least three suppliers make it to the short list. This is the list that is used as a basis for the final negotiations and ultimately for decisions regarding suppliers. In reality, the checkpoint phase, when used for small projects, is generally carried out with only one supplier, with other suppliers kept "on hold." This is one (if not the best) way, because you will reduce initial efforts (assuming a small to medium-sized project) and not lose too much time. However, negotiations should always be held with at least two suppliers capable of winning the tender. On a case-by-case basis you will decide to go through the checkpoint phase with a challenger to heat up the competition.

Ideally, the short-listed suppliers are now invited to define (ideally, the reference user stories) and implement a certain number of sprints (checkpoint phase) together with the client. The client inspects the sprints at the agreed-upon time and compares the results among the suppliers. The client may award the same or different user stories to all suppliers. After the checkpoint phase, the client adjusts the contract, the objectives of the project, the assumptions, and the levels of complexity, if required. This is presented to the suppliers in a comprehensible form based on the new findings, which were gathered from cooperation with the suppliers during this stage. This approach differs somewhat from the traditional practice. For traditional fixed-price contracts, a proof of concept should theoretically also be obtained from at least two suppliers. This often looks different in practice in traditional and agile fixed-price contracts. The checkpoint phase and proofs of concept are often completed by the first-tier supplier while the second-tier supplier is on standby, with the disadvantage that there is no genuine comparison of performance. We therefore strongly recommend performing this phase with at least two suppliers. Do not be afraid to stop a project after a not-so-convincing checkpoint phase, and get the mandate to do so!

In recent publications on "agile sourcing" (e.g., Emergyn, 2012), the strong recommendation is that no IT contract be awarded without a proper trial phase beforehand. Subsequently, all suppliers are invited to offer a binding maximum price range (see Chapters 3 and 4) based on an agile fixed-price contract for the entire project. This is based on the contract, the existing reference user stories, the remaining backlog (the entire high-level description of the scope), and the knowledge gained.

To what extent it makes sense to hold a reverse auction in this process is decided on a case-by-case basis (see the "Digression" box). It is also possible to hold auctions for individual components of the project, such as for certain standard activities, standard software, or standard hardware. To prevent dumping prices, no traditional English auctions should be held (see, e.g., Kleusberg, 2009). There can be different combinations of software vendors and system integrators for the introduction of a new software or system. When considering the short list as well as the invitation to a checkpoint phase, the client's most promising combinations according to the evaluation matrix should be kept in mind (see Section 5.3.4).

Digression: Online Auctions or Reverse Auctions

There are often elements in agile projects that are suitable for an online auction. In an agile fixed-price contract, a real fixed price (maximum price range) can be posted online in the last step: in other words, after the details of the contract are negotiated and the checkpoint phase has been performed. Note that *real fixed price* is an alternative name for *agile fixed price*, as it refers to a real fixed price without the change requests expected.

What is an online auction?

Online auctions are described in procurement as *reverse auctions*. Compared to traditional auctions, it is a question of suppliers providing a contract service to the customer. Unlike an auction where the selling price is driven up, in a reverse auction the purchase price for the contract service is "bid" low, due to the competition. This form of auction is an effective way to ensure maximum competition. The trained procurement representative selects the suitable form of auction and the corresponding awarding of the contract for the upcoming assignment.

What are the advantages of reverse auctions?

- *Objectivity.* The online auction is the most difficult but also the fairest, because it is the most objective form of awarding a tender. The decision is made under conditions that are technically the same for everyone (i.e., space, time, contacts, etc.).
- *Economic efficiency.* The objectively best customer at the best price wins the contract without subjective distortions. Emotions, interpretations, or aversions cannot affect the selection because there is no physical contact during the decision phase.

- *Low transaction costs.* Cost factors such as time and space are halted. With so-called "commodities" (i.e., clearly defined products such as screws, pallets, antennas, or servers), procurement personnel need only briefly define the minimal quality, type, and number, together with the legal framework.

Clarifying the basic principles

It is essential that the client hold a joint workshop with the best bidders of this process. They must all agree on the basic principles of the respective agile fixed-price contract: the technical requirements as well as the agile model. With an agile fixed-price contract, you should host discussions together with the business department and two or three suppliers before the auction. A reverse auction makes sense only if the following points are resolved successfully and in detail (this requires extraordinary experience in complex IT projects):

- The scope and objectives of the project and an explanation of the backlogs being verified and extended by the assumptions required
- The project environment (the client resources, software, hardware, interfaces, etc.)
- The time frame
- The agile fixed-price contract, the basis on which the project is to be implemented
- The final alignment on any uncertainties within the reference user stories

Important note: The points listed above must be incorporated into the contract or in contract attachments. The client may not start an online auction until this is done and the contract is, at least for the most part, accepted officially by the major suppliers. Otherwise, the client may receive a good indicative or real fixed price without knowing the conditions for the provision of services or for the service itself. Experience shows that it is more time consuming to negotiate the legal and technical framework after price negotiation than the other way around.

5.2.2 Comparability and Transparency

Basically, the client must specify the same commercial, legal, and technical framework for each supplier. The client should define the technical and business objectives of the project, all commercial drivers, and the legal framework before the start of each tender, to ensure maximum success. The client should notify the suppliers of all these issues in a structured RFP, including any corresponding attachments (see the original contract template in Chapter 4). Due primarily to time pressure, lack of knowhow, or a combination of both, many clients do not invest enough energy in the documentation before and during the tender. This can also happen with agile fixed-price contracts. Offers are not comparable and often lead to expensive misunderstandings between client and contractor, often making project success impossible.

In reality, an absolute comparison of offers is not possible, especially for large IT development projects in complex environments even if detailed technical (note that this part is no longer as extensive with an agile fixed-price contract), commercial, and legal documents are specified. To arrive as close as possible to a transparent and objective decision, many companies now employ a *backpack*. This assists in the event that the specified commercial, technical, or legal standards are not respected or certain soft facts are needed to influence the decision. If a supplier does not fulfill a requirement, a fictitious price is determined which will be added to the actual price. This approach is also selected by a client when conversion costs exist with new suppliers. This allows the client to include nonmonetary items in an award decision. A compliant/noncompliant list is helpful for a quick overview of those issues that are not met by the supplier. This document is presented by the client. The suppliers must enter, in a structured manner, which items they accept (compliant) and which they do not accept (noncompliant). Usually, the answer "partially compliant" is explicitly excluded in advance and interpreted as noncompliant.

In agile fixed-price contracts, the same process is proposed, the only difference being that detailed technical documentation is not available at the start of the project. Therefore, a clear distinction must be created based on the high-level detail of the backlog. This distinction should be standardized for all bidders, through assumptions and clarifications. Precisely these assumptions, principles, and clarifications will be incorporated into the contract and must be officially accepted by the suppliers before the final negotiations.

In practice, a workshop is held with the first suppliers. Here, a number of common assumptions and findings supplement the individual epics of the backlog, which up to now have been described in only a paragraph. To stress the point once again, it is important that these supplements be made jointly by the contractor and the client in the workshop. These assumptions are then introduced into the basis for discussion with the second supplier. If the client always performs one or two iterations with two or three suppliers, the greatest common multiple can be used again as a clearly defined backlog. This describes the subject of the contract more clearly (although not in as much detail as for a traditional fixed-price contract). On this improved basis, it is usually possible to start a traditional tender process. For larger projects, the supplier should be prepared to bear these indirect consulting costs within the framework of the acquisition costs.

Recently, a client who we supported in the first execution of an agile fixed-price contract–based tender remarked in the preparation phase that it seems very unlikely that the information from such an intense workshop can be passed on perfectly to all other suppliers. However, this client had the challenge of managing more than 10 suppliers in the tendering process, and there have also been quite harsh tendering rules if a supplier feels disadvantaged. We recommended hosting the workshop with all suppliers at once, which for this client was very experimental. Still the client believed us and sent an invitation to all suppliers explaining the procedure and asking that two people come to this half-day workshop. In the workshop there was the task of putting all uncertainties on the table and clarifying them by additional information or assumptions. Following that, the entire backlog needed to be estimated (first the reference user stories and then the epics). What do you think happened? It worked! The result was astonishing. Not only did the client have a clear impression as to which clients sent the right people with the right skills, but the client was also able to normalize all story point currencies among the suppliers. This example shows that it sometimes pays off to leave traditional paths and try something new (preferably under expert guidance).

Returning to the process: At the end of the tender, the client (usually, procurement personnel along with technical managers) provides a comparison of vendor prices and arguments for and against the respective suppliers, based on the jointly defined backpack. Usually, only the disadvantages of the individual suppliers are evaluated in monetary terms; that is, which "penalty backpack" do they carry with them? For example, how financially stable is the supplier? And how big is the effort to integrate a new supplier in the existing organization? However, for an agile fixed price, it is also essential to give a certain impact to the specific soft facts, such as whether the supplier is an expert in agile delivery. Based on this, the client finally reaches a decision.

An example of a supplier's price in an agile fixed-price contract follows:

- Three reference user stories with complexity values (or story points) of 5, 8, and 13 have been estimated by supplier A and offered at $13,000. These three user stories completely describe an epic, epic 1. Thus, this epic has a complexity of 26 Story points.
- The overall complexity of the three epics is estimated at 89 story points according to the analogous estimate. A story point costs (based on the reference user stories) $500. The project is therefore offered at $44,500 (assuming that no security margin is added).
- Supplier A, a supplier well established with the customer, announces that due to the complexity of the two remaining epics not yet described on the user story level with a medium risk of uncertainty, a fixed price of $48,000 is offered (a $3500 safety margin, corresponding to 7 story points, that may or may not be used in the project). Supplier A is willing to accept a riskshare of 50% if the complexity exceeds her estimate. A riskshare of 50% means that if the complexity is higher and thus the fixed price is exceeded, the price per story point is reduced by 50%, to $250.
- Supplier B, who is determined to gain market share, estimates the complexity of the reference user stories at 2, 3, and 5 story points and offers these at a price of $10,000. His estimate is based on the same backlogs

and the same commercial, legal, and technical framework. Furthermore, supplier B anticipates a total complexity of the functionality of 34 story points. He is so sure of his estimate that he offers a maximum price of $34,000 within the framework of the agile fixed-price contract, with no safety buffer. Above that he offers a riskshare of 70%.

For such divergent offers, the client must calculate a possible objective backpack for both suppliers. In addition, the client may wish to consider increasing the riskshares: for example, up to 80% for supplier B in the event that the project, for whatever reason, cannot be implemented within the agreed maximum price (real fixed price). Theoretically, the possibility exists of breaking user stories down into classes and also into activity groups. In most projects this is not necessary, however, because the client does not care how the contractor puts his or her team together to provide the required performance. Where an activity (e.g., testing) can be handled with cheaper labor (e.g., through nearshoring), it automatically results in a lower price for the person-days that might or might not lead to a reduced price for one story point or one complexity class. The contractor must therefore put together the optimal mix of resources for their teams to achieve an optimal cost structure for the team offered. Note that the agile fixed price is based on performance and results, and the client does not share any risks if the supplier's resources are not performing and therefore additional costs arise. However, what is offered here is often a product owner and a development team (including all required roles), but additional functions, such as support for the business analysis or project office support, may be appointed outside this fixed price, on the basis of time and materials, or, if requested, incorporated in the story point costs.

5.3 TENDERING STEPS WITH A FOCUS ON AGILE FIXED PRICE

In this section we describe the main steps of a tender in detail and refer to the agile fixed-price contract in each of these steps. Thus, you are able to classify more precisely how and when an agile fixed-price contract has substantial advantages or specialities compared to known forms of contracts within the tendering process. It also allows you to pay attention to any special features.

Schematically, the tender process, including negotiations, can be divided into the following stages:

- Internal goal setting and coordination
- Preparation for the invitation to tender
- Invitation to tender (for details on negotiation topics, see Chapter 7)
- Awarding of the tender (decision as to a supplier)

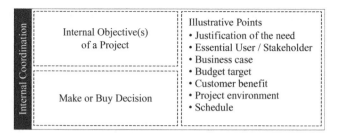

Figure 5.1 *Elements of internal coordination.*

5.3.1 Internal Goal Setting and Coordination

Figure 5.1 shows, by example, which points in the stage of internal coordination can play a crucial role in an investment decision. Internal coordination and goal setting already have a considerable influence on whether a project is a success or a failure. For example, the internal coordination serves to define the internal goals and benefits as well as scheduling and creating business cases.

The following two examples show why internal coordination is important and what impact it has if it does not take place or does not take place sufficiently. In many cases, as well as in these examples, an agile fixed-price contract helps to cope with shortcomings in internal coordination.

Example 1: End-of-year spending case
Together, the business and controlling departments come to the conclusion at the end of November that $x million of the IT budget has not yet been issued. The procurement department now typically has until the end of the year to tender for a specific project with this open budget (assuming that the budget would otherwise be cut the next year, which is a very common case). In most cases, for a complex project the time period is not sufficient to set up, tender, and award a contract in a professional manner, taking into account all technical, legal, and commercial aspects. Typically, many fundamental questions remain unanswered and thus become a risk. It would be better anyway to ignore such a budget constraint and define prepayments for clearly defined services and products, as they are used (and will come up and be described in detail) in the next fiscal year.

Nevertheless, an agile fixed-price contract can also help with such time critical tenders. A standard contract for the agile model can be set up quickly if the organization is well trained (see Example 1 in Chapter 10). A contract based on the waterfall model requiring specification of the entire project would definitely not be the correct approach, and in addition to all the other disadvantages would be too time consuming. Also, the backlog and important reference user stories can be described quickly. In such a situation, only a few especially good suppliers should be invited, so as not to waste time with experiments. After the checkpoint phase, the tender, and the awarding of the tender, the project can start immediately.

Example 2: Operation not involved

All decision makers should be involved in the internal preparation. However, quite often the department of software development develops a product for the very specific area (or internal client) that another department (e.g., the department of operations) will ultimately need to operate and maintain. If the department responsible for the operation is not involved, it can lead to costly surprises after delivery of the project. Also, with agile fixed-price contracts, all stakeholders involved (e.g., the department of operations) should be involved in the regular joint validations of the intermediate results. However, a stakeholder who by accident is not involved has the chance to claim changes at a later stage, as the scope is flexible.

5.3.1.1 Make-or-buy decision

The make-or-buy decision is made after the business case is approved and the objectives of the investment are clear. In a make-or-buy decision the client decides whether it makes more sense whether an internal department or an outside supplier implements a project or a part thereof.

5.3.1.2 Procurement engineering

For several years now in larger companies, procurement engineering departments have had the task of scrutinizing and optimizing the way in which service is provided by a supplier. For example, if a supplier uses a special procedure for the documentation of software delivery, the department clarifies whether it is suitable for the quality requirements of the company or whether a more efficient approach can be employed. Procurement engineering is similar to the role of procurement in the agile process described in this book. When a client chooses the agile model for a project, the client (and procurement) commits himself or herself to a duty to cooperate comprehensively and provide constant content and commercial optimization within the framework of agreed-upon principles to optimize efficiency.

5.3.2 Preparation for the Invitation to Tender

Many clients spend very little or no time on the process step of tender preparation (Figure 5.2) even if it contains basics such as the precise definition of the objective (scope or subject matter of the contract), technical descriptions, and a decision on the commercial and legal model. The time pressure leads to hasty, often incorrect, and expensive decisions; and very often it leads to projects that do not reach the intended goal. An agile fixed-price contract reduces the risks in a project by making it possible to make corrections along the way in order to achieve the project goal. However, basic elements of an investment should be considered and prepared thoroughly beforehand. The following list

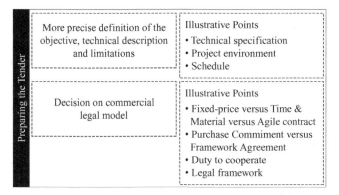

Figure 5.2 *Elements of the preparation phase of the tender.*

describes the most common reasons for rushed decisions and shows why in such cases an agile fixed-price contract is especially suitable.

- "We must utilize the budget for the current year in a timely manner; otherwise, it is lost."

  Agile fixed-price contract: Start with the overall project and exit at the checkpoint phase if the project performance (by the client *and* the supplier) turns out not to be as expected.

- "Our customers expect this application within the next three months, otherwise we will lose market share to competitors."

  Agile fixed-price contract: The start of high-level specifications according to an orderly process enables a faster "time to market." This is because it can be started simultaneously with the implementation of the first functionalities while still working on the detailed specifications of functionalities that are to be implemented later. Moreover, agile fixed-price contracts give you more security as to both time to market and budgetary goals and at the same time reduce dramatically the risk of sunk costs.

- "It is not necessary in this case to prepare the tender based on the agile fixed-price contract, because there is only one possibility as to how to do that, and nothing is unclear."

  Agile fixed-price contract: If, however, there were not only one possibility or if, unfortunately, not everything were clear, we retain flexibility.

- "Only these two suppliers can offer a solution; a tender is not possible due to a lack of precise definition of objectives."

  Agile fixed-price contract: The checkpoint period can be used to test the performance of both suppliers on just a part of the detailed defined scope (reference user stories), and based on this, in an extreme approach to achieve the best price, even in a reverse auction.

Should there indeed be too little time available, the quality of the decisions and the preparation should not suffer as a result. Instead, more, and where appropriate, external resources should be invested in the project. An agile fixed-price contract should be used to expand, over almost the entire project, the stage where the detailed specifications are written.

One essential point often not discussed in sufficient detail in this preparation phase is the cost of delay. This is a very essential parameter that could also be added to the backpack as a factor to consider in the overall evaluation. However, at least for project steering, this is an essential parameter that must be evaluated while the business case is being finalized.

Documentation as a learning tool

The tender documentation is especially important for success. Questions emerge again and again in preparing the documentation. In response to this, the specialists in the business, procurement, and legal departments discuss the content with each other and continue to refine it. This open debate has two positive effects:

1. It leads to a draft agreement agreed to by all the parties involved.
2. The various parties develop new perspectives on the project and learn more details.

Part of the preparation of the tender for an agile model is the allocation of the already defined user stories as well as the request for an indicative fixed price. As the client has already applied this to the market, we enter into the context of the next process step, the tender itself. We want to emphasize again that the client should not take the next step, the tender itself, without sufficient preparation and meticulous decisions as to the commercial, legal, and technical basics. This also applies to an agile fixed-price contract, in which the details of the scope do not need to be prepared, but the principles for implementation of the process and the legal and commercial framework must be fixed.

The tender will be postponed if the documentation is incomplete or still in dispute, or if the schedule or the project environment is not yet known sufficiently well. An agile fixed-price contract makes it possible to begin as long as the legal and commercial framework is clear, and to send out the tender after the checkpoint phase. An end-to-end specification does not need to be made.

5.3.3 Tender

With the tender, the client is requesting feedback from the market (Figure 5.3). The following types of tenders exist, each pursuing a different goal and all are assigned to a different stage in the tendering process. Depending on the project and the starting point, the individual "requests" ("calls" to the suppliers) are more or less applicable.

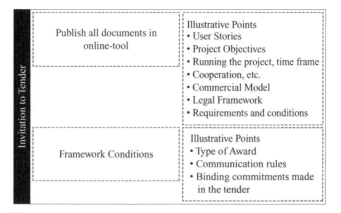

Figure 5.3 *Elements of an invitation to tender.*

- **Request for information (RFI):** a request to potential suppliers to dis-close general information about individual questions. This tool can also be used for the agile model to probe the market based on a very vague project description. Who can realistically implement this project? Who even has the resources to implement a project with a certain order of magnitude? How many employees are there, and what qualifications and experience do they have? What sites are there? Does the supplier have experience with agile methods? Is there any offshoring potential? Which certifications does the supplier have? Who is willing to work for the client even though also being involved with the competition?

- **Request for quotation (RFQ):** a request to suppliers to place an offer on the basis of fundamental information. In this way the client wants to determine which potential suppliers, on the basis of a rudimentary project description, can or even want to place a nonobligatory offer. With agile models, an RFQ would include the query of a price for the reference user stories and an initial indicative fixed price. Thus, preselection of suppliers can be reduced further.

- **Request for proposal (RFP):** a request to submit a binding offer. This step opens the tender in the true sense. With agile fixed-price contracts, a binding fixed price is requested as a last resort.

Depending on the complexity of the agile fixed-price contract to be awarded, the client may use all three of the above-defined tools, or perhaps just one or two. It is often useful to use all three tools as the scope, as the exact imple-mentation is, by definition, not fixed in agile fixed-price contracts.

Example
The objective of the project is to create new software for tracking container ships.

Step 1: RFI. In an RFI the client submits the following contents to potential suppliers:

- *The project goal:* mission and topics, so that the fundamental task is clear. This essentially includes the project vision part of the scope definition in an agile fixed-price contract.
- *The proposed course of action:* agile development and agile fixed-price contracts without a full description (mission, topics, and epics) and without reference user stories and other details. Moreover, certain questions regarding a supplier's background and capabilities (with focus on agility) are asked.

The client thereby determines with which supplier he or she can actually implement this project while remaining within the agile context. The procurement department should be informed about the RFI, but usually does not act as the driving force. Neither must all decision makers be involved. It is important, however, that even at this stage no preliminary decisions, not even emotional, are made as to a supplier. The objective is different, of course, for the client's respective key accounts.

Step 2: RFQ. Potentially suitable suppliers are selected. The client can now verify in the RFQ which suppliers are prepared to work on implementation of the scope for the checkpoint phase. This is based on the tender documents (reference user stories) and a possible riskshare in the checkpoint phase (see Chapter 3). Depending on the setting of the riskshare parameters, the checkpoint phase can range from an unpaid service (a virtually unremunerated proof of concept) to time and materials or a small fixed-price project. We recommend the latter, as it seems fair to pay the supplier if he or she delivers the requested functionality successfully by the end of the checkpoint phase. However, this payment may also be linked to a certain riskshare, which means that the client would pay only for all the work of a supplier who will continue in the process, with all others getting a sort of cost refund.

Provided that the backlog and first reference user stories exist, the client may query which nonbinding maximum fixed price the respective suppliers are offering. Based on the offers from the RFQ, the client is in a position to reduce the suppliers to a manageable number for the RFP.

Step 3: RFP. First a test run should be conducted with the suppliers listed (checkpoint phase), in which user stories are implemented (if not already done in the RFQ described above). After that, the crucial RFP is released for the agile fixed price, based on the final contract, including all attachments. In reality, for small projects, this test run is usually completed with a supplier, while a second is in the standby position. This is done in case the first supplier cannot continue the project after the checkpoint phase. On a small scale for large projects and to secure competition, it is, however, quite reasonable to carry out the test runs with two suppliers.

Alternatively, the tender for an agile fixed-price contract can also be conducted with selected suppliers without a prior checkpoint phase. This is possible only provided that the checkpoint phase is also defined in the first stage within the project with exit points (see the sample contract outline in Chapter 4). It is not an option to start a project without a clear view of a project's reality!

Let us assume that the client presents an opportunity to enter the checkpoint phase prior to the RFP. He or she can proceed with a greater probability that the suppliers of the RFP are actually in a position to achieve the goal or goals of the project, as they proved it already in this "trial phase."

A client may launch final negotiations with several suppliers after receiving all binding offers. He may also grant the contract directly to the best bidder or, for example, enter into exclusive negotiations. This is decided from case to case and on the basis of the offers and the felt level of real competition among suppliers.

Offers on the basis of RFPs must be comparable. Many suppliers try to overturn the specified commercial, legal, and technical framework to make a comparison impossible. Such an attempt may be made in various ways; for example:

- The supplier does not offer the client requested but, rather, potentially useful additional services or objectives and mixes these services in the pricing.
- The supplier offers a flat rate, so as not to be vulnerable to the single-price basis (no "cherry picking"; no comparison in detail). This approach also runs on a version of the traditional fixed-price contract, but is definitely inappropriate for an agile fixed-price contract because you would not be able to control the individual epics in their complexity and therefore not be able to retain the contractual process requested.
- The supplier tries to connect different projects or maintenance orders with the pricing for the contract currently tendered.

An agile fixed-price contract prohibits such attempts by a supplier, due to its principles. In particular, the principle that a true fixed price with riskshare will eventually be offered makes such interventions impossible or at least less appropriate.

To avoid any misunderstanding, the client should hold a question-and-answer workshop for each supplier before publishing the next mandatory RFXs. If user stories were delivered at an earlier stage (e.g., the RFQ), the workshop has a very solid foundation (as both parties have experienced their behavior in a real project setup). Ideally, the respective key account manager or procurement agent supports the technical experts. In addition, the manager or agent should be the single point of contact during the bidding process, to ensure clear communication.

It is important with agile fixed-price contracts that no daily rates generally be negotiated but, rather, units of functionality (story points or user stories, according to the complexity classes). In this respect, the transparency of the underlying planning and resources is negligible (see the example in Section 5.1).

5.3.4   Awarding of the Tender

We have already said that poor preparation of a tender is the first major error contributing to the failure of an IT project. In our opinion, based on agile fixed pricing, the second major error is to select a final supplier without having coordinated the legal, commercial, and technical framework (i.e., the contract agreed to, including technical and commercial attachments). Without this documentation of principles, it does not, in fact, even make sense to begin negotiations on the commercial parameters (real fixed price/maximum price range, riskshare, checkpoint phase, etc.).

Second, as a consequence, it must be determined, at the latest before the awarding of the contract, which legal and technical documents are accepted by the potential supplier and which are not fully accepted. (Technical documents refer to those containing certain principles, such as programming the software standard, open interfaces, hardware, etc.) If a supplier does not confirm the fundamental points in the tender as binding, the client should derail this supplier after an attempt at clarification. This includes the implementation of automated testing, and confirmation of appropriate technical tools to even develop agile professionally.

To guarantee comparability among the remaining suppliers, a backpack must be added to the total price offered. This involves all the disadvantages that would arise under the given system landscape and environment of the given project if the actual supplier were to implement the project according to the terms offered. The client can only evaluate these disadvantages with an approximate monetary value. Nevertheless, this tool is a prerequisite for an objective award involving all relevant parameters (see one discussion of parameters such as riskshare and cost per story point in Chapter 4). As shown in Figure 5.4, the award should not take place until all the content points (i.e., technical and legal) and the commercial aspects have been incorporated.

The budget for a project serves to specify the target price. Usually, this is the wrong approach, because the actual achievable lowest price very rarely corresponds to the budget value. Instead, a client must ask what minimum goals he or she wants to achieve with a minimal capital outlay. On this basis, the client must define the target price. The agile model is ideal for this, because suppliers are encouraged to name the lowest price on the basis of the necessary requirements, not based on an exaggerated condition put forth by a specific business department. The agile model generally aims at a low fixed price and a reasonable scope for the project. Thereby, for example, it can be agreed to in principle that the company's processes follow IT and not vice

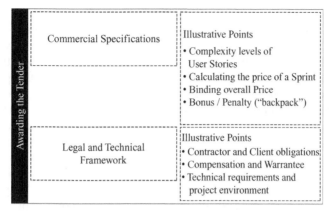

Figure 5.4 *Elements of the awarding of the tender.*

versa, as long as they are not connected to exorbitant costs (the cost issue should be defined).

Neither the budget nor the internally defined target price may be communicated to the supplier because otherwise the actual offer will never be lower than this price point. In the final stage, it must be carefully considered whether a target price operates within the context of a cooperative negotiation style. Furthermore, the agile approach based on the agile fixed-price contract process ensures that requirements which carry the highest business value and thus maximally secure the investments made are always implemented next. Thus, an optimal increase in value is ensured.

The pricing for an agile fixed-price contract is based on the following commercial items:

- **Pricing from the perspective of the supplier**
  - Reference user stories, which are presented in detail
  - Backlog evaluation for the entire project, consisting of epics in terms of an analogous estimate (if necessary, equipped with a margin of safety)
  - Riskshare
  - Margin
- **Pricing from the perspective of the client**
  - Effort for the reference user stories
  - Maximum price range
  - Riskshare
  - Backpack

As described in Chapter 3, one or two user stories should be implemented and accepted within a checkpoint phase before the auction or final negotiation with the short-listed suppliers and, indeed, on the basis of optimized costs through a riskshare. The contractor delivers the cost of the complexity points for the reference user stories proposed in the checkpoint phase as well as the price per complexity point. He or she also explains, for example, that these costs will be calculated at only 70%, in the event that one of the parties no longer wishes to continue with the project after the checkpoint phase.

During the test phase it is essential that the client include the performance of the individual suppliers in the decision over the awarding of the tender. Who does the client actually trust for the implementation? As a result, suppliers have the opportunity to better assess the work, the cooperation with the client, and the complexity of the project. In most cases, such a test phase brings more meaningful findings than an entire series of abstract workshops. Very often, in fact, these create substantial misunderstandings, because you do not specifically maintain every detail of a user story, and abstract discussions increase abstract expectations. Parallel to the checkpoint phase, the client should generally offer workshops to a selected circle of suppliers. These workshops should cover the legal and commercial framework as well as project objectives.

Even in more complex projects, it should be possible in this way for suppliers to calculate and present a realistic maximum price range for an agile fixed-price contract. The contractor will use the combined cost of all the activities and levels of complexity in calculating the maximum price range. The combined cost is based on the backlog, the already defined final user stories, and possibly epics (consisting of user stories), as well as the experience gained from the test phase. The client is usually only interested in the "team costs," which in the end results in the cost for each complexity point. The performance is assessed, not people or time!

In agile fixed-price contracts especially, the prospect of a successful and cooperative project completion is particularly important. The definition and calculation of all backpack costs (Figure 5.5) is therefore a particularly tricky and scrupulous task which should be based on a solid foundation of information. The department should calculate the backpack before retrieval of the offers, so as not to be influenced by the final result.

Important once again at this stage is the internal coordination, collaboration, and the understanding of the "new approach" among the various stakeholders on the client side. The purchaser is responsible for the process; the actual decision is usually made by top management without emotion. It is essential to communicate openly and to make the benefits of this new approach (e.g., risk minimization) transparent for all decision makers. The mindset "we will take the lowest offer" should be avoided at all levels as a basis for a decision. It is more important to raise the question of whether this supplier can support the approach that you need as a customer!

5.3.5 Price Optimization Options

To further minimize the cost at the second stage of the tender, the client can retrieve another price table for the same activities in nearshoring or offshor-

		DECISION MATRIX – SIMPLIFIED EXAMPLE				
		SUPPLIER A	SUPPLIER B	SUPPLIER C	SUPPLIER D	SUPPLIER E
	OBJECTIVE FIXED-PRICE	575.000,-	670.000,-	495.000,-	810.000,-	300.000,-
	MAINTENANCE SYSTEM	250.000,-	400.000,-	480.000,-	400.000,-	120.000,-
	SW FEE SYSTEM	50.000,-	100.000,-	80.000,-	320.000,-	100.000,-
DECISION ELEMENT	TOTAL WITHOUT BACKPACK	875.000,-	1.170.000,-	1.055.000,-	1.530.000,-	520.000,-
	BACKPACK	200.000,-	50.000,-	250.000,-	15.000,-	700.000,-
	BACKPACK EXPLANATION*	TEST PHASE WITH PROBLEMS	SHORTENED WARRANTEE	SLA LEVELS ARE NOT AGREED	ERP MODULE MUST ADAPT TO THE INTERFACE	SW IS NOT BASED ON A STANDARD
	TOTAL	1.075.000,-	1.123.000,-	1.305.000,-	1.545.000,-	1.220.000,-

Figure 5.5 Example of a decision matrix. (The explanations concerning the backpack are illustrated in a highly simplified manner. The allocation of a backpack to a supplier should be scrutinized critically by procurement, as the specialist departments can strongly influence the supplier decision by means of the backpack. This is a good thing, as long as it is not unfounded or a matter of convenience that the business department's favorite supplier is given the opportunity through force.)

ing. They may then call on the suppliers to specify what percentage of the user stories or of the established teams they can each deploy for nearshoring and offshoring. The client may also reserve certain activities defined in advance and accepted by the contractor. They can then be outsourced to third parties to achieve a price advantage: for example, testing the user stories or even the acceptance process thereof. If you follow this procedure, the client should make sure that the contract contains a clear provision to guarantee. This means that despite the involvement of a third party, the contractor will provide guarantees for the entire project, as third parties as well as the client are managed by supplier. The same applies to the liability. On the other hand, the contractor should agree to such a provision only in exceptional cases: certainly only if he or she has the possibility of reviewing and possibly rejecting the performance of the third party. Still, using agile fixed price you might find at the end that "it costs what it costs" because it is often doubted that nearshore resources, for example, really reduce the costs for a unit of performance.

5.3.6 Project and Contract Management

Even after a contract is awarded, the responsible purchaser should support the project and be part of the project team during implementation. To motivate the procurement representatives for these often labor-intensive and unpredictable tasks, the contract savings negotiated as well as the actual costs incurred in the personal goals should be fixed (i.e., an end-to-end budgetary responsibility for the project). The added advantage of having the procurement representative as a commercial partner in the project is that the technical project manager does not have to focus on commercial discussions but is able to concentrate on the project's progress, and negative emotions about commercial topics do not endanger cooperation on the operational level. This new responsibility is sometimes uncomfortable for many procurement representatives simply because it is new (and we are human). Sometimes intensive persuasion is required, and not all procurement representatives are adequate to the task. In some companies the incentive schemes for procurement representatives are already aligned to this model.

5.3.7 Effort Inherent in the Tendering Process

In our recent discussions about the topic of tendering based on an agile fixed-price contract, one of the most common arguments as to why this new process is nice but cannot be applied was that it takes so much effort compared to the existing process. We would like to respond to this argument using a simple calculation. Assume that you have a tender process to manage and we set up an example for a fictional IT project where the implementation time is approximately one year. In Table 5.1 we indicate how much effort we would expect in each stage of the tendering process (Note that we do not want to discuss the days in detail but, rather, indicate the scale of the effort.)

5.4 SUMMARY

An agile fixed-price contract can be carried out similar to the process followed for a traditional fixed-price tender but only when two special commercial parameters of the agile model are employed properly:

- Costs for the reference user stories or costs per story point
- Overall scope and maximum price range
- Riskshare

In addition to these commercial parameters, it is also important that clients and contractors verify in a checkpoint phase whether expertise and willingness to cooperate are present within the framework of an agile fixed-price contract.

TABLE 5.1

Stage	Tender Prepared and Executed Based on a Traditional Fixed-Price Contract	Tender Prepared and Executed Based on an Agile Fixed-Price Contract
Internal coordination	10 person-days Several stakeholders align. The business case is created and the basic framework conditions are agreed to.	10 person-days Several stakeholders align. The business case is created and the basic framework conditions are agreed to.
Preparation of the tender	200 person-days Approximately 20 days is required for preparation of the overall document. The vast amount of effort is invested (before the project started) in the detailed specifications where we assume that three people work for approximately three months.	30 person-days The same effort is required for preparation of the overall document (assuming that you have a template for an agile fixed-price contract). A detailed specification is not needed; instead, 10 person-days are spent to define the high-level scope with suitable framework conditions.
Sending and managing the tender	10 person-days As we assume that also in the traditional fixe-price contracts a question and answer workshop must be performed the effort for managing the process and this workshop might be around these days.	10 person-days This workshop is also required in an agile contract, as well as additional work in managing the tender process.
Awarding the tender	5 person-days The final contract setup and communication require some days of effort.	5 person-days The final contract setup and communication require some days of effort.
Effort required to create further detailed specifications during the project and for the change request process and preparation during the project	50 person-days We assume that one change request is handled every month, requiring four days until it is finally settled.	250 person-days We assume that over the course of the project three people are preparing and verifying detailed specifications (user stories) to the extent of 1.5 days for each sprint. This results in approximately 225 days. No further efforts are required. Assuming one day of scope governance every other week, this would add another 25 days.
Total effort	275 person-days The major part of this effort is spent before the project is even started.	305 person-days The effort is comparable, but the client has the major advantage that the effort is spent only if the project runs well. Additionally, the overall efficiency will increase if the effort for detailed specification is spread over the entire course of the project.

The main requirements for tendering and implementation are competition as well as comparability and transparency.

Schematically, the process of a tender, including negotiations, is divided into stages:

- Internal coordination
- Preparation for the invitation to tender
- The tender
- Awarding of the tender

It is essential that a competent procurement representative supervise the project. He or she should be part of the project team for implementation even after the tender has been awarded. It is all about an end-to-end budget responsibility and the avoidance of commercial discussions by the project teams.

6

Special Requirements for the Legal Framework of an Agile Fixed-Price Contract

In Chapter 4 we presented a template for an agile fixed-price contract with precise formulations for controlling the scope and the change-request procedures. In addition, there are brief comments on the individual regulations. At this point we need to emphasize once again that the contract templates presented in this book should in no way be accepted without further consideration. The contractual framework must be adapted to each particular project. It must first be verified that the agile model is, in fact, appropriate for the project. If this is the case, it must then be decided to what extent the agile model can be applied to the elements of the contract. For example, if the necessary hardware for an IT project is in most cases finally defined and not expected to change over the course of the project, this cost factor can be detained as a fixed amount in the contract. Even a separate procurement project can be opened for such hardware, including a more aggressive tender style (e.g., a reverse auction).

The same consideration apply to standard software. If simple adaptations of standard software are necessary, the traditional fixed price could also be

Agile Contracts: Creating and Managing Successful Projects with Scrum, First Edition.
Andreas Opelt, Boris Gloger, Wolfgang Pfarl, and Ralf Mittermayr.
© 2013 John Wiley & Sons, Inc. Published 2013 by John Wiley & Sons, Inc.

agreed upon, provided that the adjustments are defined clearly and that changes are excluded during the course of the project. On closer examination, there is no additional risk if one employs an agile fixed-price contract in accord with some more strictly defined parameters. To stress this again, it is perhaps incorrect to assume that the introduction of standard software is clearly defined and complete. Only the flexibility of an agile fixed-price contract can provide a remedy for such an incorrect assumption.

Hybrid forms of contracts are also possible for each project. For example, for the development of the actual software, both the agile model (e.g., for the implementation of special features) as well as the traditional fixed-price model (e.g., master data migration with known data content and known interfaces) can be used. Alternatively, as described earlier, all parts of an agile fixed-price contract can be regulated, thereby allowing the various parts to have different parameters. Also, a subproject can be defined for the very clear parts of the project, whereby the parties can agree that the client pays only 20% if the maximum price range is exceeded. In other parts of the project, where the responsibilities of the suppliers are not so clearly regulated due to uncertainties, the riskshare can amount to 50%, for example.

From a legal perspective, a few different features need to be considered with an agile fixed-price contract as opposed to other IT contracts. General legal explanations for IT contracts can be found elsewhere (e.g., Landy and Mastrobattirta, 2008; Overly et al., 2004; Reed, 2007; and Klinger and Burnett, 2012).

Generally, a client's legal department sets up a contract that protects the client the best it can (described very nicely by Larman and Vodde, 2010). A nice example included in their book highlights this focus, and we present it here. The International Association for Contract and Commercial Management depicted the top 10 contractual topics that corporate lawyers spent most of their time on during the period 2002–2007. The result clearly contained some old standbys, such as limitation of liability, price, warranty, or termination, but a description of the process to manage the subject matter of the contract (the scope) was not listed in the top 10. It is our experience that the legal side assumes that this topic is managed perfectly (all details included and complete) somewhere in an appendix to the contract. Based on this assumption, the corporate lawyers focus on their optimum goal, the creation of a tough, bulletproof contract. There is strong evidence that this assumption is incorrect (see Chapter 2). So it might be worse to shift some of that effort from the top 10 topics toward the legal support required to set up a contractual framework which allows IT projects to start on a high level of inclusion, then manage the scope over the course of the project.

So, it is common in traditional fixed-price contracts to provide a detailed definition of the contractual tasks based often on the mistaken assumption that this is possible. With a contractual framework such as an agile fixed-price contract, it is important to capture the reality of the project within the contractual tasks and change request procedures (scope governance and exchange for free). The reality of an agile project and the slightly modified approach has little influence on the basic legal framework (the top 10 topics) but needs some new procedures and slight modifications, as we explain in this chapter.

If you select an agile fixed-price contract for a project, at least in part, you should note some of the features of the legal issues and tools described below (the paragraph number in parentheses refer to the model contract in Chapter 4).

- Adaptable system for scope (§2)
- Warranty and damages (§9)
- Schedule and milestones (§8)
- Escalation path (§7)
- Exit path (§7)
- Obligations (§6, §7)

6.1 ADAPTABLE SYSTEM FOR SCOPE

In this section we summarize topics developed in earlier chapters surrounding legal considerations of a contract based on an adaptable system for the scope. The agile model attempts to combine two alleged contradictions. On the one hand, an agile fixed-price contract contains a true fixed price (maximum price range) for the entire project (as described by product or project vision, backlog, epics, user stories, etc.) and there are consequences if the price is exceeded. However, nothing is added to the scope without anything being taken away (exchange for free). As described in Chapter 3, a consequence is, for example, halving the complexity for single user stories. Let us assume that a client is particularly anxious that all services for the entire project be provided by the contractor selected. In this case it may be agreed that if the project is aborted by the contractor, the remaining x% (e.g., 20%) of the work to be paid for at the final acceptance will no longer be paid.

On the other hand, the price for implementation is based on an adaptable system of the final scope definition in the high-level form of a vision, reference user stories, topics, and epics, which are later specified in detail and delivered in sprints. If the contractor terminates the cooperation because the project's commercial expectations (e.g., net margin) were not fulfilled, he or she will, for example, regularly rely on the fact that the conditions for a joint agile approach have changed considerably. In this case, implementation is no longer possible at the agreed-upon agile fixed price. As mentioned in earlier chapters, this option can be made less attractive through a kind of riskshare at the expense of the contractor. However, this problem is shared between the parties and is therefore generally less problematic and cost intensive (as both parties have the same focus) for an agile fixed-price contract as for a traditional fixed-price contract. Another reason that this is less critical resides within the actual agile model and its principle that each sprint itself delivers a useful software increment. Based on this fact, the project may be resumed or developed further by the client or a third party at any stage where appropriate. The danger of an ultimate (especially a costly) failure is therefore also higher with time and materials and fixed-price contracts. Due to the penalties (riskshare) for failure to comply with the maximum price range, it is not appealing to the contractor to drag the project out. In addition, it is not actually possible because the client inspects the sprints and thus acquires a precise overview of the state of the project every two weeks (assuming two-week sprint iterations). The agile model nevertheless requires that the client be actively involved. This should be established clearly in the contract. We should therefore pay a great deal of attention to the client's obligations to participate, since the client is directly responsible for the project's success.

The adaptive scope system is formalized in a way that defines a complete high-level scope and a resulting fixed price. To ensure that this can be agreed to with less fear and uncertainty, the contract allows both parties to evaluate the estimate based on a checkpoint (a trial phase). The detailed scope is worked out jointly over the course of the project. The contract contains clear governance and processes to keep the scope within the agreed-upon high-level borders to manage this adaptable scope system effectively.

6.2   WARRANTY AND DAMAGES

Despite the adaptable scope system for delivering the project, there is often uncertainty as to how to handle the warranty and starting period for several other topics based on the time when software is accepted. Even if there might be a reason to discuss whether these time lines should begin with the acceptance of each iterative deliverable, we suggest a practical approach here. The contract should explicitly contain a single and unambiguous start date for the warranty/claims for damages period.

In addition, one should make certain that the contractor accepts responsibility for a complete position of the work or for the entire project. For the warranty and liability, it is important that the user stories be summarized in iterative sprint deliveries and that together they describe the overall functionality and therefore the detailed scope. The scope of deliverables and services, and even more important, the object of the contract, should be indicated clearly in the contract. This can be done even if these details are usually only made available via detailed specifications in the sprint preparations. You would also be able to sign a contract for a machine even though you do not know what size electric motor will be required to fulfill the contract's specifications. It must be clear at the end of the project how the deliverables are arranged and on what the warranty is based. There may, for example, be a warranty on parts of the project but not on the whole (because the client has only accepted parts). However, for everything that is accepted, the warranty period should begin at the same point in time.

For example, one may agree that each sprint is used productively, and therefore after part approval of this piece of work, the warranty period of x months begins. Suppose that 10 sprints are predicted for the complete work and the seventh sprint is not approved because there is discussion relating to a quality concern. During this discussion, sprints 8 to 10 are delivered and approved. In this case one would find nine warranty periods offset by two weeks. The warranty period for the seventh sprint would not begin until it was actually approved. In other words, there may be cases with this construct where warranty periods run for parts of the work but not for the entire span of the work.

From the perspective of the client, we need to keep it simple. A sort of final acceptance of the overall project (with the scope defined by the backlog), which follows separately after acceptance of the last sprint, offers a definite date for the start of the warranty and for the period assigned to claims for damages for the contracted services and/or deliverables. Even from the perspective of the contractor, definition of the individual warranty starting points on the basis of the individual sprints is not recommended without restrictions. If no maintenance or free service is agreed to during the warranty, this complicates, for example, calculation of the respective maintenance prices. However, for the rare cases where during ongoing projects, the client uses the first sprint commercially months before approval of lates sprints, the client should really see to it that the warranty period for individual sprints begins to run separately. As always, it depends on the individual case.

The project managers of both parties must be clear that documentation whereby they accept the detailed specified user stories before a sprint by way of their signatures, is essential for the agreed-upon object of the contract. Accurate project and contract management on the basis of an agile fixed price is a prerequisite for longterm success.

*(**Note:** Different starting points for the warranty period are also not entirely uncommon for traditional contracts in the framework of interim releases. Specifically, however, according to the agile approach, the delivery of increments as set out in an agile fixed-price contract means that these can be accepted and be binding on increments that might be in production. For such cases the warranty periods have to be defined specifically.)*

6.3 SCHEDULE AND MILESTONES

For larger projects it may be worthwhile not only to bind payment to the approval of each sprint, but to bind a portion of the payment to a set of approved sprints (called "drops" or, if larger, "releases"). This results in specific intermediate milestones: for example, partitions for the realization of a topic or epic. Generally, one of the advantages of this agile fixed-price contract with respect to milestones and the overall project schedule results from the underlying agile methodology as such. There is generally just one end milestone, and a very rough release plan is required. This plan is easily manageable, as each iterative deliverable offers great transparency as to whether improvements are needed to achieve the process required. Compared to a traditional fixed-price project, this means that permanent replanning and intermediate milestones (where documents and not working software are delivered) are not necessary, but the parties can manage scope and progress transparently. Depending on the number of milestones selected, the contract must define case by case what happens if milestones are not met or postponed (e.g., reduction of payment, specific short notice of a right to exit).

6.4 PATH OF ESCALATION

The contract template in Chapter 4 contains the appeals and decisions of an independent expert as the top level of escalation. The selection of experts is carried out jointly during negotiation of the project contract. This expert can be consulted during the course of the project in case of disagreements on effort estimations or general problems within the cooperative agreement by both parties. With the agile approach, under certain circumstances an expert may be able to clarify certain situations objectively without emotion. Contractors carrying out their first project using an agile fixed-price contract can easily be distracted by problems that threaten the project unnecessarily. For example, a non-ex ante defined "detail" in the technical attachments of an epic should not be confused with an "additional feature." Also, the importance of a detailed request relating to the project vision should not be evaluated incorrectly.

To understand this contractual feature better, let's look at two short examples.

Example 1
User stories of several epics are formulated during the project. Despite original boundaries (joint assumptions) in the epic, the details are interpreted such that the complexity of the epics are catapulted far beyond the original estimate. If this happens in an epic, this is not surprising, as the general assumption for a high-level estimation is that it evens out and that you can perhaps still compensate somewhere. However, if this happens on a massive scale, the "new" feature comes close to no longer being feasible within the agreed-upon fixed price. If escalations on the proceding levels have not yet been agreed to, the expert can simply set the newly described details in the user stories in relation to the project vision. He or she can then explain whether a detailed requirement for realization of the vision is really necessary or simply constitutes additional detail.

No IT project can realize all the details that are on a department's wish list. If the project vision is fulfilled, however, the business value of a project is satisfied and thus the project is successful.

Example 2

How quality is measured is always a topic for discussion in IT projects. Quite often, critical issues and transparency of quality are not expressed openly enough because management is missing in the project. In the early stages, an expert can usually serve each party really quickly on an escalation level. This ensures that the suppliers have an acceptable quality. If no agreement is found in this additional escalation level, the corresponding contractually guaranteed exit points are available to each party.

These examples show, based on realistic situations, how the legal framework of agile fixed-price contracts regulates specific escalation possibilities.

6.5 OBLIGATIONS

There are two philosophies. One is that limited client obligations are listed in the contract, and Appendix C (see Chapter 4) lists the general "soft facts" for cooperation. The soft facts are essential, as a project that is set up, sized, and estimated based on an agile work model can almost never be delivered with the same target conditions if one party decides not to work according to this cooperation model.

The second philosophy is that certain customers and lawyers do not like the idea of a soft-fact appendix. In such a case the essential handful of client obligations in the agile development process can be formalized and put into the contract. Compared to traditional contracts, where the essential obligation was possibly the acceptance, togehter with full-time employees who should be available at a time not specified in more detail, this is quite different.

6.6 SUMMARY

Legally speaking, there are not many fundamentally different legal features that need to be considered with an agile fixed-price contract as opposed to other IT contracts. It is common in traditional fixed-price contracts to describe the detailed definition of the contractual task. On the other hand, with agile fixed-price contracts it is important to capture the reality of the project within the contractual tasks and change request procedures (scope governance and exchange for free). The reality of an agile project and the slightly modified approach has some legal framework, particularly with relation to:

- Adaptive system for scope
- Warranty and damages
- Schedule and milestones
- Escalation path
- Exit path
- Obligations

7

Guideline for the Negotiation of an Agile Fixed-Price Contract

In Chapter 5 we presented the characteristics and requirements for the tendering of an agile fixed-price contract. We illustrated that there are very specific parameters for selecting the best bidder. In this chapter we describe the negotiation of an agile fixed-price contract as a crucial procedural step within the framework of a tender. Right from the start we would like to state that the client must comply with the different principles for a tender, especially its preparation (described in Chapter 5), in order to perform an optimal negotiation. For further reading on the subject of negotiations, we recommend the work of Schranner (2009) and Lewicki et al. (2009).

The goal in a negotiation is determined first by the business purpose of the organization and project. Second, since people come together in the negotiation, it is also determined by the persons involved and their individual motivation in the negotiation. The primary goal for both sides is usually to negotiate a successful IT project and, above all, to implement it. Behind this central goal the parties each have very different detailed goals. Even within an organization, different decision makers and managers pursue different objectives which all have to be aligned and prepared before a negotiation (generally, even before a tender is sent).

Agile Contracts: Creating and Managing Successful Projects with Scrum, First Edition.
Andreas Opelt, Boris Gloger, Wolfgang Pfarl, and Ralf Mittermayr.
© 2013 John Wiley & Sons, Inc. Published 2013 by John Wiley & Sons, Inc.

Before we will discuss details about the negotiation of this new form of contract, we summarize the most crucial points with a statement of an expert who we asked to list the major topics when looking at negotiating an agile fixed-price sort of contract.

Testimonies from the Field

Matthias Schranner founded and leads the Negotiation Institute (www. schranner.com), with headquarters in Zürich and offices in Europe, the United States, and Asia. He and his colleagues support difficult negotiations around the world. In an interview in October 2012, Schranner pointed out the following major topics and specialties regarding the negotiation of an agile fixed-price contract:

- The agreement of an agile fixed-price contract between vendor and client has as a main goal to ensuring that the project is realized in time and on budget, despite all pressure with regard to commercial and material problems emerging during realization. Hence, a cooperative negotiation style is in most cases adequate. Tactics such as information hiding and putting pressure on the negotiator of the other party should not be employed. Such tactics would perhaps lead to a better negotiation result in the short run, but during realization, often to insuperable issues, and in the end, to commercial damage.
- Cooperative negotiation of an agile fixed-price contract may be perceived of as being successful if both parties feel that the contract is well balanced, so that neither party has major advantages overall.
- Early and, in fact, permanent involvement of procurement experts before, during, and after a tender is crucial to ensure competition between vendors and no distraction of project managers by commercial issues. Often, IT managers have—due to experience— a preference for one supplier (e.g., because they have already worked with a company on the topic for tender). One of the tasks of procurement is to ensure maximum competition and the best result thereby based in a clear legal, commercial, and technical framework.
- The decision maker (normally, the CxO) determines who is commander of the negotiation and who is the most suitable negotiator [see the FBI model (Schranner, 2009)]. The negotiator should be familiar with the project requirements but must not have an emotional or material preference for a supplier.

7.1 OBJECTIVES OF THE CLIENT

First, the client must define his own objectives for the invitation to tender. This must be aligned among all decision makers to pursue a clear line in the negotiating. If you perform this alignment in detail, you often find that up until the finalization of the tender or the internal negotiation, a few questions still need to be answered. Apart from your own objectives, you must try at least to anticipate the potential objectives of the negotiation partner without focusing on possible inaccurate information. With agile fixed-price contracts, special attention should be paid to the processes on which the definition of the detailed scope of the agreement is based. Fundamental misunderstandings in this area are a major cause for failed IT projects.

The project objectives in part refer specifically to the *substantive goals*, such as: What functionality should definitely be included in the new software application? What capability is the application expected to handle? Which functions can be waived in case of doubt, and which are crucial? What principles must be followed by the application? Which principles do I wish to have secured in the project contract (e.g., if in doubt, always use the standard functionality)?

On the other hand, there should be clear *commercial objectives*: What turnover can the application guarantee? What are the maximum internal costs allowed for implementation? What internal and external target prices do I deliver to the negotiating team? How much riskshare is the company prepared to accept?

Once these project objectives are defined, the method of implementation must be decided. In principle, a make-or-buy decision is also made prior to the tender (and, of course, prior to a negotiation): Is it appropriate to implement a project with your own resources or to outsource the implementation to others? If you opt for an allocation to a third party, the commercial model should once again be defined prior to the negotiation. For example, it often happens that a traditional fixed-price contract goes out to tender but the client tends toward an agile fixed-price contract during the course of the procurement procedure. This is not negative per se, but it forces the client into a situation of having to act reactively in unfamiliar territory. This is very common these days, as knowledge of agile fixed-price contracts is not yet widespread. Ideally, of course, the IT project is awarded according to the form of contract that was tendered. For the remainder of the chapter we assume that the tender is carried out according to the agile fixed-price contract as defined in Chapter 5.

Clients should opt for fixed-price applications only when they are certain that the agreed-upon services will definitely not change after conclusion of the contract. Fixed-price tendering is a priori the best option from the perspective of classical purchasing. If, in addition to the legal and commercial framework, the specification is defined conclusively, an optimal price negotiation can be made, possibly including reverse auctions (see Chapter 5). Procurement personnel and management must carefully verify whether the risks and disadvantages of project implementation (change requests, etc.) described in eachies chapters, in fact, exclude a traditional fixed-price contract. In contrast to negotiations according to the traditional fixed-price contract, the commercial goal of an agile fixed-price contract is not only (or mostly) the lowest price but the delivery of a successful project with an optimal scope at an optimal price. These goals are achieved with the agile fixed-price contract and not with the traditional fixed-price contract. Statistics and experience as well as the ability to view the agile fixed-price contract as an evolution of the traditional contract shows that from the overall point of view of an IT project, it is usually the ideal option.

7.2   OBJECTIVES OF THE CONTRACTOR

Preparation of the negotiation is also essential on the side of the potential contractor and it also starts with coordination of the goals. To the same extent, the substantive and commercial objectives are set in which the acceptable range for the negotiation is outlined.

- *Substantive objectives* on the side of the contractor can, for example, be the clear contractual admission of certain basic principles of project implementation. Or they could be the clear definition of the team that is responsible for partial approval on the client side. The substantive objective can also be targeted to sections of the project scope.
- *Commercial objectives* on the other hand, focus on the proposed margins for the project. How can the bonus system be attractively negotiated so that profits are maximized when falling below the maximum price range?

According to the situation in the company, the setting of these objectives may also include the following aspects: How much of your margin do you renounce to win these new clients and thereby offer a more attractive price per story point (or reference user story)? As a contractor, do you want to send a clear message for an agile fixed-price contract? Do you have expertise in the team and at present have the free resources for implementation? All of this is necessary for you to take on more risk during the riskshare negotiations.

The objectives of suppliers vary immensely, depending on the market position and the significance of the contract. Providers who are not yet recognized in the industry tend to offer very aggressive pricing to gain market share. This can also happen in the context of agile fixed-price contracts. However, in this case the risk is minimized that the supplier recaptures the price difference later with change requests.

7.3 OBJECTIVES AND BONUS PAYOUTS OF THE PEOPLE INVOLVED

Once the client and contractor are clear about their goals, they should deal with the objectives and bonus payouts of the people involved on both the contractor and client sides. The contractor must also first learn the negotiating tactics of this new contract. It therefore involves tangible or intangible financial or nonfinancial incentives. These influence the objectives during negotiation preparations and also motivate the selection of particular alternatives in the negotiation itself. We consider the bonus payouts of the participating procurement representative and the key account manager of the negotiating partner. We also consider the technical project manager on the client side or the product owner on the supplier side (as long as they are already involved in the negotiations).

Incentives for the procurement representative

Previously, the most common type of incentivizing for procurement people was to compare the final price with the best initial offer. The difference was an indicator of purchasing success. The consequence of this system, on the one hand, is that the initial offer received is extremely overpriced. This makes it "easy" for procurement personnel to achieve a high savings target without any involvement. On the other hand, all that the procurement representative is interested in is achieving a relatively low price for the initial offer. How and whether or not the project is performed successfully is in this case also not the principal concern of the buyer.

We recommend a modern form of specifying objectives for the buyer. These are based solely on savings within the planned budget value of a particular project and are referred to as *on top of budget savings*. In addition, the actual accomplished savings are measured (*realized savings*). Only a clear baseline for the calculation of a saving report gives such a report a representative value.

Example

The budget for a project is $350,000, but the negotiated fixed price of the agile fixed-price contract for the project is only $280,000. No extra costs are incurred during the course of the project (in keeping with the terms of an agile fixed-price contract), and therefore the *on top of budget saving* is $70,000.

If unexpected problems occur during implementation of the agile fixed-price contract and the fixed price is exceeded by approximately $50,000, and the contractor has agreed to a 50% riskshare, the *realized savings* therefore amount to $45,000.

If this example went out to tender and was resolved according to the traditional fixed price, the project could, for example, be awarded at an amount of $220,000. However, due to changes in the project scope and unclear requirements, this could produce change requests in the amount of $150,000 (this figure is not uncommon; see Chapter 2). In this case the person from procurement would not post any savings (if measured on realized savings)!

Incentives for the key account manager

The performance bonuses of a key account manager (the responsible contact person for the contractor) are usually controlled by the net margin, sales growth, or revenue shares. But even here, many unsuccessful IT projects have left their mark. Only in very rare cases are bonuses for the key account managers based solely on sales. This would lead to the situation where the key account manager is only interested in the gross revenue and not the subsequent project reality, which leads to the sale of the lowest-priced project.

Even in this group, an end-to-end view gradually catches on and the key account manager increasingly becomes an "engagement manager." The key account manager, as well as the client's procurement representative, faces this change by stating that he or she will accompany, participate, and deal with the commercial issues of the ongoing project. These responsibilities must be supported over the entire project. Therefore, we recommend establishing the incentives for this end-to-end view as a basis for an agile fixed-price contract (and for contracts in general). This means that the parameters on which success is measured are a combination of revenue, net margin, and project success.

Incentives for the technical project manager or product owner

The objectives of the technical project manager or the product owner are unfortunately often only very vaguely attached to a projects success. At best, the parameters for bonuses in project implementation are the project's success, the net margin, or the total costs calculated. In the negotiation these people often act as a consultant in the background or might even be involved in the negotiation team. It is therefore important to be aware of their influence and motivation and to act accordingly. Their roles are crucial to project success. Depending on how motivated the technical manager already is in drawing up the contract, the less critical discussions there will be by the scope steering board during the course of the project.

As with the procurement, we suggest that both parties reward their technical leaders with an "on top of budget savings" option. The motivation of the project manager and product owner are linked to the project vision. This helps to reduce the widespread trend that the approach in IT projects always aims away from the actual project goal (the vision). Perhaps this does not fit the manner in which employees are rewarded in your company. Nevertheless, think about making changes. When employees participate in a process and are expected to comply, there must be some way or other for them to "see out of it."

At the technical level the opinion often prevails that contracts are concluded by top management and procurement personnel for their own benefit, and the technical project manager will then have to "carry the can" for the implementation. An agile fixed-price contract offers the possibility of collecting the same bonus structures up to the level of implementation, so that all parties concerned work together in close cooperation toward one common aim—a truly successful project.

7.4 STRATEGY FOR THE PROJECT AND THE NEGOTIATION

Before the negotiation or the tender begins, in agile fixed-price contract requires that principles for the project and the negotiation be defined on both the client and contractor sides. If the client selects the agile approach for the implementation of a project and the contractor accepts this, they agree on cooperative conducting of the negotiation. This presents a mutual partnership for the implementation in the foreground. Dumping prices makes no sense and is not suitable or realistic as a goal. In negotiating an agile fixed-price contract, the negotiates for the project should be encouraged to continue to support the project.

Initially, the focus is placed on the principles that apply to project implementation. The fundamental question in the background is, of course, what service and success you, as a client expect from a supplier. For example, if a client's application is to be developed and it is absolutely necessary that company-wide software standards be followed, this principle must be pursued with determination. On the one hand, it means that only those suppliers who can guarantee this come into play. On the other hand, it means that this principle is not softened in the negotiation to achieve a target price.

Fundamental strategic issues must be addressed for the negotiation; for example:

- Is the relationship with the negotiating partners important? Do we need the supplier for currently running projects? Do they expect to be awarded the contract because of a common history?
- Realistically speaking, what alternatives do we have for a strong supplier? The easier it is to replace a supplier, the greater normally is the power of the client. Especially in the drafting of contracts, the client ensures that the supplier can be replaced during the project without legal or technical problems. The agile fixed-price contract approach presented in Chapter 4 includes this principle.

These are just two examples, but the range of strategies is large and depends very much on the situation, the project, and the parties. It is important to establish principles in the strategy that support the success of the project and at the same time specify a clear and ambitious commercial framework (see earlier chapters).

7.5   TACTICS FOR THE NEGOTIATION

Once the objective and strategy are defined, you should consider exactly how to reach your goals. What negotiating tactics are therefore necessary? For both parties, the negotiating tactics for agile fixed-price contracts are not particularly different from those featured in traditional contracts (with possibly one major difference by really aiming at a real "win-win" situation). It is, however, essential that the negotiating team internalizes the previously fixed principles and rules. For a successful IT project, it is just as important that the scope management process be guaranteed as negotiating a 5% lower cost per story point. If one regards the outcome of a project, the former is even more commercially feasible than a price reduction.

The approach to negotiations that we now introduce leans heavily on standard operating procedures and is equally valid for both parties. The party that excels in mastering this "game" will also find it easier to use agile fixed-price contracts, despite the focus on cooperation in the project.

Negotiating team

Basically, the negotiating team as well as the circle of all stakeholders should be as compact as possible. The reason for this is to avoid jeopardizing the confidentiality of the objectives of the project, the negotiation strategies, and the tactics [see also Schranner (2009)]. The negotiating partners will naturally try to obtain confidential information (even in cooperative negotiation, this helps a lot). A popular way is to hold talks with disgruntled employees, who are flattered to be questioned on specific points by a supplier. Such conversations may well provide fruitful information when the client's confidential data are spread too far internally.

These conversations may, for example, involve the experience with decisions taken previously on the project. For example, should the contracting authority learn that the contractor is under heavy time pressure to make a decision, the contractor can use this to his or her advantage. The contractor would thus make sure that he or she is not being overly flexible during the negotiations for accepting additional riskshare.

Also interesting for the client is, for example, the information that the top management of the supplier has not adequately supported projects in the past. In this case it should be clearly noted in the agile fixed-price contract that the top management must be involved in the scope or executive steering.

The following summary of the negotiating team is based on the *FBI model*. According to this model, negotiation takes place in a team with strictly assigned roles. There are three main roles [for more details refer to Schranner (2009)]:

1. Negotiating leader or negotiator
2. Commander
3. Decision maker

Negotiating leader or negotiator

Even with agile fixed-price contracts, only one person should act as the negotiator and thus be the only voice of the negotiating partners. He or she focuses on the negotiation and tries to identify any possible misunderstandings and optimization of all relevant topics regarding the project. Within the framework of agile fixed-price contracts, the negotiator for the most part chooses a cooperative negotiation style after he or she is convinced that the negotiation partner does not set traps or hide information. Primarily in the initial phase, the negotiator attempts to test claims by the negotiating partner and secure information.

One of the greatest challenges of the negotiator is the emotional task:

- Highlight the strengths of your own technical team for implementation of the agile model and put that of the supplier into perspective to force the partner to accept the cooperative model contractually.
- Provoke the emotional errors of the negotiating partners but do not allow yourself to be provoked.
- Communicate your demands as being important in order eventually to redeem them against actual important supplier concessions.
- Offer no compromises, but obtain compromise proposals with any issue.
- Exert a convincing powerful position and do not allow yourself to be intimidated by the negotiating partners.

On principle, the negotiators never decide on essential issues alone but obtain the freedom of action in a predefined framework. The negotiator must coordinate with his or her team on all decisions outside the scope of action. This allows for more time and prevents rash or emotionally influenced decisions. In this way the negotiator is prescribed a target framework for pricing that does not reflect the actual minimum goal.

Commander

The negotiator is supported by a commander. He or she never intervenes directly in the negotiations but, instead, always communicates only through the negotiators. The commander follows along with the negotiation, always retains the big picture, and pursues the strategic objectives while the negotiator is involved in the actual negotiation. If the negotiator needs support, the commander does not immediately climb into the negotiations. He or she first obtains a break in the negotiations to provide guidance for the negotiator.

Decision maker

The decision maker always remains in the background and makes the fundamental decisions without being influenced emotionally by the negotiation. This team position has the advantage that the negotiator can only exploit the freedom of action that he or she actually has, and maintaining concessions are thereby limited. Ideally, the negotiator negotiates with the decision maker of the other party because the negotiates has no confidence in his or her own negotiators. There can be many reasons for this lack of confidence, including:

- The decision maker believes that he or she can help in any situation. The decision maker is provoked by the negotiating partner to intervene (false information about the negotiator is spread, workshops on "future issues" are held with the decision maker, etc.).
- The fixed-price offer should be examined without emotion as to its feasibility and attractiveness in the context of the overall package, especially with agile fixed-price contracts. The negotiator of a party therefore has advantages over a decision maker in a face-to-face negotiation, not only because the decision maker has wides freedom of action (he or she must not stick to any given frame), but the impact of essential details cannot be assessed as well (knowledge of details is essential in a negotiation under time pressure).
- The appointment of the negotiator and the commander should also take into consideration the team positioning and the assumed motives of the negotiating partners. Therefore, all efforts are made to know the decision makers and the motives of the negotiating partners.
- The negotiating style for an agile fixed-price contract should in principle be cooperative. Time games or demonstrations of power by a party are in most cases counterproductive and are also not a good basis for the implementation of a project. The integral roles in the negotiating team remain.

Documentation and agenda

Even with an agile fixed-price contract, you have a decisive advantage: the setting of the contract and therefore the technical, legal, and commercial framework. Here, one must be especially certain that after the conclusion of the contract, as few as possible open issues are brought up for discussion. On the other hand, the initial draft contract should contain some items that can again be considered in the negotiation. It is also important at the end of the negotiation not to fixate on a point: for example, the fixed price. It is better to have a certain bunch of negotiation points in order to help with negotiations. Generally, you should aspire to determine the agenda and thus the content of the negotiation by yourself. If the negotiating partner suggests an agenda, you should respond with counter agenda.

Unlike other contracts, with an agile fixed-price contract the restrictions imposed after conclusion of a project are not so massive. Therefore, if a party is in this position of power, it is also not effective to gag the contract partner too much during the negotiation. Finally, any party may leave the project at any time after the agreed-upon procedure. Even when the sabers are rattled, hard words are falling and the competition is felt. The goal is a balanced contract, encouraging cooperation and consequently ensuring the success of the project.

For example, it would make little sense if an error was made by a contractor due to being too harsh when negotiating with a client's optimally selected negotiating team. This would cause the reference user stories to be offered at an economically unreasonable price. These loss-making areas would become transparent to the contractor sometime during the project and he or she would then end the project after an appropriate lead time. Alternatively, the contractor might assign cheaper, not-so-qualified experts to the project, thus provoking the client to opt out, thereby jeopardizing project success.

Strategy and negotiation tactics must ensure that the core principles of an agile fixed-price contract are not being diminished or eliminated. For example, if the exit points are too restricted (e.g., due to penalties) or the scope control process is not clearly defined, this can lead to fundamental drawbacks.

7.6 PRICE DETERMINATION

Basically, the pricing of agile fixed-price contracts, and thus the commercial factors within the negotiation, can take place only on the basis of the following parameters (for details, see Chapter 5):

- A comparison of the estimated maximum fixed prices of each supplier
- A backpack for the supplier's technical, commercial, and legal insufficiencies
- The unit price per user story and complexity level or story points and reference user stories
- The project riskshare, cassied out during the checkpoint-phase (if this has been carried out under contract and not in advance as a proof of concept)

Pricing for agile fixed-price contracts is usually associated with intense negotiations on the project content, the commercial drivers, and ultimately, the maximum fixed price. This gives the negotiation itself great significance. Even if one of the parties could exert great power over the other, it is usually not conducive to overflex one's muscles during negotiations. This does not, however, mean that the process should be run without tough negotiations and tenders.

7.7 CONCLUSION OF THE NEGOTIATION AND PROJECT STEERING

For an agile fixed-price contract, the first negotiation is complete after agreeing on legal, commercial, and technical documentation and a maximum price range. However, not all hoped for objectives are achieved. User stories and sprints (i.e., the prioritization of user stories), as well as the relationship of the content to the overall project vision, must be negotiated constantly. With agile models the negotiations should, in fact, not be regarded as complete until the project has been implemented successfully. Therefore, it makes sense to involve the respective procurement representative or key account manager in the project steering group, as these people know the spirit of the contract. More-over, the technical project managers can focus on their core job, successful implementation of the IT project, without losing time over commercial dis-agreements. A clear set of rules is extremely beneficial for each IT project—before and after contract and price negotiations. It could even be an option to have the same negotiation team for the overall contract part of the scope governance group, as this group steers the further detailed content and com-mercials for the project.

7.8   CONCLUSIONS

This chapter shows that an agile fixed-price contract can, in fact, be negotiated. The agile model places emphasis on cooperation. This principle must be reflected in the approach through all the necessary severity and objectivity during the negotiation and at the time of the contract award. However, there is still proper negotiation, which is intended to lead to an optimal commercial framework. The following major commercial parameters can be negotiated:

- Price per story point
- Riskshare

This, in conjunction with an appropriate set of rules and principles, provides adequate flexibility for the project reality, thereby ensuring a successful IT project within an optimum scale and at an optimal cost.

8

Advantages and Disadvantages of Agile Fixed-Price Contracts

So far, we have introduced the agile fixed-price methodology and answered questions regarding where the agile aspects should be incorporated in the contract, tender, and negotiation. We have provided comments and described in detail a template of the agile fixed-price contract as a possible solution. But what exactly are the pros and cons of this new type of cooperation (i.e., this new contract)? How does it compare to the models currently available: the traditional fixed-price contract and time and materials contract (also called a cost-plus contract or cost-reimbursement contract)? We answer these questions in this chapter by analyzing and comparing the advantages and disadvantages of the three types of contracts. Each is documented from the perspective of the client, the supplier, the consultant, and the Scrum team. The motivation of each party for or against the agile contracting model will become much clearer. This chapter can also sence as a platform for discussion, enabling you to make objective changes in your organization's approach to contracting.

There are also other contracts normally seen as variations on these contracts: cost-plus incentive fee and cost-plus award fee, which have slightly different advantages, although our general conclusions in this chapter are not

Agile Contracts: Creating and Managing Successful Projects with Scrum, First Edition.
Andreas Opelt, Boris Gloger, Wolfgang Pfarl, and Ralf Mittermayr.
© 2013 John Wiley & Sons, Inc. Published 2013 by John Wiley & Sons, Inc.

affected by these slight variations. In the same manner it is not relevant whether one of the ratings for a topic might be seen differently by a reader, as, again, the overall conclusion remains untouched.

We have gathered together many possible aspects that are relevant when considering an IT contract. Even if such a list can never be complete, it still embraces a lot of the pros and cons of various types of contracts for IT projects. The following topics are described in detail:

- Budget security
- Requirement flexibility: flexibility with regard to changes in the requirements
- Detailed requirements: flexibility with regard to missing details in the requirements
- Negotiation costs
- Security estimates
- Quality risk
- Price elevation tendency
- Probability of winning a project tender
- Cost risk
- Security to deliver the awarded project as a whole
- Acceptance efforts
- Pricing transparency
- Progress transparency
- Controlling capabilities/permanent regulation
- Securing the investment (early business value/client benefits)

8.1 DETAILED ANALYSIS OF THE PROS AND CONS

To understand arguments as to the advantages and disadvantages of agile fixed-price contracts and traditional forms of contract, we first declare what is meant for each aspect. We then describe how these issues are expressed by various forms of contracts for the parties involved. For a quick overview, the individual advantages and disadvantages are assessed according to the following rating schema:

- Sizable advantage: + + +
- Advantage: + +
- More beneficial: +
- More detrimental: −
- Disadvantage: − −
- Serious disadvantage: − − −

The *client perspective* is not limited to the view of a single party within the client group (e.g., procurement), but represents a total consideration for the client. The *view of the supplier* is limited primarily to the sales management or project management. For the *Scrum team*, the view is based on the assumption that the project is delivered according to an agile approach, such as Scrum (the situation that arises when this is not the case is described in Section 8.2). The *view of the consultant* represents some controversy here. In reality, it is true that large IT projects are almost never prepared or performed without a consultant. The crucial factor here is that the consultant, with his or her vast experience, is often able to influence the decision making.

It should be clear that you should consider carefully where the benefits of each type of contract lie for the consultant when seeking consultant advice. In the tables that follow we always refer to the consultant who supports the client (whether in preparing for the invitation to tender or in the project).

The parameters are themselves, of course, often closely related, such as the estimate security with the budget security. However, each of these 15 parameters is a key issue and therefore important to the overall balance and worse to discuss separately.

8.1.1 Budget Security

In budget security we refer to the possibility of securing the end-to-end costs of a project; in other words, this indicator judges how well the final real cost of a project matches the initial estimation in the contract. In theory, budget security is best for a traditional fixed-price contract. However, in practice, a fixed price that looks very nice in the contract is often very different from the actual cost to bring the project to a successful end. But let's look at the details in Table 8.1.

8.1.2 Requirement Flexibility

Requirement flexibility refers to the ability within a current project to respond to changing requirements without causing massive additional costs. Changing requirements can, for example, have the following characteristics:

- Due to a new market situation during the course of a project, a new feature is needed.
- A feature planned previously is no longer needed.
- A feature planned previously must be modified. At the time the client receives the first feedback in the form of working software resulting from his or her requirements, the client often realizes that features planned previously should be described differently or lack some functionality.

Requirement flexibility does not mean inherently that each new request can be implemented without additional costs. Instead, it is assessed as positive in terms of reducing complexity when the exchange for free approach allows for changed requirements to be implemented with zero or minimum extra effort. It is assessed as negative, compared to the complexity of the request, when new requirements can only be implemented at high costs (in addition, influencing the delivery of the overall project). The question is whether the parameters available in each project are or are not in the "genes" for this type of contract (see Table 8.2 and Chapter 2).

8.1.3 Detailed Requirements

Evaluation of the detailed requirements topic here shows which specification level of the scope is required for each type of contract at the point in time where the contract is signed. This is an important point in reference to the client's costs prior to the start of the project (costs that have not yet produced much business value). It also carries the disadvantage that these detailed requirements will be forfeited in actuality. The counterpart to this is in relation to the "lean development" of a production process, in which only the information currently required, with its corresponding effort, is prepared in detail (see Table 8.3).

8.1.4 Negotiating Costs

In negotiating costs we refer to a parameter that describes how much effort is needed for each party to negotiate a project commissioned according to a certain type of contract. During discussions it is often argued that an agile fixed-price contract is not an option because it is too expensive to negotiate. Table 8.4 shows the details and hence also that the agile fixed-price contract is anything but difficult to negotiate. It is clear that it is something new and for this reason alone presents a particular challenge for the organization and procurement. A traditional role perception and traditional processes need to evolve for this type of contract.

8.1.5 Estimate Security

Estimate security is the security that both sides will position the actual project cost on or lower than the estimated cost (see Table 8.5).

8.1.6 Quality Risk

Quality risk is the risk that during a project, for whatever reason, the supplier produces poor-quality work. Contractually, you can ensure against this in different forms. However, additional overheads and delays may be created at a later stage in the project to address the lack of quality. Of course, a quality risk also occurs when serious communication problems are discovered too late in the project or when these problems cannot be improved iteratively (see Table 8.6).

8.1.7 Price Elevation Tendency

Including a cost margin for the supplier is actually required, and certain contracts encourage the submission of higher prices for a service for security reasons. The reasons for this might be:

- There is uncertainty in the definition and delimitation of the scope of the contract.
- There is uncertainty in the effectiveness of the cooperation.
- The scope of the contract is complex. This can result in the supplier offering a rather high price for self-protection. Or the complexity is so great that the client is not able to recognize that the price offered is excessive.

From the perspective of the suppliers, the price elevation tendency is something that optimizes their margin. Contracts that provide this possibility are therefore preferred (see Table 8.7).

8.1.8 Probability of Winning a Project Tender

The probability of winning a project tender refers to the general view of the supplier to win a project based on a particular type of contract. The basic assumption here is that the project is still not advertised according to a particular type of contract, or you have adapted the required form of contract in a discussion with the client. The nature of the invitation to tender from the client is therefore often not very professional, due to a lack of comparability (see Table 8.8).

8.1.9 Cost Risk

In cost risk we consider the view of the client, supplier, or consultant in suffering a commercial loss on a project with a certain type of contract. This consideration includes the point of view of a client who fails is to meet the positive business case for the project (see Table 8.9).

8.1.10 Security to Deliver a Project as a Whole

The security to deliver as a whole a project that has been awarded grants security to a supplier where signing a contract to deliver the entire job. This job security is synonymous with a promised delivery. In software development, as in other industries, the discount is directly dependent on the size of the

TABLE 8.1 Budget Security

	Traditional Fixed-Price Contract	Time and Materials Contract	Agile Fixed-Price Contract
Client	–	–	++
	Many clients have discovered that the price delivered during a fixedprice offer has little to do with the actual budget. Budget security does not exist, and the planned budget is based only on an estimate of the amount by which the cost of the original fixed price will be exceeded. By 50% or by 200%? We do not know and hope that we do not experience a "black swan." The risk of budget security is shared, as the need for additional effort is usually discussed and must be approved. It is stronger on the client side, however, as the supplier often demarcates skillfully.	The client can control the effort in detail within the budget in this type of agreement. Disadvantages: High control costs to secure the resulting quality and to ensure no dependency on the supplier in a later phase of the project. The entire budget security risk lies on the client side.	The client determines the budgetary constraints and the riskshare in cooperation with the supplier. The quality remains traceable throughout the project, and the client can control the work within the budget.
Supplier	–	+++	++
	The budget security of the client is probably a disadvantage here. The supplier must try to obtain an optimal price with the best coverage through contractual assumptions. Attempts are often made by the supplier to keep the excess low for the fixed price offered. However, increased turnover is, of course, not bad in order to sustain the client. Because of frequent nonsensically low fixed prices, this additional revenue is often actually necessary; otherwise, a margin is lacking.	From the perspective of the supplier, this type of contract is of great benefit since it carries no risk. However, there is a danger that failure will still reflect on the supplier even if the client manages the project incorrectly.	The supplier can support the client in adhering to the budget. The budget constraints established are not based on an unreal price battle but on traceable costs for the client. The supplier bears the risk of budget security and can help to shape a truly successful project.

Client's Consultant	+	+	+++
	Based on his or her experience, the consultant must correlate the contractual assumptions and the price submitted to establish comparability between suppliers. The role actually makes sense because there is often a lack of detailed knowledge on the client side. The assumptions are complex and the requirements are volatile. It does, however, remain a form of damage control.	In these contracts, the consultant often has the role of project manager or is responsible for quality assurance. Of course, it should be noted that the consultant is a supplier who accepts that the "politics" between the parties in critical situations is a hindrance to the project.	The consultant can clearly support the path to maintaining the budget through transparent pricing and budget control. Experts who can contribute to optimization of the scope are especially required in this type of contract (i.e., "What can you do minimally to enable the client's business processes?"). Did you ever hire a consultant in a project, who should always tell you as a customer what is not needed or can be done more simply? This is possible in an agile fixed-price contract.

Supplier's Scrum Team	–	+	++
	At the beginning, the implementation team must master an often impossible task at the stated price. The challenge is to generate technically optimal minimal overhead and to develop a feature that possesses the functions described and defined. The better the Scrum team, the easier it can participate in the optimization. The Scrum team usually enters far too late in the game. It is designed to help squeeze into the framework incorrectly estimated topics which have not yet been set. In this case, the team can only respond with poor quality.	The Scrum team can control the estimate and delivery output without too much pressure from outside the sprints. Of course, the pressure should otherwise be kept from the Scrum team, especially in this type of contract, which succeeds in terms of the budget considerations. Theoretically at least, there is a risk that the Scrum team will "rest." They have all the time in the world, and the sprint content is defined in such a way that they have it very easy. In practice, however, this behavior is actually rare. Another point is that there is no time frame in which something must be completed. The team can theoretically develop solutions that far exceed any budget. Here it is important that the agile process ensures the integrity of the increments delivered and prevents overachievement.	A greater emphasis is placed on the Scrum team for what can be done and how to jointly implement the functionality required by the client within the given budget. The Scrum team (i.e., the project organizes and the development team) is incentivized to achieve the goals set by the client. There is interest within the team to comply with the general guidelines agreed to with the client. In this case the Scrum team acts as an entrepreneur.

TABLE 8.2 Requirement Flexibility

	Traditional Fixed-Price Contract	Time and Materials Contract	Agile Fixed-Price Contract
Client	– – –	+++	++
	The client is under the impression that he or she describes the contract scope at the beginning and it does not change during the course of the project. If it still was so, additional efforts would be incurred, in the form of expensive add-on efforts. The hidden problem with the client is that he or she must think of everything (and know everything) he or she wants. The client must then describe in detail what he or she wants. This results in high costs for the client before the project has even started. These efforts must be allocated to the project, however, and can drive the project costs up. If changes are necessary, the client must make these change efforts in the course of the project, by creating new requirements. But there is often no time for this and the costs are not recorded in the budget.	This contract provides all the flexibility needed to change the requirements during the project. However, it is important that the overall budget frame be transparent (i.e., closer to the elements of the agile fixed-price contract). Unfortunately, this often leads to loss of focus on the client side, especially during longer projects. New features that arise during the course of the project are necessary because it only becomes clear later that these things are also still needed.	This form of contract provides the client with a set of rules to change requirements, minimize the resulting extra costs, and not lose sight of the relation to the overall project vision and guiding principles. The client and supplier each have the goal in mind at all times. They must constantly negotiate with each other and decide together which changes are useful additions or amendments. Detailed requirements are generated timely to their actual use in the project.
Supplier	++	–	++
	Through skillful assumptions and clever project management, you can exploit the fact of changing requirements for significant additional revenue to the project price. The work required for these change requests, in the sense of directorial effort, is no longer calculated so closely and is very profitable. Design efforts can be charged for functions that have not yet even begun.	In this contract the supplier has no risk regarding changes in the requirements. However, the sword of Damocles of damaged reputations continues to hang overhead. Since the supplier is not included in the control, he or she is not able to counteract in a timely and efficient fashion.	This form of contract provides the client with a set of rules to change requirements, minimize the resulting extra costs, and not lose sight of the relation to the overall project. Ultimately, the supplier carries the risk within the riskshare. However, the project success may be enabled together with the client.

Client's Consultant

−

Consultants can unfortunately also not predict the future. Therefore, they must accept the additional costs for changes to the requirements. The specification phase and the changes in the scope are often identifiable projects for consultants; however, steadily changing requirements do not shed a good light on the consultant who prepared the RFP and most of the detailed requirements.

+

Consultants can play a major role and often carry a lot of risk on the side of the client (at least in terms of their reputation).

++

Consultants can make use of the rules to optimize client benefits and minimize their own risk. Consultants should possibly also participate in riskshare and incentives in order to send all the parties into the race with the same motivation.

Supplier's Scrum Team

++

The Scrum team is unaffected as long as the changed requirements do not affect the already implemented functions or the functions that have just been implemented within the sprints. This is the exception, however. The traditional fixed-price problem is also relevant for Scrum teams. The fixed-price project is calculated in such a way that a minimum of rework is incurred. Late changes in the architecture, however, often have fatal consequences for the overall architecture. One should prevent these at all cost.

++

The Scrum team is unaffected as long as the changed requirements do not affect the already implemented functions or the functions that have just been implemented within the sprints. This is the exception, however.

TABLE 8.3 Detailed Requirements

Traditional Fixed-Price Contract	Time and Materials Contract	Agile Fixed-Price Contract
Client		
– –	+++	+++
The client must prepare the detailed requirements before the conclusion of the contract. This has the following disadvantages: You must invest effort, with the knowledge that at the point of implementation, the detailed requirements may already be out of date—that a long time will pass before the end of the project, making the amount of knowledge decay considerable.	In this type of contract, the client does not have to prepare the requirements in detail beforehand. It is advisable to create a rough picture of the requirements at the beginning of the project, as with an agile fixed-price contract. For the next features to be developed, the details should then be defined as soon as possible.	The client should only define the requirements at a high level and simply describe the details for a number of reference user stories. This saves time in the preparation of projects and allows flexibility and timeliness of the specifications during the project. In addition, it allows the client to improve communication problems iteratively within a "high-level" framework (vision, topics, and epics).
Supplier		
++	+++	++
It is helpful to the supplier to have a detailed picture in mind at the start. Less expertise is required in estimating the costs. All that is unclear is deferred in assumptions and subsequently paid by the client as a change request.	The supplier should not provide a binding estimate or control the project. Thus, in his or her view, the detailed requirements can be provided at short notice.	At the start, the supplier has only a rough picture of the contractual object. However, he or she has the opportunity to demarcate exactly where to move the detailed specifications, through the use of suitable assumptions for each epic. The advantage for the supplier during the actual editing of the specifications is that the client still knows exactly what he or she wants. The client is always "better" able to assess precisely what will result from the specifications. The client will see from the iterations what was produced by the supplier at the last sprint on the basis of the specifications.

Client's Consultant

++

Clients gladly assign implementation of the specification phase of the project to consultants. This project assignment for preparation of the detailed specification is thus a good argument for the traditional fixed-price contract.

−

The consultant can also take on the specification of requirements. In practice, this task is less distinctive and rarely transferred to a third party in time and materials projects.

+++

The consultant can also take on the specification of requirements. An additional benefit is the possibility of short-notice responses and adaptations of the quality.

Supplier's Scrum Team

−

For the Scrum team, this point has somewhat negative implications. The client's requirements often lack the appropriate form in order to implement the corresponding wishes effectively. It describes what to do or what is currently being done, rather than what you want to do with it. So according to the agile process, another iteration is performed with the client in order to cast the requirements in the user stories.

++

The Scrum team or the product owner in the specification team manages to accomplish being involved from the beginning. In this way, they can work better toward ensuring that the requirements have the appropriate form and quality.

+++

It is a regulation, as part of the contractually specified processes, that the Scrum team receives high-quality requirements on time in the form of user stories.

TABLE 8.4 Negotiating Costs

	Traditional Fixed-Price Contract	Time and Materials Contract	Agile Fixed-Price Contract
Client	+	+++	++
	The negotiation is quite simple. Closer examination shows, however, that it can become very difficult to make the different assumptions in the offers reasonably comparable. However, buyers are generally very experienced in this discipline.	The negotiations could actually not be any simpler, because it is only about "quantity multiplied by price" and no adjustments to the content are necessary. The question of what represents content and quality for the individual resources or their representation in a résumé is usually not discussed any further.	Compared to a traditional fixed-price contract, the effort to negotiate an agile fixed-price contract is about the same. Workshops are also necessary to achieve a common understanding as to comparability. The slight advantage is that the negotiations are transparent (and even allow win-win situations) and the risk to the client is not as massive (riskshare). In this way we are perhaps able to keep the costs down because we do not "sell our soul."
Supplier	+	+++	+
	The supplier is accustomed to these negotiations and attempts to achieve an optimal price with optimal assumptions. If the buyer is very conscientious on the client side, the negotiating efforts require a variety of complex iterations in order to gain maximum comparability within the existing level of detail.	The negotiating efforts are minimal, because it is all about quantity, skill level, and price.	The effort for negotiation is similar to the traditional fixed-price contract as long as comparability is also provided for conscientiously.
Client's Consultant	++	− −	++
	Given that a role already exists here for the consultant, his or her experience is also useful in supporting this process.	The effort on the consultant side is minimal for these negotiations, and the support of the consultant is generally not needed.	Given that a role already exists here for the consultant, his or her experience, too, is useful in supporting this process.
Supplier's Scrum Team	*Not applicable*	*Not applicable*	*Not applicable*

TABLE 8.5 Estimate Security

	Traditional Fixed-Price Contract	Time and Materials Contract	Agile Fixed-Price Contract
Client	– –	– –	++
	The client has little insight into the estimates and their security. They can indeed verify it internally but can do little to secure it. If necessary, a list of person-days per topic level is specified. Verification is difficult, however.	The client must estimate the efforts of the entire project. Due to the fact that he or she has sole responsibility, it is more difficult to coordinate the security together with the supplier.	The client is involved in the estimate and configures the assumptions together with the supplier, thereby ensuring maximum estimate security. The supplier riskshare provides extra motivation for improving security.
Supplier	+	+++	++
	Based on available details, the supplier may indeed often estimate accurately. However, whether this effort will appear in the offer depends on the situation.	The supplier must, in any event, have security in the estimation. The reason is that he or she carries no risk and can calmly accept the estimates and the naturally resonating assumptions.	The supplier indeed accepts riskshare for the estimate but is able to secure the estimate perfectly through open discussions and the common set of assumptions.
Client's Consultant	+	+	++
	With his or her experience, the consultant can contribute to verification of the estimate security.	With his or her experience, the consultant can contribute to verification of the estimate security as well as the estimate itself.	With his or her experience, the consultant can contribute to verification of the estimate security. In workshops with both sides, the consultant can serve as a mediator to further increase the estimate security (i.e., the quality of the assumptions and the shared understanding).
Supplier's Scrum Team	– –	++	+++
	The team may indeed estimate the detailed requirements presented. However, the room for interpretation is usually still very large and must be covered by assumptions.	The team can either assist in the overall estimate (without risk) or first estimate roughly and then later estimate in detail before each sprint (as with agile fixed-price contracts).	The contract process and the contractual framework dictate the process by which the Scrum team can contribute optimally to the estimate.

TABLE 8.6 Quality Risk

	Traditional Fixed-Price Contract	Time and Materials Contract	Agile Fixed-Price Contract
Client	– – –	–	+++
	It is only at a late stage that the client has the opportunity to review real results and thus the quality. Even with early concerns, the possibilities of interventions are limited.	The client pays here according to effort and not performance. It is therefore particularly difficult with this contract to reduce the quality risk. It is usually possible only through strong dependence on methods that follow the direction of agile fixed-price contracts.	The client is involved in a predictable and clearly structured process of partial acceptance in the early stages of quality assurance.
Supplier	–	+	+++
	When an agile project is delivered, the client is involved at an early stage and the quality can be verified. Unfortunately, this does not happen here very often, since the duty to cooperate is not handled as strictly as with agile fixed-price contracts, where they depend on the cooperation.	The supplier does not have to meet any contractual claims on quality here. Of course, this may also be to the detriment of the supplier. If the project fails, especially for reasons other than the quality of delivery, it is often not easy for the supplier to reject the blame in a credible manner.	The supplier and the client successfully negotiate a contract framework in which the quality assurance process is also guaranteed.
Client's Consultant	–	+	++
	Depending on the approach, the consultant can assess and ensure the quality at an early stage. The fixed-price construct leaves little room to employ a transparent and efficient advisory role.	The consultant can play a vital role here in quality assurance. This must, however, be established in the time and materials contract and is often found again in formulations that resemble an agile fixed-price contract.	With his or her knowhow, the consultant can play an essential part in this process by supporting and cooperating in the mode of cooperation for the common goal. The contract framework prevents tactical maneuvering between the parties.
Supplier's Scrum Team	–	++	+++
	The duty to cooperate is indeed regulated in the contract but is not an essential part of the process. Therefore, the team often has to forego the active participation of the client in quality assurance through discussion and clarification. Often, even with efficient internal quality assurance, the communication problem is not quite overcome.	Depending on the client control, the Scrum team may be able to secure the quality at an early stage, through partial acceptance and client presentations. This strongly resembles the procedure that is defined in the agile fixed-price contract.	The clearly defined contractual process ensures quality with regular votes and allows the Scrum team to demand the right to the client's duty to cooperate.

TABLE 8.7 Price Elevation Tendency

	Traditional Fixed-Price Contract	Time and Materials Contract	Agile Fixed-Price Contract
Client	−	−	+
	The rise in price is at least added in the margin of safety. The actual price elevation comes only during the course of the project. As the options for the client are limited, an excessive price is usually paid for the change requests during the project term. The initial fixed price (i.e., the fixed price in the traditional fixed-price contract) is, however, usually very attractive—although this does not often mean very much, as illustrated in Chapter 1.	The client cannot recognize the elevated price at the beginning. Over the duration of the project, however, resources are usually exchanged, and after a few months, the same price is paid for less output. As a result, the client must constantly resist to keep the price elevation under control.	The client purchases output, receives completed deliveries, and may terminate the contract. In this way he or she can counteract price elevations much easier than with time and materials.
Supplier	+	+	−
	The supplier will attempt to make the initial price as attractive as possible to remain competitive. However, with security surcharges and expected change requests, the prices are placed on realistic scales. The supplier can argue a higher premium if specific reasons exist for a price elevation (e.g., unclear scope).	By exchanging expensive resources for cheaper ones, the supplier is able to optimize his price elevation (his margin).	The client receives deliveries in small intervals, checks the quality and interacts with the team. The possibility to optimize the internal costs during the project is thus limited. In exchange, the risk of being replaced by competitors is lower as the value per dollar rises during the course of the project.
Client's Consultant	+	+	++
	The expertise of the consultant can help to minimize the price elevation for this type of contract.	The consultant can help the client to reduce change within the team of suppliers but cannot, however, prevent this.	The consultant can help the client to measure output and to optimize costs (i.e., counter price elevation).
Supplier's Scrum Team	*Not applicable*	*Not applicable*	*Not applicable*

TABLE 8.8 Probability of Winning a Project Tender

	Traditional Fixed-Price Contract	Time and Materials Contract	Agile Fixed-Price Contract
Client			
	Not applicable	*Not applicable*	*Not applicable*
Supplier			
	+++	+	+
	The best chance for winning a project exists with this type of contract, due to the fact that it is the most widely used form of contract and still often required in the tender. In addition, there is the possibility of defining and minimizing the initial price of the proposal, which increases the chances of an order. Statements such as "no problem, it's a fixed price . . ." are unfortunately still alive.	Responding to a required fixed-price offer with time and materials is not usually appreciated. If time and materials is already stipulated, the chance of winning can naturally be reversed drastically by appropriate pricing pressure.	In this type of contract you must make the client recognize that you are doing him or her a favor. The agile fixed-price contract is primarily a benefit to the client (see the summary at the end of this chapter). If this persuasion does not succeed, it is difficult to afflict the mostly lower-priced traditional fixed-price offers, which are equipped with hidden costs. This also entails more responsibility for the buyers.
Client's Consultant			
	Not applicable	*Not applicable*	*Not applicable*
Supplier's Scrum Team			
	Not applicable	*Not applicable*	*Not applicable*

TABLE 8.9 Cost Risk

	Traditional Fixed-Price Contract	Time and Materials Contract	Agile Fixed-Price Contract
Client			
	– – –	–	++
	The client has little transparency and few opportunities to influence the project approach. As the statistics show, the risk here is significant.	The client may indeed do the controlling personally and thus minimize the risk of costs. However, in the case of problems due to "knowledge hiding" and poor quality, his or her options are very limited.	The client has full transparency, regular quality control, and constant protection of the investment transacted. The cost risks are thereby reduced.
Supplier			
	–	+++	++
	The supplier attempts to minimize the cost risk through price, security surcharge, and additional effort. However, unsuccessful projects based on fixed prices are often a losing proposition, even for suppliers.	The supplier has no responsibility and is difficult to control with regard to performance. He or she can extend the profits even further, for example, through "knowledge hiding." Therefore, the cost risk is minimal.	As part of riskshare, the supplier is obviously involved in cost overruns. For this reason, an agile fixed-price contract follows a clearly regulated process with defined exit points. This limits the cost risks sharply and offers better prospects for a successful project.
Client's Consultant			
	+	+	+
	With his or her expertise, the consultant can assist but is not usually involved in the cost risk.	With his or her expertise, the consultant can assist but is not usually involved in the cost risk.	With his or her expertise, the consultant can assist but is not usually involved in the cost risk.
Supplier's Scrum Team			
	Not applicable	*Not applicable*	*Not applicable*

order. Clients who can guarantee a long project comprising a lot of effort get a better price based on unit costs (see Table 8.10).

8.1.11   Acceptance Efforts

Acceptance efforts are often an issue when the disadvantages of agile fixed-price contracts are discussed. There are "constant" acceptances due to the partial acceptance after each sprint (or at least drop), and the appropriate resources on the client side as well as on the supplier side, are bound by them. It appears to be easier to perform six weeks of focused acceptances every nine months after each release, for example. In theory this is a reasonable opinion. However, in practice we see that the possibility of constant quality control and the iterative optimization of the communication between the client and supplier are key factors for successful IT projects. Of course, even for a traditional fixed-price project is supplied in agile form, partial acceptance is defined. In practice, this is not usually handled as clearly as when the entire contract construct promotes the agile methodology (see Table 8.11).

8.1.12   Pricing Transparency

Pricing transparency describes the transparency of the supplier's work to benefit the client. This transparency helps the client to gain confidence in the services offered and to avoid a tendency forward price elevation (see Table 8.12).

8.1.13   Progress Transparency

With IT projects, you need to know about the actual progress of a project in order to take appropriate action in case of problems or to initiate changes in direction. The progress transparency parameter indicates to what extent a supplier is obliged and encouraged to disclose actual progress (see Table 8.13).

8.1.14   Permanent Regulation

An IT project is a long journey that we embark on together. On this journey it sometimes helps when either party can grant changes to a certain extent to motivate the opposition to progress. The permanent regulating therefore describes the possibility of regulating and motivating the supplier upon completion of one of the contract types on the client side. This issue affects primarily the client side because it is assumed that the supplier, regardless of the type of contract, can establish enough regulatory measures (see Table 8.14).

8.1.15   Securing the Investment

The cost depreciation (sunk costs) of a failed IT project is known to most companies but is still an extremely unpleasant situation. When selecting the

TABLE 8.10

Traditional Fixed-Price Contract	Time and Materials Contract	Agile Fixed-Price Contract
Client		
++	+	++
From the client's perspective, a large body of work is awarded to achieve a better price for the "part." This must be taken into account by the next add-on effort, in the form of change requests. The commitment of the overall contract ensures job security, and thereby the initial achieved discount is leveled out.	The client secures certain order quantities. However, this cannot be guaranteed in advance with respect to time and materials assignments. As a follow-up, the client negotiates a volume discount or yearly reduction.	The checkpoint phase is short, but it offers the client the further advantage of awarding the entire work and obtaining a corresponding discount on team costs. Unlike the traditional fixed-price contract, the mass of change requests are not such a cost factor.
Supplier		
+++	–	+
The supplier receives the entire contract and issues appropriate discounts. This is maximum job security, as the value of the contract, including a significant amount of change requests, is secured. After all, the client no longer has an option after the contract has been awarded.	Job security is limited to the respective order cycles (e.g., quarterly). However, even these are sometimes not fully recalled with a project stop or other incidences. Nevertheless, the client demands appropriate discounts.	After a successful checkpoint phase, the supplier receives the contract for the entire project, which minimizes his or her own risk. The possibility of generating additional orders through additional change requests is minimal. Furthermore, the client has the option to terminate the job at a specified point in time, leaving the supplier with very little job security. However, the supplier is in control of this.
Client's Consultant		
Not applicable	Not applicable	Not applicable
Supplier's Scrum Team		
+++	+	+
Long-term planning is possible with the Scrum team. Continuity in the project increases their performance.	The Scrum team works in short intervals. Accordingly, the planning security is also acceptable in quarterly orders.	After the checkpoint phase, the agreement is generally to finish the project with a lead time of at least two or three sprints. This at least creates sufficient planning and/ job security from a development standpoint.

TABLE 8.11

	Traditional Fixed-Price Contract	Time and Materials Contract	Agile Fixed-Price Contract
Client	+	++	+
	The effort for the acceptance is minimal. Thus, for example, for a 1.5-year project, each of the two releases can be inspected in six weeks. At best we could say 12 weeks, but in reality it is often much longer than that. The client only sees for the first time after nine months how many of the specifications were actually understood by the supplier. In practice, it is a wish rather than a reality that the client is able to plan the use of his or her resources. This is due to frequent shifting of milestones.	The effort for acceptance is not given explicitly in this option. The resources of the suppliers operate under the control of the client. There is the normal quality assurance of the project, but there is no acceptance of the delivery performance of the supplier.	Assuming that for a 1.5-year project, every second sprint is delivered as a drop, there will be 18 subapprovals. If any part of the acceptances last a week (one to two days in reality), it is indeed comparable to the 12 weeks requested for the acceptance effort of a traditional fixed-price contract. However, you have dramatically reduced the risk of exceeding the 18 weeks. The predictability for the resources is maximized because sprints always take the same length of time. The content may vary, but certain functions can be inspected at a scheduled point in time.
Supplier	+	+++	++
	The supplier can work undisturbed on the first release. However, in many projects it is also a surprise to the supplier's project manager what happens at the first acceptance or the week leading up to it. This is when the client provides feedback on the functionality for the first time. Even for the supplier, the risk is significant to virtually generate an essential project delay and additional acceptance efforts within a theoretically short turnaround time of acceptance.	From the perspective of the supplier, no acceptance effort is necessary here.	Regular acceptances are accurately predictable, and regular feedback improves the quality. The risk of taking the wrong path for the implementation of time-consuming software requested by the client is minimized.

Client's Consultant

++

Support during acceptance is difficult to plan because in practice there are often displacements. A blocked commissioning for quality assurance is, however, beneficial for consulting support.

+

The consultant often supports quality assurance, but an actual acceptance in itself does not exist.

++

Through iterative acceptances, there is no continuous block for consulting support during the acceptance. In return, the days and weeks can be planned meticulously.

Supplier's Scrum Team

−

The single acceptance at the conclusion of the entire project may reduce costs on the client side. It is generally also true that the effort increases for the elimination of the errors found during this acceptance. This depends on the distance in time from the function implemented originally. For example, after a project duration of 18 months, the risk is already very large because the distance in time generates higher total effort.

+

It is difficult to quantify because no acceptance takes place between suppliers and clients. Assuming that the resources of the suppliers constitute the Scrum team and the client represents the product owner, the acceptance and its efforts would be similar to those of agile fixed-price contract.

++

The contract construct regulates the process of regular partial acceptances. This makes continuous and timely cleanup of errors possible. It also corresponds to the optimal deployment of Scrum teams because the people do not need to refamiliarize themselves with the "old" issues that they implemented a few months ago.

TABLE 8.12

	Traditional Fixed-Price Contract	Time and Materials Contract	Agile Fixed-Price Contract
Client	++	–	+++
	For most fixed-price offers, calculation of that work required, as well as statements of the applied security surcharges, are required from the client. If the client provides clear guidelines for a detailed price sheet, the pricing is comparable and transparent (if the supplier wishes). It is not handled here in the exception that it is not required by the client (in this case no transparency is provided). However, the disadvantage is that the comprehensive list of assumptions that is provided within the supplier's proposal weakens the actual transparency.	The pricing is based on a nonbinding estimate of the effort by the business department. It is therefore transparent on the basis of person-days. However, the actual person-days often differ from the initial estimate.	The reference user stories are described and estimated in detail. Maximum transparency is ensured through joint discussions in the cooperation workshop on the work and assumptions involved. This transparency is maintained over the course of the project (open books). It is recommended that the costs be limited simply to "team costs."
Supplier	++	+++	+++
	The supplier delivers transparency according to client specifications. Most will not proactively create transparency since with a fixed price, you are of the view that the details of the pricing are not a concern for the client (it is, after all, a fixed price). The assumptions are used to put the transparency into perspective.	Transparency is easy to achieve on the basis of time and materials: Which resources are allocated to the client for certain tasks, and how long are they available?	An advantage for the supplier is the possibility of bringing the reasons behind the estimate closer to the client and verifying the assumptions. After all, unlike a traditional fixed-price contract, there is less danger that the client will draw incorrect conclusions.
Client's Consultant	+	–	++
	The consultant is usually effectively appointed to review the pricing according to the client's specifications. His or her expertise helps in the assessment of individual items.	The consultant has no job here, as only person-days are represented.	The consultant can actively participate. Due to his or her experience, the consultant is required to verify the estimate based on complexity and team composition.
Supplier's Scrum Team	–	++	+++
	The client specifications often differ from the Scrum Team's estimate (e.g., overall design cost, implementation, testing and documentation). Therefore these efforts must be converted. This is not clear transparency in terms of what is "really" estimated.	The Scrum team can support the estimate efficiently.	The estimate is based precisely on the elements required by the Scrum team in order to work (epics, user stories). Consequently, a direct mapping is possible and maximum transparency is provided.

TABLE 8.13

Traditional Fixed-Price Contract	Time and Materials Contract	Agile Fixed-Price Contract
Client		
– –	– – –	+++
The client obtains little insight into the actual progress. Weekly status reports that set out the progress of individual high-level milestones according to percentage values are, according to experience, very unreliable. Usually, there are a few surprises for a progress of between 80 and 100%. The Pareto principle, which declares that the last 20% of the progress is responsible for 80% of the effort, is not very helpful for progress transparency. Even if agile is the underlying approach, it will unfortunately not be utilized.	Progress is verified only by the client. The client is therefore dependent on the notifications of the time and materials working resources. Time and materials often does not support transparency, because the suppliers want to represent themselves in the best light and conceal certain shortcomings.	The client has contractually guaranteed the process of "open books." It is desirable that the client be integrated as much as possible. The scope is divided into clear units and allows the client easily to keep track of actual progress.
Supplier		
– –	–	+++
Even if the supplier wants to ensure transparency, it is often difficult internally to query the actual status. Even the project manager is usually surprised by the problems that still tend to arise at the end of large releases. To actually make the progress transparent, the contract also stipulates milestones instead of a process.	From the perspective of the supplier, the progress transparency in this assignment is merely incidental, as the client is responsible for the project. The supplier is responsible for a good reputation so that he or she is assured of further assignments. A commitment and policy in the contract for progress transparency does not usually exist.	The binary measurement of progress is based on small units (finished or unfinished user stories, and not percentage values). The supplier is obliged to comply with certain requirements of the "open books" process. Acceptance occurs after each sprint to ensure that there is little risk of the transparency being lost somewhere.

(Continued)

TABLE 8.13 (Continued)

Traditional Fixed-Price Contract	Time and Materials Contract	Agile Fixed-Price Contract
Client's Consultant		
– –	+	++
The consultant has few possibilities to control the actual progress of a project. Clear protocols and governance do indeed help to document the failures in hindsight, but provide little support for progress transparency.	In terms of quality assurance, the consultant can verify deviation from the reality of the progress report by means of samples. This is useful to ensure a certain progress transparency.	The consultant can support the process very efficiently and verify progress transparency for the client.
Supplier's Scrum Team		
–	–	+++
The Scrum team has the exact progress status on the current sprint and also its relation to the overall project. Certainly, in a traditional fixed-price contract, the client's contractual obligations in comparison are not so clear and transparency is probably prevented. In addition, massive change requests at the end of a project are sometimes responsible for ensuring that the overall progress is difficult to estimate, even from the perspective of the implementation team.	The Scrum team is usually in the situation of having good progress transparency, at least over a portion of the project. But even with this type of contract, there is no clear commitment to this transparency.	This contract supports the Scrum team's approach. Openness and cooperation are essential elements and also provide transparency at this level. This is made possible through the contractual process.

TABLE 8.14

	Traditional Fixed-Price Contract	Time and Materials Contract	Agile Fixed-Price Contract
Client	- - -	+	+++
	The client can regulate the price at contract completion as part of the competition and negotiation. Subsequently, the IT project's journey begins, without the client being able to perform further regulating. On the contrary, he or she is even forced into additional efforts in the form of change requests, without having an influence.	The regulator is constantly given on the price per unit of resource. The control is really quite complex. Due to "knowledge hiding," the ability to employ other resources for the task is severely restricted. The further the project progresses, the more dependent the client is on the supplier.	The contract specifies that fully functional increments are delivered after the agile process. The project can also be terminated relatively quickly. After each sprint the client is in the picture about the actual performance of the suppliers and may intervene to regulate. Further incentives are established through bonus systems in the contract.
Supplier	+	++	++
	For the supplier, this is a comfortable situation, as he or she can work over a large part of the project flow without the client's influence. However, this usually has the disadvantage that the supplier often works in the wrong direction because of a lack of feedback and control. From the supplier's perspective, the first regulator is so great that later change requests are necessary to conclude the project positively.	In practice, work is carried out in the direction of optimal client satisfaction at the beginning. However, the behavior of the supplier changes once the specific project knowledge of some introduced resources increase where the lack of documentation cannot be exchanged. Through optimization of resources (i.e., introducing cheaper, less efficient staff into the project), the regulatory element of the client is turned off for the most part.	The supplier adheres to the contractually agreed processes. The supplier attempts to make himself or herself indispensable to the client by increasing his or her corresponding performance over the course of the project. The supplier is not open to blackmail, however, because he or she can also use certain exit points.
Client's Consultant	- -	-	++
	The consultant can probably provide only toothless support in both the status meetings and the process. Even in this role the consultant cannot provide a regulatory climate in which the contract could be defined.	The consultant can slow down but may not stop the process that the supplier makes irreplaceable in the project.	Through clear measurement criteria and transparency, the consultant can support the client in reviewing and regulating performance through the course of the project.
Supplier's Scrum Team	*Not applicable*	*Not applicable*	*Not applicable*

181

TABLE 8.15

Traditional Fixed-Price Contract	Time and Materials Contract	Agile Fixed-Price Contract
Client		
– – –	–	+++
Results that are recyclable are contractually guaranteed at the latest at the time of the milestones. In practice, for traditional fixed-price projects, functionality that is still simple and has little business value to the client is often implemented in the first release.	Depending on planning by the client, the securing of investments falls higher or lower. Contractually, however, it is by no means guaranteed.	A usable increment of software is delivered at the end of each sprint, due to the underlying agile approach as well as the contractual guarantee of these processes (perhaps with the exception of the first sprint). With corresponding prioritization, the next respective increment always includes the maximum business value to be achieved for the client for this investment.
Supplier		
Not applicable	Not applicable	Not applicable
Client's Consultant		
Not applicable	Not applicable	Not applicable
Supplier's Scrum Team		
Not applicable	Not applicable	Not applicable

type of contract to employ, care should be taken as to the extent to which a contractual form secures the investment made over the course of a project. By securing the investment, we refer to the efforts incurred so far that have led to recoverable and usable results that benefit clients (Table 8.15).

8.2   SUMMARY AND OVERVIEW

In Tables 8.16 and 8.17, respectively, the pros and cons of each of the foregoing topics are summarized in detail from the client and supplier perspectives. Although the views of the consultant and the Scrum teams have been included above, they do not affect the core message but only reinforce it. Thus, these views are not summarized again below. As indicated above, the client perspective reflects not only the view of procurement. From a procurement perspective, the traditional fixed-price contract would probably be the most attractive option, provided that the bonus payouts were governed only by the final price negotiated and not by the actual project cost. What we are trying to illustrate here is an overall consideration of the views of top management, implementation, project management, legal, and procurement personnel.

TABLE 8.16 Client Perspective: Pros and Cons of Various Types of Contracts

Topic	Traditional Fixed-Price Contract	Time and Materials Contract	Agile Fixed-Price Contract
Budget security	−	−	++
Requirement flexibility	− − −	+++	++
Detailed requirements	− −	+++	+++
Negotiating costs	+	+++	++
Estimate security	− −	− −	++
Quality risk	− − −	−	+++
Price-elevation tendency	−	−	+
Opportunity to place orders	/	/	/
Cost risk	− − −	−	++
Job security	++	+	++
Acceptance efforts	+	++	+
Pricing transparency	++	−	+++
Progress transparency	− −	− − −	+++
Controlling/permanent regulation	− − −	+	+++
Securing the investment	− − −	−	+++
Total	6 positive points 23 negative points	13 positive points 11 negative points	32 positive points

TABLE 8.17 Supplier Perspective: Pros and Cons of Various Types of Contracts

Topic	Traditional Fixed-Price Contract	Time and Materials Contract	Agile Fixed-Price Contract
Budget security	−	+++	++
Requirement flexibility	++	−	++
Detailed requirements	++	+++	++
Negotiating costs	+	+++	+
Estimate security	+	+++	++
Quality risk	−	+	+++
Price-elevation tendency	+	+	−
Opportunity to place orders	+++	+	+
Cost risk	−	+++	++
Job security	+++	−	+
Acceptance efforts	+	+++	++
Pricing transparency	++	+++	+++
Progress transparency	− −	−	+++
Controlling/Permanent regulation	+	++	++
Securing the investment	/	/	/
Total	16 positive points 5 negative points	26 positive points 3 negative points	25 positive points 1 negative point

8.3 CONCLUSIONS

If you consider the client as the decision maker in selecting the type of contract to employ, you can see in Table 8.16 that an agile fixed-price contract brings the mostly positive parents and no negative points. Detailed reviews of the individual points can certainly be discussed, but the trend will not change. This is because an agile fixed-price contract is the type of contract with which a client can achieve the greatest benefits. The realistic observations of earlier chapters also testify to the online of an agile fixed-price contract.

Looking at the summary of all the parameters, the client has even more significant benefits than the supplier within an agile fixed-price contract. Nevertheless, the fact is that it is suppliers who are currently promoting the move toward this type of agreement because of the huge impact that a successful project has on a supplication reputation. In addition, the agile model is not very widespread on the client side, opening up a way to bring additional value to clients.

With support from an agile fixed-price contract, a client can build strategic partners. You receive software of higher quality through essential improvements in efficiency and with the help of constant regulators. After partnering your first project under the umbrella of an agile fixed-price contract, new projects with manageable negotiation efforts can be placed. This fact has been largely ignored so far.

As reflected in this chapter, we have always assumed that even projects based on a traditional fixed-price contract can be delivered through agile methods, although in practice it seems to mean a break in the methodology and, as we described from the viewpoint of the Scrum team, the client assumes some of the benefits of agile project implementation. The primary obligation of an agile fixed-price contract is to deliver in an agile fashion.

Offering a way out of the current paradigm break between the agile development methodology and the traditional fixed-price contract is one of the driving forces behind this book. However, in no way does this mean that a traditional fixed-price contract works exclusively with the traditional waterfall method. On the contrary, Scrum is also an appropriate approach to traditional fixed-price contracts. The full spectrum of benefits of agile development can, however, be enhanced only by optimum structuring of the agile model, starting with the contract.

9

Toolbox for Agile Fixed-Price Contracts

The path to an agile fixed-price contract is not always easy. In earlier chapters we identified the principal issues. In this chapter we illustrate how you can take this path without stubbing your toes too badly. The tools in this toolbox, shown in Table 9.1, should make the path to an agile fixed-price contract easier. Above all, you should find the support here to gradually change attitudes toward the agile model within various departments and decision makers.

Initially, it is important to recognize that the transition to a cooperative framework contract, such as an agile fixed-price contract, does not constitute a purely organizational change. It is not treated through the introduction of new contract templates and a new process. To work in an agile framworks and particularly to work across department boundaries, calls for a new way of thinking. This requires a new mindset in the past of all participants, which in many companies is still not very well developed. Gerald Haidl, CEO of the System-Integrator Newcon, explained the situation in an interview in February 2012 as follows: "Agile project execution requires agile processes from both the client and supplier sides, or at least a certain base culture for such an approach. For very large clients or corporations such a base culture scarcely exists, because very often the processes tend to resemble steel production, even in engineering and IT."

This chapter should help you to create a positive and accurate attitude regarding the Agile model within your own company or with a client. Earlier

Agile Contracts: Creating and Managing Successful Projects with Scrum, First Edition.
Andreas Opelt, Boris Gloger, Wolfgang Pfarl, and Ralf Mittermayr.
© 2013 John Wiley & Sons, Inc. Published 2013 by John Wiley & Sons, Inc.

TABLE 9.1 Toolbox for the Path to an Agile Fixed-Price Contract

Laying the groundwork	Stimulate interest with arguments
	Open an exchange of experience
	Establish a common language and shared experiences
Discussion of the form of contract	Feature shoot-out
	Discuss the Black swan scenario
	Conduct a workshop on the contract setup
Reports and metrics	Create a KISS Backlog view
	Establish team metrics
	Focus on a common single goal

chapters serve as a basis and show that the transition to an agile fixed-price contract is not a "switch to uncertainty." It clearly provides an opportunity to deal with reality and minimize risk (quite often you can find comments pointing toward a switch to uncertainty: for example, http://bit.ly/Jp0Mjv, last accessed on 4/22/12). Depending on the company that you are dealing with, whether it is a "learning" organization or a traditional organization, the effort and approach are different (Cobb, 2011), But the benefit of an agile mindset is the same for every organization. There is already a lot of literature on the transformation (e.g., Schwaber, 2007), so we focus on a few key principles that were either very useful in our practice over the last few years or are critical to the contractual part of the agile process.

Generally, it is strange that the effort to initiate a change in mindset with respect to the overall process for IT projects is difcult to get approved and that even if other entities in today's organizations (e.g., a typical sales organization) already employ empirical processes, applying this also to IT projects often requires some education and extra motivational effort.

9.1 STIMULATING INTEREST BEFORE THE NEGOTIATION

To be able to lead successful negotiations and ultimately set up a good contract and a successful project, all parties involved must understand the general advantages of agile methods and how an agile fixed-price contract supports these advantages. Creating this understanding should be made top priority if awareness is not (yet) sufficiently present. The other side will not respond to the perceived "uncertainty" of a new type of contract until they also recognize the benefits. If a company is already working with agile methods, or has at least experimented with them, you can build on this experience. In most cases, the operating units know more about the agile methodology, as Scrum is often implemented bottom-up. The management and the procurement or overall finance departments many still be sceptical or even hostile to the new methods, even though the development teams are already working with them.

Scrum can essentially be implemented bottom-up or top-down. In the bottom-up (viral) approach, the developers decide to deviate from the existing process model and use agile methods. They are trained in the necessary knowledge, and Scrum is simple tried out. The experience and success is then communicated upward and some problems are solved at other levels. With the top-down method, the executive management usually already has an understanding of why Scrum or another agile process model is to be used.

This message usually meets fundamental resistance from middle management (procurement or project management), as processes that have been practiced for many years must be changed. Experience shows that middle management tends to allow an agile approach only when an individual manager is convinced or has already experienced significant advantages. Therefore, it is very important that the transformation process toward a more agile approach always includes some thought as to what each party has to lose and how to demonstrate the benefits for the individual.

Whether you meet with open or deaf ears in terms of agile methods depends on the "maturity" of the partner or the type of organization. There are different arguments that can make the agile model interesting. We propose some of these arguments and challenging statements, as they are used repeatedly by us. Communicate some of the benefits of agile fixed-price contracts at the next informal meeting with your clients or your own organization. It is interesting to observe what happens in the right circle of participants. These arguments can also be used as a basis for preparing elevator pitches. So you should work on the bait that triggers an "aha moment" in your contacts, and increases their curiosity for more information.

- **Argument 1: "In currently IT projects, only what has been specified is implemented, not what is really needed."** In the current procedure, the client first attempts to specify exactly what is to be done. Subsequently, the supplier delivers the same or even a slightly reduced (e.g., due to technical constraints) content in the project or product specifications. That which is described is then implemented. Would it not make more sense if the client says what he or she wants to do or wants to achieve, and the expert makes that request possible? Should experts not focus on pursuing the best and most technically efficient possible way to bring clients to their goals?

  The fixed-price method supports the traditional method and is somewhat reminiscent of the battle of Don Quixote against the windmills: The developer should implement exactly what the client requests, knowing that the client is not a technical expert and realizing in the end that this is a battle that he or she probably cannot win. But the agile fixed-price contract lays a foundation for crushing this method. The client should not focus on the "how" but rather on the "what". The supplier then has the freedom to decide how and thus gets a chance to implement the "what" within the agreed-upon maximum price range. This engine the strong advantage that the development teams get away from the plain implementation of some detailed requirements to a much more sophisticated role where they have to think how to implement the "what" in the most efficient way.

- **Argument 2: Striking statistics.** Try to memorize some of the data from Chapters 1 and 2, or take advantage of the extent of your Smartphone in order to have such data easily available. Ask your contact on the client's side if he or she is aware that the scope and thus the detailed scope of a two-year IT project usually changes by more than half. Also, ask the contact whether he or she has perhaps already experienced a disastrous "black swan" (Flyvbjerg and Budzier, 2011). Would this not, in fact, suggest verifying whether the company is still healthy or if any of the fixed-price IT projects running currently might become a "black swan"? (See Chapters 1 and 2.) No? Then you should save the flexibility and have a go at trying a new form of contract that minimizes dramatically this risk of stranded investments.

- **Argument 3: Bonus schemes.** At the beginning of the discussion ensure that all parties agree to live out and affirm the model "structure creates behavior." Discuss the current incentive schemes of IT procurement and what impact they actually on your IT project or IT budget, have on the basis of a fixed-price project.

- **Argument 4: Transparency.** Are you aware of this situation: Close to the completion stage, the status of IT projects is frequently depicted as green, or perhaps yellow. Shortly before the end of the project, everybody is suddenly very excited and surprised. All that is discussed at this point is delays and a red status, even though up to a completion of 80% everything seemed more or less fine. The rule that 80% of the effort lay in the last 20% of completion of IT tasks very often comes true. Unfortunately, this usually happens at a point where the remaining time is insufficient to repair any errors by new actions before the project ends (with its original time lines). On the other hand, in the agile model you see what is completed and what is not, after two-weeks and every two weeks thereafter (assuming a two week sprint cycle). This information is quality assured and transparent. You should also not settle with predictive project progress of, for example, 80%. There are two possible reasons for these distinctions:

1. In the traditional approach, there are easier ways of deliberate coverup than with an approach in which progress is communicated based on

    binary-measured user stories (finished or unfinished, based on your definition of done, see Chapter 4).

2. Since most of the parts are not tested until the last third of a project, at this time the client or tester can only see what the state of the quality really is. If, at this stage, poor quality is found throughout the software, the information is usually too late. Here, too, an agile approach offers the advantage of binary inspection of finished increments. Finished means that *everything* is finished.

9.2 IDENTIFYING ISSUES OF THE OTHER PARTY

Wolf et al. (2010) describe very clearly that practices such as Scrum are all about identifying a problem and trying something new. Often, this happens due to an emergency situation, and the statistics show that many clients are in regular emergency situations with their IT projects. An ideal starting point for the discussion is when the client his already acquainted with the problems of traditional IT project contracts (which should be the case with almost every client if you look openly and honestly at the most recent IT projects). The starting point can, of course, also be current software development problems of the client concerning, for example, delivery dates or the quality of a ongoing project. Both statistics and our own experience show that most clients bring such a "problem basis" with them.

    The climate of the conversation must, however, allow an open exchange of experiences. The "pub atmosphere" described by Wolf et al., is, of course, a practical environment in which to place the first ideas. But it is important that the clients also have the opportunity to develop the benefits themselves. With an agile fixed-price contract, if you explain exactly how a checkpoint phase proceeds, even the minimal risk of a project becomes more vivid and tangible (or it is exaggerated, as described in Chapter 1: "If you don't like it, you don't pay"). From this stage on, you should offer a trial project. Without the client's cooperation, there is, however, no point in having a trial. On the client's side, the employees of the trial project must be familiarized with the idea. If the client wishes to run a risk and try out the new contractual arrangements, the benefits described in Chapter 8 will play into his or her hands. Thus, the first step in the transition to an agile fixed-price contract is successful. It is, however, important to set the expectations right. Every change to a new approach is bound to the Deming cycle (plan, do, check, and act). The more support there is by experts in this first phase, the faster the client will tend to use the agile fixed-price contract as a basis for IT projects.

9.3 ESTABLISHING COMMON LANGUAGE AND EXPERIENCES

After a common awareness of a problem is present, work begins to create additional foundations for a successful implementation. Mutual understanding requires a common language and a shared vision of the benefits of agile methods. We assume that it will become easier in the future to talk the same and possibly to think the same, because a knowledge of agile methods is distributed rapidly. With this book we also aim to spread the idea of an agile fixed-price contract faster to create a common ground in discussions with legal and procurement departments. Currently, however, it may still be necessary to work intensively. We have had very good results with two-hour workshops. In the first 45 minutes describe the basic idea of agile methods and at the same time, set the realistic expectations.

Following is a list of the principles of agile methods and the motivation to carry out IT projects according to these methods:

- IT projects have an extremely high failure rate, and constant change is one of the main reasons for this.
- The ability to adapt to change is a fundamental pattern of success in nature: "It is not the strongest of the species that survives, nor the most intelligent, it is the one most adaptable to change" (Darwin, 1860).
- Adaptability requires rapid feedback (plan, do, check, and act).
- Inefficiency due to switching a context too rapidly sets a lower limit.
- "Strictly time boxed" protects the supplier from an excessive rate of change as the detailed scope is fixed within this time box. Agility is often thought of as "I can change anything and everything at any time." This is not what agility means and is not how an agile fixed-price contract ensures the delivery of a "whole known (high-level) scope" within a certain time frame and budget.
- Analogous estimates are fast and efficient, as explained our description of the planning poker exercise.

Planning Poker and Ball-Point Game

After the first 45 minutes of a workshop, there is group work. The team must, for example, estimate the cost of a three-week vacation trip to the Bahamas with the planning poker. A weekend city break serves as an example reference user story. The team members with the highest and lowest values estimated must explain their arguments (Gloger 2011).

This exercise raises the attention span enormously. The participants can really sense the agility, because they have had a successful experience. After the feedback, we go from the estimate to the implementation. Here, a production game with stress balls has been established successfully. Trainees receive a box full of stress balls and a task with just a few instructions, such as:

- A ball counts as 1 point when each participant has touched it at least once.
- The ball must stay in the air between the participants.
- The ball may not be passed to neighbors on the left or right.

The aim is to "produce" as many points as possible in a given time.

The team now each receives, for example in six iteration cycles, 1 minute for planning and feedback, and 2 minutes to produce points. Typically, you can reach tremendous production improvements (400% +) after a few runs. Even if you change the conditions during the game, a team adapts very quickly to these changing conditions through continuous feedback.

Ideally, one of several groups is entrusted with the task of carrying out this exercise in the traditional fixed-price mode. The group may plan comprehensively for 6 minutes and then produce for 12 minutes. Here as well, after half the time has passed, the conditions are changed while production continues.

Experience has shown that this exercise provides a good incentive to try out what has been learned and to increase awareness that it might be necessary to change current contract models.

9.4 FEATURE SHOOT-OUT

Chapter 8 provides a very detailed picture of advantages and disadvantages of various types of contracts. Invite your clients to a feature shoot-out, a weighing against each other of the benefits of the various methods, which gives everyone a "shot" at an advantage. The person still standing at the end is the winner. When the appropriate experts for IT contracts and IT projects on the client side enter openly into this discussion, it will cause debate about individual advantages and disadvantages of the various types of contracts, But in the end, the person upholding the agile fixed-price method should naturally win.

If employed skillfully, the tendency is clear that the benefits of agile projects come to light for a client with a correspondingly complex IT project (see Chapter 8). This is also evident in this discussion. Visualize and use flip charts and colors to document. Illustrate results in a clear picture on a flip chart at the end of a two-hour session. Each type of contracts may have its place. However, the picture developed, jointly during the discussion, shows that you have to address the agile fixed-price contract if you do not wish to ignore the benefits of this contract. Use the opportunity to convince a wider circle of the client's employees of this jointly developed result. For IT, where innovation has always been a top priority, the resistance against a new method should soften. The same is true where one business department is not keen about the idea but all others are. After all, why not try something significantly better, even though you know little about it?

9.5 THE BLACK SWAN SCENARIO

Many decision makers in IT projects are not aware that their ongoing or planned IT projects are actually much riskier than they believe them to be. Flyvbjerg and Budzier published an article on this theme in 2011 (see Chapter 1), the central elements of which are called black swans. These are projects that, due to their failure, not only devour vast sums but can also end careers and, in the worst case, destroy companies. This is a central argument to raising awareness of necessary changes. IT managers must submit their projects for risk analysis. What can happen in our respective environments when the largest IT project ends up 400% over the projected budget? What can you do to avoid this? Is the client aware of the extent of this risk, and does he or she carry out a risk analysis? Regardless, a switch to agile fixed-price contracts should be considered, specifically in cases where failure would have a great impact on an organization. With traditional fixed-price projects, the risk of damage grows from a certain "point of no return". As a first step in this process, the agile approach and the agile fixed-price contract maximize the transparency and the value added. This causes the risks to be minimized, and extreme damage becomes almost impossible.

9.6 WORKSHOP ON CONTRACT SETUP

The old saying that "a picture is worth a thousand words" is still valid. So together with the client of an IT project, drawn up a case based on an agile fixed-price contract in the form of a specific example (possibly as contrasted to a traditional form of contract). You can consult the examples from Chapter 10. Preferably, choose an example in the appropriate context for this client. It is possible to establish this example in a one-day workshop, which also shows that this model is quite efficient.

With your specific example in hand, the first theoretical issues adopt practical forms within a few hours for the "agile (contract) newcomers." Before the workshop, because you understand for which IT projects this agreement offers significant advantages and for which (highly standardized) projects the traditional fixed-price contract is still a valid—but not necessary—option.

The workshop is divided into the following parts:

1. **Sketch of the example according to traditional methodology (about 150 minutes)**
   (a) The vision, the underlying issues, and, in brief, the epics that come to mind within the specified time frame are all noted. Use three or four

flip charts or a large whiteboard for this exercise. Keep a tight hold on the effort necessary to sketch the vision and initial topics and epics (e.g., 20 minutes). Jointly estimate how much is still needed to properly complete this high-level description of the contract (e.g., 8 hours).

(b) Next, a small section of the example, or part of an epic, is singled out and specified precisely (in detailed user stories). To do this, select a suitable form of visualization (e.g., flip chart, projector), so that all participants can understand what is being done. Give this exercise 20 minutes and estimate what still needs to be done to specify all the user stories for an entire epic (e.g., two days).

(c) Then proceed to estimate the effort required to perform these detailed specifications for all parts of the project scope with the work necessary to ensure that everything is included at the highest level of detail (e.g., 200 days).

(d) Question critically for which parts the client still detects uncertainty or a potential for change over the duration of the project. Note the answers in percentages in the topics and epics (e.g., 40% on average). Try to obtain realistic values here with targeted questions. It is best to select a topic with the client, where you know that you can ask the right questions. For example, this could mean not choosing a quite easily standardized rollout project for 500 workstations of Windows 7 in the company, but rather, a migration project with many interfaces and little documentation.

(e) Add up the cost for the specification and the percentage of still open uncertainty values. Make a bold note of the effort (e.g., 200 days from above) that must now be provided to create a value that will change by $x\%$ (40% in the example above) over the course of the project. The goal here is obviously to make the workshop realistic, so that high values occur.

(f) Demonstrate using examples of assumptions in the supplier's offer, as he or she can easily maneuver away from this risk [e.g., the assumption that each interface is fully in accord with the specifications, provided and test data will be provided at the start of the project (where experience shows that the specification is either incomplete or changes and that the test data are almost never ready at the start of a project)].

(g) Estimate an overall price that a supplier could deliver with a fixed-price proposal and a possible delivery period. It is not a matter of achieving the real cost but, rather, to have a dollar value and months of lead time for further illustrations.

(h) Sketch critical situations in the project (for examples see Chapter 10), and stipulate how inflexible the traditional fixed-price contract is in finding solutions for an actual project. Overturn additional costs and delays due to these critical situations. How do they deal with changes of x%? What happens if the quality of delivery to the client does not meet expectations?

(i) Calculate the x% of change and uncertainty for an assumed total cost. The cost of changes in the project compared to the costs in the scope of the contractually agreed-upon, fixed price should be reported as twice as high. (This means that, if you have agreed on a fixed price of $2 million and you change 25% of the scope, the additional costs are not $500,000 but actually twice as much, that is, $1 million). Directorial work is definitely more expensive in traditional fixed-price engagements!

(j) Conclude by summarizing the facts. "We have specified a project according to the traditional fixed-price contract with y days of effort. We are aware that the details of x% of the scope are not yet sufficiently known or will change. We have thus carried out a project on the basis of a contract that has not supported the project's reality and its success. Subsequently the project delivered exceeded the time frame by the approved percentage in point (e), and overdrew the cost of the resulting values in points (e) and (i)."

(k) Present a brief statement of what could have happened in the worst-case scenario: much higher costs, massive effort, loss of revenue, additional costs for the existing system (refer to the cost of delay), and so on.

(l) Finally, ensure that the most relevant information is summarized and is available on a flip chart.

2. **Scope in an agile fixed-price contract (15 minutes).** Describe here how the work in point (1a) was actually already done and estimated. Point (1b) shows what effort would be necessary for a few reference user stories (e.g., two days). Keep a tight grip on the work involved in for drawing up the specifications (again visible to all on a flip chart).

3. **The main components of the agile fixed-price contract for this sample project (45 minutes)**

(a) Use the contract template and explain the individual components. (Chapter 3 should support you in this argument.) The client should get the feeling that simply described meaningful processes already exist here.

(b) Setting the main contract parameters of an agile fixed-price contract (assumed riskshare, etc.)

4. **Don't forget to take a break!**

5. **Go through the standard situations of the project with examples (30 minutes).** Consider project development according to the agile approach with the help of Chapter 10. The client should see how well the contract process supports the agile development process. Do not be too tired to emphasize, based on this example, the instruments used for the compli-

ance of the budget and time frame, such as exchange for free and quality assurance.

6. **Construct and run through specific exceptional situations (60 minutes).** From the many examples found in Chapter 10 and supported by the arguments in this book, you can prepare exceptional situations that can easily be applied to a specific project. Demonstrate here, for example, that no additional work exists if they do allow emerging requirements to be replaced with less important requirements during implementation. Outline the fact that if a quality problem has crept in, it is already recognized in the project after two weeks. (It is best to look at the same situation as in point 1). Once again, write down each default and the overhead that results. Point out how the implementation can be set back on the right track, by means of the agreed-upon basic principles of cooperation as well as the scope (the vision).

7. **Simulate the end of the project according to the new approach (30 minutes)**
   (a) Summarize in what time frame, with what effort, what quality, and what added value the project can be concluded. Also illustrate, however, what can happen in the worst case: if for example, the project is canceled or transferred to another supplier after an investment has been made and a business value already delivered.
   (b) Summarize the essential information again on a flip chart.

8. **Retrospection among the participants of the workshop and conclusions (60 minutes).** Allow enough time so that each participant of the workshop is able to submit his or her opinion on the subject. Use standard techniques of group dynamics to position the questions accurately and get started with the proper team member. Better still, invite a professional who can assist in moderating the workshop.

The outcome of the workshop is to represent in a simplified form the entire agreement set up according to the agile model. In addition, the client is now equipped with an arsenal of sample arguments that are familiar to him in here. This also helps the client to explain comprehensively the new procedures and their contractual basis within the organization. Some of the examples clearly show how an agile fixed-price contract can sharply ease frightening scenarios with use of the traditional approach.

With the simulation of the end of the project, you can give the client a good feeling about a "positive outcome." In addition, the significant advantages of an agile fixed-price contract only manifest themselves at the end of a project, for example:

- The quality is always transparent and is secured at the end of the project.
- The focus is placed on the important features, including generating the maximum business value.

- The project may even be completed successfully ahead of schedule as well as below budget.

The retrospective will help you to capture the atmosphere and to identify and address uncertainties. Being an "ambassador" for the agile fixed-price contract, each retrospective provides you with additional knowledge and different approaches that are vital for successful transitions.

(**Note**: *Adjust the proposed time periods according to your moderation style, the group, and the knowledge of the participants. The workshop can also last for two days!*)

9.7 REPORTS AND METRICS

One of the key aspects of the agile model is that the client is always informed about the current status of the project. By this, we do not mean high-level project status reports where three to 10 milestones are marked with approximate progress percentages. We are talking about a development methodology which allows the progress to be measured in small binary units (finished or unfinished). Based on this, the reports that are submitted on a regular basis are agreed upon contractually. Here we offer examples of how such open-book approaches can work in practice.

9.7.1 KISS Backlog View

The backlog is the key element of agile software development. All parties from top management downward have a glimpse into this. Following the motto KISS (keep it simple, stupid) the status can be viewed directly on the basis of the backlog. Table 9.2 illustrates this method. The backlog items are assigned to the planned sprint. A "conversion rate" for story points to team expenses is stipulated contractually. The contract is necessary if the Scrum team continues working purely on story points. The exchange rate that is derived from the team costs is, of course, relevant contractually. After all, clients are interested in what it costs them for a team to implement a certain complexity unit within two weeks. Who is on the team and where they sit might be interesting for the

TABLE 9.2   Backlog Representation for the Status Report

Priority	Backlog Item	Type	Story Points	Sprint	Accepted
1000	Create user	User story	8	03-2012	Yes
995	Search user	User story	5	03-2012	Yes
990	Delete user	User story	3	04-2012	
985	Manage user requests	Epic	21	05-2012	
980	Manager user roles	Epic	13	06-2012	

selection. However, it is irrelevant during the project and a problem that the contractor must take care of.

You can see from the table at any time what functions have already been delivered and what the client has already accepted. Thanks to the story points, the expenses can be forecast. If you like, two additional columns can be added showing which parts have been finally described (in detailed user stories) and additionally, which detailed user story specifications have been approved by both parties.

In addition to this table, the velocity of the final sprint and the person-days used or team costs should also be displayed. An open discussion must be made possible if, for some reason the actual use of person-days or items lies above the planned rate of use (e. g., because the team has few experienced developers). The steering board reaches a decision on this sound information basis. Through riskshare, both parties are affected by the commercial consequences of this decision.

Team metric

At the team level, IT tools can support the capture and presentation of expenses in the project. The example in Figure 9.1 shows the client clearly the extent to which the team has been working on project-related tasks. It also indicates where the team, for example, participated in product improvements that were not covered in the billable services of the project.

9.7.2 Focus: There Is a Single Goal!

In IT projects, an entire series of goals are often pursued. Many project members with many objectives inevitably cause a decrease in efficiency. In

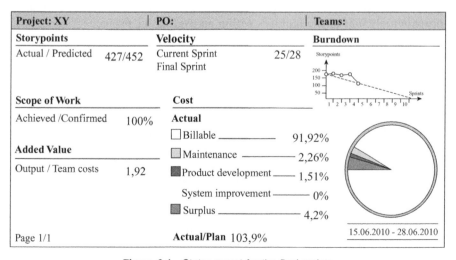

Figure 9.1 *Status report for the final sprints.*

addition, with an approach using the agile model, prioritization of topics becomes more difficult, and interests and politics come into conflict. One way to solve this problem is to fix one common goal—exactly one, and only one goal! The goal should have the highest business value and be crucial to the project's success. Often the goal is to go live with the new software (and turn off the old system), which fulfills a simple project vision by a certain date. Thus, we have suddenly found a tool with which you can quite easily distinguish between "must haves" and all other priorities.

We have experienced projects where many features were of the nature of increasing the degree of automation and comfort in handling the software. For example, "this administration task should run via a click on a button in the administration cockpit allowing entry of the possible parameters." However, if you challenge these features against the one common goal, you might find that this is not a procedure done 10 times a day but rather 10 times a year and can also be performed using the command line and a well-documented procedure call.

This does not mean that this one goal defines the contractual scope as a whole or in any detail. It does, however, concentrate forces on a clearly defined common direction of impact. With such a simply formulated goal, the various levels in the project governance can reach decisions. The importance of one goal can be explained in 5 minutes, whereas explaining the most complex relationships often never leads to a single goal.

If your client or you as a client are not able to create a project vision that is less then half a page, you should question whether you are really ready for the project and have the right standing to push such a project through. Our experience is that nobody is empowered to make a decision to compress the real value of a project down to a simple goal—from a fear of missing even one of the less necessary details. Unfortunately, these are features without which a project would still be able to generate the relevant business value, normally approximately half of the features within an average IT project.

The client is usually not willing to reduce complexity if it is unclear whether and what can be removed from the scope of the contractual object. On the other hand, the supplier can earn more through change requests. This makes things even more difficult. With the question of whether individual items actually are essential to the fulfillment of the primary project objective (e.g., going live with the new system), the discussion can be reduced to facts and solved in this way. What's more, both parties are involved in the riskshare. They have not completely committed themselves irrevocably, but they agreed contractually on a process. Therefore, all are heading toward the same common goal.

10

Practical Examples

In this final chapter we illustrate to you the benefits of an agile fixed-price contract, based on two comprehensive practical examples. We decided to include two complete examples as case studies in addition to some smaller examples throughout the book. We believe that the practical value of such end-to-end examples provides a valuable complement to the small practical hints that we gave in earlier chapters.

First, we describe the client's situation. Next, we present the contract design and project progress from the perspective of the traditional forms of contract. How does the project proceed under a traditional fixed-price or time and materials contract? Then we change the perspective and answer the following question: How can this project be drafted on the basis of an agile fixed-price contract? For this purpose and on the basis of actual facts, we discuss a slight variation on the use of the sample contract or key points of the contract template from Chapter 4.

We also take a look at the benefits of working cooperatively on a project. Despite the similar structural organization of the contracts, we introduce you to other facets of the contract types in each example. This creates clarity because not all aspects have to be compressed into one instance. You will discover interesting points in each example that are perhaps directly relevant to your specific work situation.

Agile Contracts: Creating and Managing Successful Projects with Scrum, First Edition.
Andreas Opelt, Boris Gloger, Wolfgang Pfarl, and Ralf Mittermayr.
© 2013 John Wiley & Sons, Inc. Published 2013 by John Wiley & Sons, Inc.

10.1 EXAMPLE 1: SOFTWARE INTEGRATION IN A MIGRATION PROJECT

This example was based on a real situation. To maintain confidentiality and allow an easy understanding of the key facts, we have, of course, significantly simplified, adapted, and slightly modified the contents. The migration project, which was the central issue in this example, was appropriately implemented according to agile methods based on an agile fixed-price contract. The same migration project was carried out a few years earlier (one software life cycle earlier) according to the waterfall principle and delivered on the basis of the traditional fixed-price contract. In this way we were able to see what could be done with different procedures and contract terms and conditions. We know that different people in a different setup at a different time make this comparison not too exact; however, the trends and key facts are comparable and provide an overall impression for applying an agile fixed-price contract and agile delivery model.

10.1.1 Initial Situation

A known problem: An international group used specific software to adapt the data formats in different countries and to normalize the data and deliver them into a central system. For the purpose of harmonization in this case, a central department at group level was trusted with this service for all national offices. The existing software attained the current version at the end of the life cycle, and the functionality therefore had to be migrated to new base software. A main reason for the migration was the projection that for some countries, within a few months, the performance of the software was no longer able to withstand the growth of the data that would have to be processed.

However, this software played a central role for the company. Ultimately, a large portion of the turnover of the group depended on the fact that the data were processed correctly and on time.

The central department at a group level consisted of an innovative team of experts in this field. Over the years, the maintenance of releases of the software for each country was carried out very carefully. Several times a year, changes were necessary in each country for each interface because of the special importance of this software. Most of the time, the specification of these small projects was a delta specification for each change. Some content in these specifications was not described explicitly enough or well enough for a third party to understand. The team finally built up a high level of expertise over the years.

When considerations for a migration began, the situation was as follows:

- There were no complete specifications for the interfaces, which could have helped the third parties to understand the current system (interfaces) in its entirety.

- The existing specification for each interface was distributed in dozens of delta documents.
- The time pressure for migration was large. A missed deadline would have disastrous consequences, as the existing solution would no longer be able to process the data. This means that the cost of delay is enormous, as additional hardware (and the system required costly high-end hardware) would have to cover this performance gap.
- The risk of errors had to be reduced to an absolute minimum because the contents transformed via these interfaces was essential for the business of the group.
- In terms of migration and changes, development of the existing system had to continue until just before the cutover, as this planned project was not permitted to block the existing business (i.e., update of the existing interfaces based on business requirements).
- There was a rare opportunity to very "easily" test the results by comparing the old and new systems.
- A particular challenge in this project was the role of the central department. This internal service provider was under enormous pressure, and political standing hung by a thread for successful migration.

The schedule in Figure 10.1 shows the critical sequence from 1 to 18 months divided among countries L1 to L5. Kickoff was allowed to take up to four months beforehand. This included the tender and intense contract negotiations. Therefore, the tender had to be sent within a maximum of three weeks.

What were the major challenges in the coming months?

- Implementation based on time and materials was not an option, as an assured budget limit had to be adhered to and nobody wanted to take the risk of managing this project without having the proper experience in this new software tool. The budget limit had to be approved by several committees of the general manager of the national subsidiaries.
- How could you describe the exact scope of the project in a few weeks if there were hundreds of pages of delta specifications for each of the

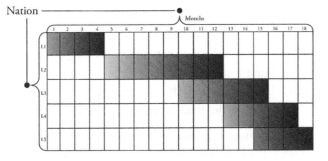

Figure 10.1 *Schedule for the Migration Project.*

national interface group? In addition, it was already known that even these documents would not be sufficiently detailed for an external supplier, in order to come close to clearly defining the scope of the contract. Top management exerted pressure, however: Standard software should be adapted, thereby allowing an interface to be clearly defined (i.e., it may actually be defined already).

- How do you find a supplier who can deliver in a transparent manner, who can ensure the quality from the start of the project?
- The cost pressure was immense, and you had no leeway for intercepting a reasonable extent of the risks with security premiums, as in similar projects.
- The existing team was used presumably in daily operations and could not concentrate on the development of the technical requirements of a request for proposal (RFP).

10.1.2 Contract and Procedure for Traditional Methodologies

We look first at how this project proceeded from the tender to completion according to the traditional fixed-price contract. This illustration is simplified, of course, and we highlight some distinctive points.

10.1.2.1 Tender stage

The employees of the central department at the group level had no alternative and therefore also no choice: Due to the fact that the amount of data threatened to increase and the current situation was inefficient, a fixed-price project had to be put out to tender immediately.

For the tendering phase, the following plan was drawn up and predefined:

(A) Weeks 1–3: Describe the technical requirements of all five countries.

(B) Weeks 1–3: Create the commercial-legal framework and the invitation to tender.

(C) Week 4: Review the tender including the commercial-legal framework, release, and send out to potential suppliers.

(D) Weeks 4–8: This is the time period for the tender response being prepared by the suppliers.

(E) Weeks 9–10: Review the offers and create a short list.

(F) Weeks 11–12: Lead a workshop with the first two suppliers on the short list.

(G) Week 13: Obtain a supplementary offer.

(H) Weeks 14–15: Negotiate with the first two supplies and make a decision.

(I) Week 16: Negotiate the final contract and conclude the contract.

Very tight time frames were necessary in steps (A) to (I). The people involved, all of them professionals, saw this plan as "challenging but possible." They did not consider the exact preparation of a tender to be a good investment in this time-sensitive situation (see Chapter 5). Three to four people were involved in steps (B) to (I). The most time-consuming was step (A), which was the basis for all other steps. The following problems existed:

- The software in principle could not be specified clearly and completely (not even in this relatively "simple" context of interfaces).
- Neither three weeks nor three months would be sufficient to achieve a complete and adequate specification. You would probably need a year to do this (if possible at all), and during this time the interfaces would probably change again.
- Even though everyone was already aware of the problems at this point, they simply had to make the best of it because there was no clean alternative.

Of the 60 employees from the central department at the group level, 40 were assigned for the specification phase, which lasted three weeks plus one week for the review. This was possible only because the individual countries had to accept the delays in the interface changes for ongoing projects. Even at this early stage of the project, the central department was aware of the unwillingness of the countries and the critical situation the countries faced with each delay. In this example, 40 employees multiplied by four weeks multiplied by five days resulted in an investment of 800 person-days. This was before the tender was even shipped for a task that was difficult to achieve, if it could be achieved at all.

Many traditional fixed-price projects present this picture in the early stages. This is before there is even a project and significant efforts are invested already (if the monitoring of efforts is already transparent at that stage). Compared with other IT projects, however, this was not a very big project, and the preparation phase especially was extremely short. (Efficient or too short? See Chapter 5.) The experience in practice showed that sometimes 20 people work for months to prepare the specifications of an IT project. In this way, thousands of person-days are invested in a commodity whose timeliness, and thus value, was permanently forfeited and whose benefits are later questioned. We will not provide details regarding the tender documents at this point for this specific example. We assume that you know the nuances of a traditional fixed-price tender.

In response to the RFP, the offer was prepared by the supplier and a fixed price was estimated according to the following criteria:

- What was clear could be estimated.
- What was not clear was bound to a minimum effort by assumptions as inconspicuous and nonalarming to the client as possible.
- As the price was to be minimized, additional assumptions were introduced to reduce the effort, even if the parties believed that some of these assumptions were very likely not to be met in the project.

The client determined the two highest-ranked suppliers based on the evaluation matrix specified in the tender preparation. These suppliers were both invited to a two-day workshop to discuss the details of the offer. The aim of this workshop was to clarify technical details and agree on interpretations in order to establish comparability. In such workshops, a protocol is often written but is not worked directly into the scope document. The results are then incorporated somewhere into the revised offer without the required specific formulations, as in this case.

The outcome of these workshops: a technically coordinated scope to a certain extent and an adapted offer from the supplier. Let us once again remind ourselves about the initial situation: This offer was based on an incomplete and constantly changing description of the scope of the contract and has now been enhanced with assumptions, that are somewhat difficult to understand (are one-sided). The question that often arose in such situations for all parties involved was: "Who expresses this openly?" The client or the supplier? The staff on the client side knew that they needed this project and therefore did not want to confuse anyone, "because it's always this way anyway." The supplier wanted the job and therefore tried to work more competently "because there are always assumptions to minimize the risk."

10.1.2.2 Negotiation

The last step before the start of the project was the final commercial negotiation. As usual, the first two on the list were invited since they had now submitted a bid that was technically comparable (see Chapter 7), and in the view of the commercial negotiator, covered a fully described contractual scope. This was also the case in this example. It was nevertheless possible to acknowledge that this offer was not perfect and the experience at the level of the buyers also showed that things could and will still change. Thus, for internal budgeting, another 20% of the total fixed price was reserved as the budget for change requests. However, in the entire budget framework the client had to reserve even more for change requests in this particular situation in the migration project because in addition to unplanned changes and events, the current platform had to be developed further, and an amount for adapting these planned changes had to be included. Once again the client was assumed to cover that with an addition of 25% of the effort, based on verification from the internal experts on the existing system.

This scale is consistent with the values in Chapter 2, in which it is suggested that you go out with a change in the scope of around 50% for an 18-month project. What is not correct in this calculation, however, is that you ever obtain the additional work required for change requests (directing services) for the same price as that for the original scope and that this would not impact your timeline. Defining the costs of directing services based on complexity points (which we refer to as story points) could be anchored within each fixed price (Brooks, 1975) as well. In practice, this is often not done or is implemented insufficiently, as is evident in the sample project discussed below.

This means that you should already expect that the adjusted budget is to be set much higher than the price negotiated in the commercial agreement on a fixed price that is to be achieved during the negotiation. In our example, the commercial offer was structured so that the expenses and costs were disclosed for each country and each interface. With an additional block of overheads (e.g., for the project management) and a safety margin, the supplier was able to sum up the final price offered, [i.e., the (traditional) fixed price].

As usual, discrepancies between suppliers in different positions, stored daily rates, and the level of security supplements were discussed and negotiated. The buyer received a bonus based on an outdated but still popular model: namely, on the basis of the difference between the best initial offer and the final price negotiated at the conclusion of the contract.

Also in this example, with skillful assumptions and limits, the supplier was able to create the potential for a satisfactory negotiation (i.e., the supplier reduced the price to a level where he or she counted on massive change requests already, due to clever assumptions) between the buyer in particular and the client in general. Thus, negotiations could be completed within the plan. In addition to the ranking based on the evaluation matrix, the final price was now crucial. What was unfortunately not critical was the cost at the end of the project and who would bear the risk for it. The responsible buyer withdrew from the project at the end of this process and sold the detailed scope for the minimum price achievable.

10.1.2.3 The traditional fixed-price contract
The traditional fixed-price contract concluded included the following components (with reference to those relevant to the discussion in this book):

- **Full detailed description of the scope of the contract.** The contract itself comes first in the order of contract-related documents. The contract includes the legal and commercial aspects (see more below) but not the actual description of the scope of the contract. As usual, the supplier's offer was referred to in the final contract. This latest valid offer contained a description of more than 100 pages on what was included in the scope of the contract and what was not. Few people were capable of really understanding the details of this complex representation. In this example, a description of all interfaces was compiled in the RFP document in that short time based on the documentation available. For safeguarding it was, however, noted in the RFP that the results from the new interfaces must be equal to those of the old interfaces. In the supplier's offer, however, it was clearly stated that exactly what was defined in the specification was to be implemented (and that is not vicious but the only way it can be from the suppliers and a traditional fixed-price perspective) and that no changes were possible after the contract. This also involved changes that originated from variations in the comparison data. This assumption was clear, as no supplier would offer a fixed price proposal allowing the original RFP assumption to be valid, as the supplier would therefore fix a price for something unknown.

- **Complete delimitation.** Each offer includes a section on assumptions. Sometimes more obvious or implicit assumptions are incorporated elsewhere in the document. This chapter with assumptions is a collection of dozens of points accurately determining exactly where the contractual scope ends. Therefore, the client does not obtain a simple comprehensively description of what services will be received. Instead, the project scope is defined by supplier-selected assumptions interwoven with complex representations. Usually, the offer is referenced in the contract, and this offer together with the assumptions becomes part of the contract. In addition, of course, any deviation in the contract and change to the specifications of the contract are ruled out after contract completion. Strangely enough, we meet again and again with clients who assume that the scope of a contract is what was originally specified in the RFP. Clearly, this is usually not the case and if it were, the supplier's offer, including the assumptions in order in contract-related documents, is preferred.

- **Effort.** The estimated effort expended by the supplier, with 500 person-days for country L1, resulted in a corresponding price. The effort for the other countries, L2 to L5, was adopted with 900, 700, 600, and 500 days. (***Note:*** *The values were changed for simplicity in this example; however, the statement of the facts is thereby not affected.*)

- **Obligation to cooperate.** The obligation to cooperate is also defined in the traditional fixed-price contract. This is usually kept very generic and is found often in a similar formulation, as in this example. Here the client was obliged to support the suppliers throughout the project duration with an average effort of five full-time employees. In the faithful representation of this obligation to cooperate in the contract, the performance may still be specified toward tasks such as a review of specifications, acceptance, and testing, and thus be somewhat more concrete. However, based on these formulations the client could not specify what resources to block and when (i.e., his or her exact scope of the obligation), based on this obligation to cooperate. In this example the obligation to cooperate was limited by the approval of designs and the software solution delivered, as well as support during questions regarding the specification.

- **The project plan and milestone plan.** The project and milestone plans contained in the offer were very high-level, and simply presented the major steps in the project, as is very often the case in fixed-price offers. Information that can be derived from such project plans is, for example, when the entire project is to be completed. A more accurate project plan is, however, usually defined as the first activity in the project, as it was also the case in this example. You enter into an agreement for a fixed-price contract and you know when it will be completed. However, you still don't know exactly who will do what and by when. Admittedly, we are not in favor of detailed project plans for IT projects. These plans usually consume half of the resources solely for updates and changes. It is, however, always interesting to see which unrealistic plans are signed and thus contractually binding. In this specific example, the project plan included a linear distribution for each country in the phases of design, implementation, testing, and acceptance that was not so realistic that the first part of the project would surely take much more effort, as cooperation has to be established.

- **Payment plan.** The following payment milestones were agreed to for each country:
  - ○ 20% at project start
  - ○ 20% upon approval of the design
  - ○ 30% upon completion of the implementation (i.e., when declared ready for acceptance)
  - ○ 30% upon acceptance

  This sounds familiar and reasonable, but it means that the client has already made 70% of the investment before he or she is even able to inspect the quality of the software for the first time, and thus there is the risk of spending 70% for work for which doubtful business value has been created. Of course in case of failure you could try to get this money back, but have you ever tried that or witnessed some company doing so? It is normally not so easy.

- **Part payments.** The contract included part payments in the event that the scope was reduced. Should one of the interfaces be made easier to represent or cease in general due to changes in the business, 80% of the cost would still be paid in the context of the fixed price. The supplier would then argue: "Such a price can only be offered for large-quantity orders." Basically that's right; after all, one cannot order 100 laptops at a discounted price and then buy only one at the same price. To compare with the agile fixed-price contract, we want to emphasize, however, that as a client, at least at first sight, you can indeed get a good price but you responsible for paying for scope *reduction*.

- **Delays.** Delays caused within the responsibility of the client were regulated by an additional cost of x euros per week of delay. In return, a penalty of 0.5% of the contract value per country and per week was agreed to in the event that the supplier would not meet the deadlines due to reasons caused mainly by the supplier.

- **Change requests.** A precise procedure was determined for how change requests would be handled. It was also clarified which daily rates would be charged for resources used by the supplier. In this example, as with many other projects, it was not, however, put into a binding relation with some reference points: It was not defined that a function that the supplier has delivered within the original fixed price for a certain effort should cost about the same amount in a change request. No, instead, a "directing scope" was invoiced without the possibility for the client to do something about excessive prices.

- **Acceptance.** The key element is the acceptance or the interim approval of design documents. A clear set of rules dictated that each country must be accepted by the client within four weeks from RFA. The supplier had to fix errors from class 1 within a day and these from classes 2 and 3 within five days. This ensured test progress. Approval would be granted at the end of the four weeks only if no class 1 errors and no more than three class 2 errors remained. (*Note: Of course, we have greatly simplified the acceptance procedure. Nevertheless, we can show that it concerns a standard regulation which communicates clearly what needs to be inspected and how.*)

- The points on warranty, damages, and other legal issues are almost similar in both contract types and thus are not discussed in this example. For details on this topic, refer to Chapter 6.

- Most readers will be familiar with many of these issues, as they represent the key meaning of the traditional fixed-price contract. There are no surprises, and in the next section we illustrate this specific example through the course of the project. You will see how inefficiently this contract has supported the actual project work and how "toothless" the regulations were in critical situations.

- With traditional fixed-price contracts, it is usually assumed that the specifications can be processed according to the waterfall principle, and the implementation is estimated in this way. In this example we want to highlight briefly the fact that the fixed price supports an established practice from the last decade in which the client describes exactly what he or she wants from the experts (suppliers). Sometimes the client even describes exactly what needs to be done. The supplier accepts this request and sees it as his or her duty to implement it accurately. This seems strange, as you would normally not tell a baker how to bake bread; you would roughly specify what you want and leave the expert to do the rest.

- If we later consider the same project within an agile fixed-price contract, we will realize that it is much more useful for an expert to optimally enable the goal that the client wishes to achieve. This means the project vision should be, for examples, "The new system delivers the same result as the old one, only with x-times the performance." You can then use the expertise to embark on the best technical solution for implementation. Basically, this is a problem of procedure, which is, however, supported strongly by the type of contract, or, in the case of an agile fixed-price contract, the problem is eliminated.

10.1.2.4 *Project progress, the teams, and critical situations*

The project began with a pompous kickoff and with it, the motivation of all those involved to make this project one of the successful projects of this company.

It began with country L1. The first two weeks elapsed for various ramping activities, but above all, a meticulous project plan was prepared. During this time, in the project status report and the project steering, the supplier expressed concern that some of the specifications were not yet detailed enough. Nevertheless, the steering board decided to begin the detailed technical design phase anyway. How is the project represented right from the start if we take all these concerns seriously?

The technical design was created in the next four weeks and presented to the client for approval. Of course, the supplier pointed out immediately that he was no longer obligated to deliver to the client what was within the original specifications but what was in this technical design. Once the client approved the design, he was committed to the delivery of what was described and approved in the design. Often, the clients are not accurate enough in their acceptance (often also due to a lack of time and plan-able tasks) or could not recognize every facet of implementation in the complex design documents. Even among those interfaces that were verified intensively by the client's staff, although their comments were accepted, because of the time pressure, the comments were not incorporated properly. On the client side, the work required for the reviews of seven interface designs amounted to approximately 18 days. The turnaround time for approval of these designs was limited to one week. Meanwhile, seven of the 20 weeks available were consumed without a single line of code, and thus no real business value was generated. The design accepted was then handed over to the developers who implemented their interpretation of the design. Quality assurance measures such as unit testing or test driven design were not heeded. The developers began implementation with the aim of delivering software after a further six weeks for the module tests phase. One week was planned by the supplier for the module tests. This time line was already exceeded for some interfaces, because after six weeks the interfaces did not function as well as expected. In two of the interfaces, the specifications were so unclear that more demands and discussions resulted in a delay of two weeks.

In the next step in the test phase, a comparison test was conducted. Here, the same test input data for the results of the existing interfaces were compared with the results of the newly implemented interfaces. One week was planned for this. However, it was found that the results were not close to being the same for any of the interfaces. Analyzing the data differences was not easy: The causes of the errors could be in development, in the specifications or in the test data, even in in the current implementation. With the increasing delay, more and more of the changes carried out in parallel to the existing system piled up, to be implemented as change requests in the newly developed system. This backlog, which should have been incorporated in the past two weeks based on change requests, had become increasingly larger. Escalations due to delays had also now begun.

How had the contract helped to find more effective solutions to this critical situation? Not even all the interfaces passed the comparison test, and the project for country L1 was already at week 16 of 20.

- **Failure to meet the obligations to cooperate**
  - The supplier claimed that the client did not fulfill the obligation to cooperate, as the additional effort in the comparison of data should be

performed by the client. Also, due to a lack of resources, the project supported ambiguities in the specification, design approval, and comparison tests. On average five full-time employees were planned for in the contract. This was not the case, however, according to the supplier's calculations.

○ The client assumed the position that compared to the original project plan, the displacements at all corners allowed no planning, and the client did the best he or she could do. For the comparison tests it was obvious to the client that major software defects caused the deviations, and thus it was not clear to the client that he or she should bear the major part of this additional work.

- Delay
  ○ The client was of the opinion that the delay had been caused by the supplier. The software quality was poor (defects found in the comparison tests), and this was not recognized until the end of the project. The client demanded the appropriate compensation in accordance with the contract (penalty).

  ○ The supplier reported the incomplete specifications and the differences in the comparison tests as a reason to delay the milestone. The supplier also demanded the appropriate compensation in accordance with the contract (price for additional week for delays caused by the client).

- **Change in scope**
  ○ Due to the delay, the client found him- or herself in the situation that the existing system changed more and more, which in turn forced the client to pay for expensive change requests. This major change concerned in particular the other countries already specified in the contract, which then had to start with delays, which hinted of further problems. However, an interface in country L2 was dropped, which seemed to relieve the budget and so should be accepted by the supplier to.

  ○ The supplier saw an opportunity here to receive compensation for the very closely estimated fixed price and argued from the contractual point of view that scope changes must be compensated.

The contract could not help the parties find a common solution during these escalations. The camps were divided, and the additional costs grew and grew. No longer was anyone pleased over the originally well-negotiated fixed price, and the buyers no longer felt responsible for this process, as the trouble was caused by incomplete specifications and implementation mistakes, not by contractual issues.

A conclusion to the first part of the project.   Still, after weeks of escalations, country L1 was finished after seven instead of four months, with an additional 100% added to the costs.

10.1.2.5 Project completion

Country L2 began after seven instead of four months. The client's options to change this were zero. The additional compensation indeed tarnished the reputation of the supplier, but the supplier was at least able to polish his sales figures. In addition, the implementation for country L2 lasted 20 instead of the scheduled nine months. Overspending meanwhile was 200%. This was a strange situation as everybody knew from the experience of the first country that the approach is not optimal; they stuck to the already agreed-upon contractual approach.

It was decided to eliminate the previously mentioned interfaces for country L2 only after the design phase had started because the release management in complex IT environments often does not allow such simple and long-term decisions to be taken in a timely fashion. So 80% of the expenses had to be paid according to the contract. This was supported by the waterfall process, according to which the work had already begun. The discussions ended with the fact that where there was a page design and a small project plan, 80% of an interface would be paid for. The situation was similar in the other countries. After more than three years and exorbitant costs of +300%, the project was completed.

But let us not forget the performance of the existing systems. Hardware and software worth several hundred thousand USD had to be purchased due to the delays. Hundreds of person-days were invested in the installation and handling of load distribution. In this way at least the operational running of the business was protected.

Contractual compensation and other contractual provisions could at no point be used for anything other than threats. Oddly enough, you move away from threats in most fields of activity in which teams and parties work together. It is only in IT projects where there is still a strong focus on intimidation.

The consequences were significant. The responsibilities were redistributed, and some of the staff had to vacate their positions regardless of the fact that they had done their best in the initial situation according to the contract. Staff members who have been punished were those who had tried to move the project from a poor initial position to a conclusion, and according to certain criteria, some of these were even successful. Many such brave heroes get nothing but blame in the end, causing us to ask who really enjoys the job of project manager in a non-agile-developed IT project?

Summary

Even though it sounds dramatic, this project was not a real "black swan." Of course, it was not a model project, but basically it would not especially frighten or surprise IT professionals. On the positive side, the project could be completed with additional costs of "only" 300%, despite the unfortunate initial situation.

What were the fundamental problems associated with the traditional fixed-price contract used for this project?

- An early attempt was made to create exact specifications for something that to date had not been specified. Decision makers often do not believe that it is possible that quite major changes can take place over time.
- The time set aside to prepare the tender was not enough to describe and verify the detailed scope and most of the circumstances (e.g., that the comparison test will show that the specifications and real data deviate).
- Although the quality problems were due partially to incorrect specifications, they were always discovered very late in the project for each country, as well as throughout the country's entire delivery performance. There was no way to counteract this at an early stage.
- Although the contract offered formulations for all eventualities, there was no way out and no motivation to cooperate. Thus, there was also no road back to efficiency.

When using in the agile approach it is often noted that the effort required to meet the client's obligation to cooperate is very high. Is the effort significantly lower in this example of a traditional fixed-price contract? Let's take a closer look at the obligation to cooperate in the project for country L1 (we contrast, the agile fixed-price contract in the next section):

- Discussions on unclear specifications: 10 days
- Design approval: 18 days
- Questions during implementation: two days
- Support during the comparison test: 80 days
- Approval acceptance: 100 days
- Project management, etc.: 120 days

The project was very profitable for the suppliers, especially because a total of 600 days of change requests were invoiced for country L1 alone. This was made possible because:

- The detailed specification was not sufficiently current.
- There were delays due to the poor quality of comparison data and specifications and therefore an obligation to cooperate for longer.

Changes to the interface that had occurred since the start of the project had to be reworked in the last few weeks on the basis of change requests. This was aggravated, of course, through the total delay, because it involved permanent changes in the existing interfaces.

10.1.3   Contract and Procedure for Agile Methodologies

A few years have passed and we see now, in the same context, how the same functionality has been migrated again onto a new software product for all different countries. However, this time the decision was made to use an agile approach, based on a slight variation of an agile fixed-price contract. Our experience is that clients who already use the agile fixed-price contract idea or even the template from this book generate their own slightly adapted contract template. This is fine, of course, as it is not the detailed formulation (which can always be questioned or improved) but, rather the general ideas and processes that create the value of this new contract form.

10.1.3.1 Tender stage

Again the data volume threatened to increase. The current solution had become increasingly more inefficient, since it was getting a bit old (a common life cycle for software products). The employees of the central department at the group level again had to prepare the tender for a migration project. Not all employees had to step down after the first fiasco a couple of years ago. Therefore, there were still vivid memories of the last migration project, which required increased attention to the following pitfalls:

- Strictly speaking, software cannot be specified completely and unambiguously.
- To achieve anything near this state, much more than three weeks would be necessary to revise the existing documentation.
- Migration of the countries planned for later was so far away that massive changes would arise in the specifications (due to a natural evolution of these interfaces over time).

The experience gained from the project a few years ago encouraged the client to put the migration project out to tender, this time in the form of a slight variation of an agile fixed-price contract. In this example, preliminary work and discussions on "mindset" were also necessary to steer the process in the right direction. So another plan for the tender stage was created. The fact that this process was not initiated earlier was due to the cumbersome processes involved, which often enable decisions only at the last minute. Have you ever been responsible for achieve a decision in a large company by aligning all countries that had a certain degree of freedom? Then you know what we are talking about!

- (A) Weeks 1–3: Compile the detailed technical requirements for one country and the high-level requirements for the other four countries.
- (B) Weeks 1–3: Create the commercial-legal framework for the tender.
- (C) Week 4: Review the tender, release, and ship to potential suppliers.
- (D) Weeks 4–8: this is the time period for the tender response.

(E) Weeks 9–10: Review the offers and create a short list.

(F) Weeks 11–12: Lead a workshop with the first two suppliers on the short list.

(G) Week 13: Obtain a supplementary offer.

(H) Weeks 14–15: Negotiate with the first two suppliers and make a decision.

(I)   Week 16: Negotiate the final contract and conclude the contract.

The key difference was that in the three weeks set aside for step (A), 10 people directed their complete attention to a more precise specification for the first country, L1. Another two employees did high-level analysis of the other countries in order to create one more stable reference point from which to derive analogies (complexity estimate of the functionality based on number of fields, lines of code, etc.) for the other countries. The reference specifications for the overall project for country L1 were thus created in only 180 days, and there was a projection based on analogies to the other countries.

The plan was to continue during the course of the project to invest in the creation of the detailed requirements for another 600 days, in time, however, for the latest release version of the interfaces. Information needed at short notice (first country) was created immediately. For long-term information, it was proposed that this would be developed before reaching the implementation of this part of the project.

The invitation to tender included the following parts:

- **Reference user stories.** Country L1 was one of the smallest of the five countries with regard to the overall scope. But based on the interfaces of country L1, a possible detailed specification was developed and included in the tender in step (A). The requirements included conventional interface specifications as referenced in the user stories and defined according to the agile approach. With these user stories the suppliers could calculate the effort very closely and make an appropriate offer. Significant portions of the user stories were grouped into epics for each respective interface. In addition, some user stories were also defined from the perspective of operations and maintenance.

- **Analogous values.** The respective epics for the individual interfaces of the remaining four countries were specified in the tender documents. In addition, a relation to at least one interface/user story from country L1 was prepared with a brief rationale for each of the epics. Furthermore, one or more epics were held for each country in the form. Whether or not this was in addition to the interfaces, more functionality could be expected from the perspective of operations and maintenance. A practical example related to country L2:

    ○ Country L2 contains the following interfaces X1 through X7.

    ○ For each interfaces, the following definition was specified:

○ Interface X1: Accepted up to 5 million records from system A (10 fields) and converted these, through simple format changes, into a format for system B (eight fields). There were no further enhancements of data, and no aggregation of records was carried out. In the event of an error, one would have to revert to the functions created in country L1. The complexity was twice as high as that of interface Z from country L1. The main reason was the much higher volumes of data and the additional data fields.

○ For the remaining requirements, the following frame conditions were defined:

○ For country L2, processing must be performed for one day's data in 8 hours instead of 12 hours as in country L1.

○ Two additional operating functions must be created for the automatic display of the processed records in the application, specifically for country L2.

- **Requirements regarding the pricing.** The suppliers were asked to indicate the work involved in the reference user stories and justify the structure. In addition, a list of the daily rates for the individual engineering levels were included, which resulted in an average daily rate for the supplier-selected team. Furthermore, the necessary planned effort was specified for the product owner. In essence, therefore, the cost of the team and its (initial) structure was requested. Furthermore, when implicitly required roles in the project were considered necessary by the supplier, these were to be listed and offered as an option. Within the scope of an agile fixed-price contract, the supplier also had to declare and justify a margin of safety for the individual components and argue where he or she sees uncertainty.

- **Contract template.** The tender was accompanied by a basic description of the agile approach and a contract for the agile model. This was then included by the providers in the key items in response to the RFPs. The contractor had to emphasize in his or her offer a willingness to sign an agile fixed-price contract.

- **External subject experts.** The supplier had to propose an external expert in his or her offer and in return accept the external expert who was proposed by the client. In the final contract negotiated they would then agree on one of the experts.

- **Project plan.** The procedure prescribed had to define how the final milestone was to be maintained. There also had to be a guarantee that the first quality-assured partial delivery could be supplied to the client not more than four weeks after the project started.

- **Quality.** At this point, the following questions were asked: In what form would the software be tested? How many tests per interface would be implemented, and how many of these would be automated? Furthermore, the software environment in the development department of the suppliers had to describe what was to be used for these automated tests.

- **Delivery.** The supplier had to confirm that he or she was able to deliver working software in short iterations.
- **Next steps.** The suppliers had accepted the fact that the expenses would be discussed openly in two one-day workshops within two weeks. The degree of the riskshare that the supplier was willing to take had to be confirmed in the proposal already.
- **Software licenses and software maintenance.** A proposal for when the software licenses had to be paid, and when the software maintenance would be carried out, and how one would deal with any payments already made if the project were terminated (which would be a valid possibility in the cooperative model of an agile fixed-price contract) was required of the suppliers in the offer.

For a detailed look at the invitation to tender for agile fixed-price contracts, refer to Chapter 5.

10.1.3.2 Negotiation

From the suppliers who answered the RFP and were fully able to meet the requirements, the clients were now guided by the following key messages:

- The effort required for each reference user story, including a description of what was to be done in this implementation to increase the transparency of the expenses.
- The effort planned for the product owner: Depending on the design, one or more product owners were provided, as well as an "owner of the product owner" ("similar" to a program manager).
- The projection of the effort on the basis of analogies and under consideration of the security surcharges resulted in the maximum price range within which the agile fixed-price contract would move.
- Acceptance of the individual components of the agile approach and the agile fixed-price contract.
- Quantitative statements on quality assurance.
- Statement regarding experience with the agile methodology and the ability to deliver regularly.
- Statements regarding dealing with software licensing costs and software maintenance.
- Proposed riskshare of suppliers.
- Daily rates for individual roles and teams proposed to implement the required functionality within the time specified, according to the suppliers.

The negotiation could be carried out based on these parameters (see the details of negotiating an agile fixed-price contract in Chapter 7). In this example and based on these parameters, the client tried specifically *not* to reduce the costs of the team to an unrealistic degree. Of course, there was still the assumption that the price must remain very attractive, as the best suppliers lined up to date who could meet the sum of the basic criteria, such as competence, references, and price, were going to be selected. In this approach the goal of selecting the best bidder was pursued thoroughly, but with caution. Instead of reducing the costs immediately, the first round of negotiations ensured that the actions of the highest-ranked suppliers were comparable. Subsequently, two workshops were held with each of these suppliers. Here, the acceptances and work required were determined and specified together with the client's specialists from the central department at the group level. This resulted in:

- The final maximum price range, which included the client's understanding of the work involved and the common basis of possible acceptances of defined security surcharges per user story and epic.
- The riskshare that the supplier was prepared to accept based on clarifications and acceptances incurred during the workshops.
- An assurance that the suppliers had understood all the other parameters of the agile fixed-price contract.

The last and genuine round of negotiations proceeded relatively unspectacularly, because the requirements were considerably more relaxed and not intended to be confrontational. The client no longer had as a goal pushing the fixed price submitted originally. High levels of transparency and understanding on both sides were more important. These were unusual statements for experienced negotiators, but on closer acceptance were very functional. In addition to optimizing prices through competition in the tendering process, the negotiation manager made sure that the project had a good chance of success! The procurement representative and the responsible senior managers on the suppliers' side considered themselves part of the steering board for the project.

10.1.3.3 The agile fixed-price contract

For this example, we have included in Appendix A a sample agile fixed-price contract in which is close to the contract used originally. This illustrates that the contract template from Chapter 4 can be employed and that even with slight adaptations, this new type of cooperation remains much the same. The content in the sample contract was modified accordingly and was comprised of examples only. It shows clearly that a corresponding agile fixed-price contract can be formulated efficiently and completed given all the necessary components. Thus, a contractual basis is laid for a successful IT project to be executed in a cooperative mode and not in a mode based on hope.

However, the contractual template was not available in this form at the time the project was kicked off. Still most of the essential aspects that are now formalized in the template in Chapter 4 were incorporated in the contract at the time this project was negotiated. The tendering phase was already forcing these essential aspects, as described above.

For the second example provided at a later stage in this chapter, such a sample contract is not provided again but we simply highlight specific parts of the agile fixed-price contract. This is done because the contracts differ only in the expression of the parameters and through slight adaptations of the formulations.

10.1.3.4 Project progress, the teams, and critical situations

Based on an agile fixed-price contract, the project began in a slightly calmer atmosphere than that of its failed predecessor. Of course, this time the kickoff was also celebrated, and everyone was motivated to make the project one of the few successful IT projects at the time. Unlike the first project, everyone knew that the euphoria was controlled on a sensible path by the reservations of the new methodology. If it were to be discovered in the checkpoint phase that it no longer worked as planned, both parties could then pursue a different path.

The project again began with country L1. Unlike the first time, no time was wasted with project plans; instead, implementation began immediately with the already well-specified reference user stories (the high-level release plan was known). The first tested functionality of a simple interface was completed after only two weeks, and after another two weeks, the first interface was delivered to the client. At this time further actions were planned and user stories aligned in detail, prioritized, and discussed between the contractor and the client.

The client used the opportunity during the individual sprints to follow the progress on site with the supplier for one to two days and, simultaneously, to optimize the flow of information. Compared with traditional fixed-price contracts, in which several days were already invested in the approval of designs, the effort required was now minimal.

After another six weeks, the client had already gained a good impression of the operation and was able to measure precisely the progress of the deliveries received. A verification of effort after the four weeks of the checkpoint phase had shown a slight correction upward of 5%, which was understandable to the client. Based on the binary measurements, it was indicated that after the first two sprints, progress was not sufficient. This was then compensated for in week five by assigning two more people to the team. Through early recognition one can sometimes bypass Brooks' law, which states that additional labor only further delays an already delayed software project (Brooks, 1975, p. 25), as Brook did not have agile delivery methodologies available. At this point we would like to note the following: With agile fixed-price contracts, the client does not have the freedom to add more and more changes on top of the original high-level scope, which then causes the supplier to compensate for this scope overhead at his or her own expense, or in the context of risk-share. The supplier may compensate at his or her own risk only when the team does not provide as planned!

Comparison test. Once again, a comparison of the results of existing interfaces with those of the newly implemented interfaces was the next test step on the program. One week was planned for this test. But it turned out again that none of the results were approximately equal for any of the interfaces. Once again, the data differences were very expensive to analyze. In contrast to a traditional fixed-price contract, the parties were able to realize this very early in the project.

After intense debate, a solution was found: As early as the next sprint, the experts of the central department at the group level worked directly with the development team on a specified day in the course of the implementation of a new user story. This ensured that the client was able to eliminate ambiguities and verify the results during development. Most points that would cause explainable errors during the comparison test had been highlighted early in the development cycle. Confidence in the quality of the software increased due to the cooperative involvement of the client in the development mechanism. There was very little discussion regarding the fact that, depending on how you choose to see it, this was due to not-yet-explainable deviations with a high probability of error in the specifications or errors in the existing system.

Let us observe a few critical project situations and analyze how the agile fixed-price contract has contributed to resolving these situations.

- **Failure to meet the obligations to cooperate**
  - The client was informed clearly about his or her obligation to cooperate and plan fixed tasks on specific (fixed) days over the long term. In this project there was also misconduct, but it could be precisely identified and cleaned up by means of the clear cooperative structure. To sum up, in this case the client exceeded his obligation to cooperate because he was able to recognize his own benefit.
  - None of the parties could hide in the position that project delays and uncertainties on what to do led to the fact that the obligation to cooperate was not fulfilled. In the agile process a sprint always takes two weeks. Sometimes the content changes slightly, but the key points and tasks agreed upon are fixed.

- **Delay**
  - At this point we came to realize that after the positive experience of the first six weeks of the comparison tests, there would be some delay in the project. However, both parties remained focused on the solutions due to the riskshare model and the type of cooperation. The contractually committed involvement of the client in the development process also ensured cooperation and confidence in the quality.
  - The supplier was largely correct in saying that the origin of the problems lay in the specifications and the comparison data. However, through intensive cooperation a solution was found to make the working methods of the suppliers more efficient, thereby compensating for the additional work that resulted from this fault.

- **Change in scope**
  - ○ This time, despite the slight delay, the client was not faced with the problem that the existing system kept changing because these requirements were still not specified in detail. In this case, the majority of the changes involved real changes and not an increase in complexity. Again, it became clear that one interface in country L2 would no longer be necessary. This was discussed openly and ultimately was used as compensation for additional effort in the comparison tests.
  - ○ The supplier was willing to accept each new change, within the assumptions of complexity, before the date when the implementation was planned. The supplier did not succumb to the temptation to charge too many change requests because the assumptions concerning delimitations were defined together with the client, and the client had little understanding when something was suddenly presented in a different manner. It was different when assumptions that were defined together were changed. To sum up, the supplier endeavored to keep within the budget limit, as she would otherwise have been involved in the loss of riskshare. There was also no "contractual obligation" to blackmail the client, as exit routes were stated clearly in the contract documents.

- **Disagreement on efforts**
  - ○ Following the implementation of country L1, there were discussions during further assessments of the details of country L2 that additional work was claimed by the supplier. This additional effort resulted from the comparison tests, in which the supplier recorded increased work in feedback and analysis. After arduous discussions this was also confirmed by the technical experts from both sides. In steering board meetings the client could also verify that the efficiency had been increased due to the close cooperation, which minimized the risk, and a solution was found.

In this project, escalations usually ended with the parties falling back on the processes set out clearly in the contract. In this way, during critical times, a path to cooperation was once again sought.

Country L1 was completed after five months instead of four, at a 15% additional cost. Since this exceeded the 10% margin of safety, the additional overhead was reported to the steering group at an early stage. Close attention was again paid to obtaining budget overspending during migration of the other countries.

10.1.3.5 Project completion

Country L2 was begun after four months. Although migrating country L1 was not yet complete, the process strengthened confidence in the quality and the process. This enabled migration of the next country to be tackled with additional resources and without any concern about starting before L1 was finished. The other countries were concluded with similar values of approximately 15%. The additional effort of 5% (over the 10% security buffer) divided the riskshare accordingly. Taking into consideration the fact that the 18 months planned were exceeded by only one month, it was, nevertheless, clearly a very successful IT project for both sides.

The intensive cooperation led to the employees of the central department being well trained at the group level for all further modifications to the interfaces in their daily work. Nevertheless, for some time the staff of the suppliers were hired as experts to make the entire team "self-sufficient" after only a few months. The need for training was not exceptionally high, however, and due to the strong integration of the client's employees during the project, no software was "taken over," as the staff already viewed it as "their" software.

With the hardware planned, the performance of the system was even above the expectations of the client, which was also a result of the tight collaboration between the client's expert, who discussed the performance critical functionality during the implementation, and the developers.

The consequences of this project were also significant. The responsibilities were redistributed, and some employees had to leave their positions and were appointed to higher-level duties. This was due to the fact that even in large companies with hundreds of IT projects per year, there are not many projects that can be completed successfully.

Summary

This example clearly illustrated the benefits of an agile fixed-price contract as a link between a fixed budget and agile development. The main advantages were:

- There was no attempt to specify the changing needs precisely at an early stage. Ongoing changes on interfaces still in operation were thus not a problem.
- The problems of unexpectedly high deviations in the quality of the data compared to the specification could be discovered early. Thus, it was possible to implement timely counter measures, easily adapt the working methods, and minimize the impact.
- The contract offered no theoretical formulations but, rather, practical advice and guidelines for cooperation. In this way, the efficiency during the project actually increased significantly.

We reiterate the assumption that the effort for the client is significantly higher with the agile approach, due to its obligation to cooperate. Let us summarize this on the basis of country L1:

- Discussions about unclear specifications: 20 days
- Discussions during implementation of the design: 40 days

- Questions during implementation: 20 days
- Support during the comparison test: 20 days
- Acceptance: 80 days
- Project management, etc.: 100 days

With 280 days, the client's effort lies well below the 330 days that had to be invested in a traditional fixed-price project. In addition, the number of change requests was very low. Some of the assumptions for country L1 were not correct and could not be compensated by "exchange for free." The steering board approved 50 days for change requests. This value was much less than the effort expended in change requests for a traditional fixed-price contract.

10.1.3.6 Summary

Although this example was presented in a highly simplified manner, it still indicates clearly that the agile model has significant advantages and can pave the way to a truly successful IT project. The client's work in preparating a tender is dramatically lower. For the detailed specifications the effort is postponed. The advantage here is that the information is timely and created properly, which has a noticeable effect on quality and cost. Contrary to frequent claims, when setting up a traditional fixed-price contract, an effort similar to that in the case of an agile fixed-price contract must be invested in workshops.

10.1.4 Contract for Example 1

Contract for the Software Project

Example 1

concluded between

Software Delivery GmbH
hereinafter the "contractor"

and

Telekom Atlantis GmbH
hereinafter the "client"

and both referred to as the "Parties"

Preamble

According to the requirements (backlog in Appendix B) for this project and the current state of technology for software development, the parties agree to an agile approach in the implementation of this project. The following principles in particular apply:

(a) Maximum cost transparency for both parties

(b) Maximum price security for the client

(c) Permanent commercial and technical control of the contract progress by both parties

(d) Partnership cooperation of the project team:

- Timely and practical specification of requirements through user stories, whereby the client is actively engaged and responsible for the definition

(e) Maximum flexibility in the realization of the project:

- One of the parties may consider it necessary, for whatever reason, to change the scope during the course of the project. In this case, each respective party should verify whether this request can be met without altering the maximum price range agreed to. This can be done, for example, through complexity changes in the forthcoming sprint.
- Where appropriate, the software project can be completed without major effort or transferred to another contractor: for example, in the case of insurmountable problems in the cooperation between the parties or with third parties.

§1 Definitions of terms and clarifications

(a) **Definitions of requirements.** All existing requirements are collected in the backlog. Requirements are specified in varying detail at the conclusion of the contract: The first backlog defined in Appendix B consists of various topics. These in turn are classified into various subtopics in the detailed epics. For the actual implementation, an epic is divided into the required number of user stories during the course of the project.

- **Backlog.** This is a list of all topics with appropriate prioritization and complexity or effort rating. It includes the epics and user stories contained therein, where already defined. At least on the level of detail of the epics, the backlog is a complete description of the project scope
- **Topic.** This comparises a group of requirements, from a business perspective, whereby each topic is on a very high level of abstraction and is described concisely in a short paragraph. The description is sufficient for experts to assess the complexity and thus also the scope of work. For the avoidance of uncertainty, each topic can be extended by a list of limiting assumptions.
- **Epic.** A topic consists of functionally related groups of user stories, or subtopics, called epics. An epic is described concisely in one paragraph.

- **User story.** This is a description of a specific functionally independent application case as well as a sufficient number of test cases (at least three good and three bad cases) to verify the correct functioning of the application.

(b) **Further definitions**

- **Services.** These are services delivered by the contractor in the course of the project to support the delivery process and create the deliverables; defined in Appendix B.
- **Deliverables.** These are deliverables created and delivered by the contractors defined in Appendix B.
- **Product owner.** This person plays a role in the agile delivery methodology as a sort of project manager, with deep knowledge of the content of the requirements.
- **Project vision.** The basic project objectives to be achieved from the customer's perspective to ensure a projects benefits constitute the project vision. It includes the nonfunctional requirements and constraints that govern the interpretation and realization of each user story within a project.
- **Documentation.** This includes software source code with inline documentation, user stories, and the design document. The documentation allows the client to continue developing the project at any time without the contractor, and possibly lead it to completion, given that the appropriate relevant expertise is available. However, it is agreed between the parties that this is sufficient documentation and the realization should focus on high-quality software instead of many pages of descriptions.
- **Exchange for free approach.** In the course of a project a requirement can be exchanged against a requirement that is not included in the project scope, provided that the scope for their implementation is equivalent and the requirement exchanged has not yet been implemented.
- **Good case.** This is a description of a desired result for a user story.
- **Bad case.** This is a eq. description of an unwanted result for a user story.
- **Sprint.** This is a two-week iteration during development in which the client delivers to the contractor the highest-priority user stories from the backlog. The contractor develops and tests the functionality and hands it over to the client at the end of the sprint. The project managers of both parties sign the user stories for a sprint before the transfer, confirming its completeness and clarity. The project manager approves each sprint deliverable in writing. The performance content defined in a sprint should be compiled and approved within two weeks unless agreed to otherwise.

- **Project manager:**
  - ○ Max Wheeler (on the client side)
  - ○ Maria Namarra (on the contractor side)
  - ○ The project managers of both parties are empowered to make all decisions for this project independently as long as the steering board does not make certain decisions subject to their consent. A provision must be agreed upon between the project managers and steering representatives before the project begins.
- **Scope steering board.** This panel consists of the following individuals:
  - ○ John Smith (manager of the IT sector) as a decision-authorized representative of the client
  - ○ John Doe (head of delivery) as a decision-authorized representative of the contractor
  - ○ Max Wheeler as the project manager of the client
  - ○ Maria Namarra as the product owner of the contractor
  - ○ Each meeting of the scope steering board results in a binding protocol signed by both parties.
  - ○ Each decision of the scope steering board requires the approval of at least one decision-authorized representative of each party of the steering board.
  - ○ Executive Steering Board: This panel consists of the following individuals:
  - ○ Jack Johnson (manager of the central department at the group level) as a decision-authorized representative of the client
  - ○ Karl Klee (CEO of the supplier) as a decision-authorized representative of the contractor
  - ○ Each meeting of the executive steering board results in a binding protocol signed by both parties.
- **Written form.** A written form exists when an authorized person signs a document (PDF transmission possible). All declarations of intent (e.g., acceptances, specification of sprints.) must be in writing according to this contract.

§2 Scope of the contract and document hierarchy

The project vision and the backlog, both listed in Appendix B, define the scope of the contract: interface migration scope. The backlog consists of all epics and user stories for the scope of the migrating interfaces of the first country to migrate and the epics for the other countries with contractually binding assumptions for the complexity compared to the first country's interfaces.

The minimum standard for execution is the current industry standard of information technology at the time of order placement. This is in terms of recognized industry standards and takes into account the contractual purpose. The hierarchy of the documents is as follows:

(a) Decision of the independent expert signed by the expert and the decision authorized representatives of the steering board

(b) Steering board protocol signed by all decision-authorized representatives

(c) Sprint signed by both project managers

(d) Epic signed by both project managers, as long as this differs from the original epics in Appendix B

(e) This contract

(f) Appendix A: Commercial Provisions

(g) Appendix B: Technical Provisions—Backlog

(h) Appendix D: Definition of Done (not attached in this example; refer to Chapter 4)

(i) Appendix C: 12 Principles of Cooperation (not attached in this example; refer to Chapter 4)

The documents defined above constitute the entire agreement of the parties. Verbal collateral agreements are not valid.

§3   Usage rights for the scope of the contract

The contractor must transfer to the client all foreground IPRs that have been developed within the scope of this agreement. This includes the resulting software, copyright, and usage rights resulting from this project or acquired by the contractor within the scope of this agreement. In addition, the contractor commits to providing information on the extent of these rights at any time at the request of the client by submitting the appropriate documentation. The contractor keeps all rights on background IPRs (methods, tools, etc.) which existed at the start of the project or were adapted within the course of this project. The client is entitled to pass on to a third party the rights that were awarded to him is here, for free and unrestricted use. The moral rights of the contractor remain unaffected.

§4   Transparency and "open books"

The contractor is obliged at all times to document the project, including the source code, during implementation of the project. This ensures that the client can continue to develop the project further or even use the project at any time up to the state to which it was completed by then in production, or with an operative third party with the necessary expertise.

The contractor undertakes to forward a detailed report to the client every 14 days. The report should include the costs already incurred, the project progress in comparison to the plan, and a forecast as to overall cost and duration of the project.

Furthermore, the client is entitled to participate at any time in the development process and in on-site meetings with the contractor. This allows the client to create a picture of the cost and of how the contractor operates. The client is actually encouraged to participate on-site in the development process, within the framework of the procedure agreed to.

The contractor agrees to hold daily standup meetings (daily meetings of the development team) that can (as can all other project meetings) be attended by the client.

The contractor agrees to maintain an impediment list (a list of things that impede the progress of development), which is freely accessible and is discussed at least every two weeks between the contractor and the client.

The contractor agrees to bass on all to the executive steering board unsolved impediments older than 48 hours, to reinforce the fact that a speedy solution is required.

The client must name a contact person on his or her side who is responsible to provide suitable and timely solutions to impediments.

The contractor must provide the client with full insight into the development progress at any time, in addition to the two-week deliveries.

§5   *Interim or partial acceptance*

The agile approach provides both parties with prompt quality assurance and inspections on the intermediate software deliveries (sprints). This is ensured by interim acceptance of the increment delivered from each sprint. These interim acceptances are completed and signed accordingly by both project managers and are binding with regard to the functionality accepted. The scope of a partial acceptance includes the source code, documentation, and functionality of the software increment delivered.

Subsequent changes in the scope of any user story may, however, lead to changes in a partially accepted functionality. These expenses are compensated for either by reducing the scope of the maximum price range or by additional scope outside the control of riskshares. Still the parties agree that the scope governance group will investigate each such case, as the user stories should generally be independent, whereas the parties are aware that this might not always be possible.

A final inspection follows upon completion of the overall performance and concerns verification of the integrative components of the system (i.e., functions that can only be verified through complete integration and capability of the overall system). A functionality that has already undergone interim approval can no longer be withdrawn.

Both parties understand that inspections are required during a sprint in order for new ideas on functionality to emerge. These new ideas are welcome, but it does not mean that they will automatically be included in the scope of the project. These ideas are discussed by both parties in the follow-up review (inspection) and it is decided whether these new functionalities should be added into the backlog as new entries. If new functionality is added, it will be estimated by the development team. The steering board can then decide if this functionality should be included in the scope of the project and, alternatively, which functionality could be removed from the scope of the project.

§6 Cooperation in project development

The client has cooperative duties in the iterative cycles (sprint cycles) a described below. The project manager fixes these dates at the start of the project parallel to the sprints (the project manager can make other arrangements by mutual agreement):

(a) **Specification of user stories.** The client specifies the user stories in advance in the format prescribed (at least in the scope of the delivery performance of the next sprint; see Appendix B). During a workshop, the project manager discusses and finalizes the user stories for six hours; this represents the definition and prioritization of the next sprint. Before the start of a sprint, both project managers accept each user story specification jointly in writing. This delivery capacity is to be regarded as a likely delivery capacity, as the actual delivery capacity is agreed to only after estimation and commitment by the team (in the sprint planning). If, however, the actual delivery capacity in a sprint is below the scope agreed to between the project managers (the projected time frame regarding the scope necessary for a sprint to achieve the end milestone agreed to), analysis is carried out as to whether the scope has been changed silently in the context of this sprint. Consequently, the scope governance process in Appendix B is performed. If the scope has not changed, the contractor must expand the implementation team within four weeks so that the corresponding speed can be achieved in the implementation. This only affects the delivery performance, based on the agreed-upon scope, not on additional scope. In the case of additional scope, the process described in Appendix B is initiated.

(b) **Availability for feedback.** Within a development cycle (sprint), the client's experts are available for queries and are contactable either by phone or will answer written questions within [**one**] business day (in the country of the client with respect to business days). If changes to the scope of the requirements are reported by one of the parties during this discussion, the change is valid only after written approval by the project manager (product owner) for cases where the overall effort is not extended, and by the scope governance group otherwise.

(c) **Intermediate acceptances of project progress.** Within a period of two days, the project manager leads a binding intermediate acceptance after every two sprints. In a joint meeting, the project manager is then able to verify the functionality according to the agreed-to good and bad cases per user story. With intermediate acceptances, resulting errors are adjusted by the next interim acceptance by the contractor, and are verified again in the interim acceptance of the next two sprints. If after being double checked, functions are still recognized as defective, they are sent on to the steering board.

(d) **Final acceptance.** The acceptance has to be performed by the client and supported by the contractor according to §9.

The contracting parties agree to be transparent and to communicate openly and objectively, even in the case of differing opinions about the project.

§7 Client's obligations

(a) The client is obliged to approve the number of user stories agreed to within 10 calendar days after jointly defining these user stories.

(b) The client is obliged to participate in the joint preacceptance workshop after each sprint and to ensure that the defects are documented accordingly.

(c) The client is obliged to declare the final acceptance within 15 calendar days after the contractor has fulfilled all final acceptance criteria.

(d) If the client fails to comply with its obligations of cooperation (from this paragraph and §6), the contractor must grant a reasonable grace period in writing to the client to satisfy the client's obligation of cooperation. Furthermore, the contractor's project manager must escalate the issue to the executive steering group without undue delay.

(e) Insofar as the contractor is prevented from performing services due to the client's failure to comply with the obligations of cooperation and provision as agreed, the contractor is not responsible for resulting delays or reduced quality of the deliverables arising from this specific failure of cooperation, provided that the contractor has informed the client in writing without undue delay of the failure to duly cooperate and the impact of such failure if foreseeable.

(f) The client is obliged to highlight any nonconformities in quality at the preacceptance workshop, to allow the contractor to react in a timely manner.

(g) The client must inform the contractor of any risks and issues of which he or she is aware, to ensure that the contractor has the necessary transparency to steer the project within the contractual boundaries.

In addition to these detailed obligations, the parties agree to work cooperatively within the project according to the principles of Appendix C.

§8 Escalation to the steering board and the independent experts

Either party can appeal to an independent expert in the following situations:

- When there is no agreement within the steering board on the work determined by a sprint or specific requirements or effort for user stories.

- When there is no agreement within the steering board on the approval of a sprint or the intermediate or final acceptances.

The parties agree that the following expert will support the project in its decision: Dr. Kurt Sedlatschek, 5th Avenue, New York, sedlatschek@it-consult.us, 001/(0)1 44554433. The cost of experts will be shared equally between the parties on each occasion. The parties are not bound by the decision or recommendation of experts; however, they may reconsider their position based on the new information. If an expert is not available for whatever reason, the steering board will appoint another suitable expert. For the sake of clarity, it is noted that the decision of the expert is not legally binding, and none of the parties are prevented from contacting the ordinary courts. To avoid doubt, it is also noted that the client may terminate the project at any time when complying with the notice period of four weeks, without stating a reason.

The contractor is obliged to fulfill the project under the commercial conditions as long as the steering board or the expert does not come to the conclusion that due to subsequently amended requirements from the client, the complexity of the user stories is predictable and lies in the acceptances defined in Appendix B. This will exceed the agreed-upon safety margin, and the client will not appoint these additional expenses within a period of two weeks.

This is an acceptable regulation for both parties, since this approach ensures the client that any functionality delivered previously is delivered ready for use. Also, the contractor will be compensated for the work already expended in accordance with the intervals agreed to in Appendix A.

§9   Final acceptance
In addition to the services created for the client by the contractor within the context of this project, and the agreement on interim approval encountered in §6, the following applies for the final acceptance:

(a) The client will perform acceptances to verify whether the performance results substantially satisfy the contractual performance content (the "specifications").

(b) The client is obligated to accept or partially accept (in the "acceptance") the performance results, as long as these comply fundamentally with the contractual specifications.

(c) Provided that no other period is agreed upon, the client has to carry out the respective acceptance within 20 days from the notice of completion.

(d) If the performance results differ considerably from the contractual amount due (i.e., there is a "defect"), the client must notify the contractor in writing within the applicable acceptance period.

(e) The contractor must immediately make all reasonable efforts to eliminate any discrepancies at his or her own expense and must inform the client as to when the faults will be corrected. Test data that were processed during a failed acceptance test are handed over to the client in electronic form at the request of the contractor.

(f) The client will reexamine the process and the performance results after the successful correction of faults within the planned period of 10 calendar days.

(g) The work is considered accepted by the client if the client does not notify the contractor of significant discrepancies within the acceptance period; or the client appoints the work within the framework of production or in other ways as part of his or her normal business operations; or the client accepts or uses work despite deviations from the specifications.

(h) The client is entitled to withdraw if the contractor, after receiving written notification, fails to eliminate the discrepancies within the limit of what is reasonable within four weeks or another agreed-upon period. In this case, the contractor's liability is limited to reimbursement of the fees and expenses the client has paid for the work or for poor performance results.

(i) Provided that in accordance with the provisions of this contract, the work was approved in any phase of the service delivery by the contractor and has been approved or exonerated, or considered as accepted by the client, the contractor is entitled to rely on this approval for the purpose of all subsequent phases of the provision of services by the contractor.

(j) Final acceptance has to be declared if no priority 1 defect, no more than three priority 2 defects, and no unreasonable high number of priority 3 and 4 defects are reported as open. For all unresolved priority 2, 3, and 4 defects, a list must be provided by the contractor with a schedule as to when the defects will be fixed (within a reasonable time).

§10   *Time lines and milestones*

Scheduling will be agreed to according to the following delivery dates for the final acceptance per country:

- Start for country L1: 5/1/2008
- RFA (start acceptance phase) for country L1: 7/31/2008
- Final acceptance for country L1: 8/31/2008
- Start of country L2: 9/1/2008
- RFA (start acceptance phase) for country L2: 3/7/2009
- Final acceptance for country L2: 4/30/2009
- Start for country L3: 2/1/2009
- RFA (start acceptance phase) for country L3: 6/20/2009

- Final acceptance for country L3: 7/31/2009
- Start for country L4: 5/1/2009
- RFA (start acceptance phase) for country L4: 8/22/2009
- Final acceptance for country L4: 9/30/2008
- Start for country L5: 7/1/2009
- RFA (start acceptance phase) for country L5: 10/1/2009
- Final acceptance for country L5: 10/30/2009

§11   Warranty and damages

The warranty period is nine months. The warranty period begins for each part of the software that is used in production, or, as a part can not be seen later as separate, the period begins with the final acceptance. The burden of proof is applicable within this warranty period, and the regulations for statutory damages apply.

§12   Limitations of liability

Under this agreement, the contractor's liability for claims of damages may not, to the extent permitted by law, exceed USD$2 million.

§13   Force majeure

Should the occurrence of force majeure lead to an interruption of the work, the parties shall be released from their obligations under the contract for the period of interruption of their service obligation. In the case of force majeure preventing the fulfillment of service entirely and on a permanent basis, the parties shall be entitled to terminate the contract. Claims for damages in this case are excluded.

In particular, the following events are considered to be force majeure: war, instructions from higher authorities, sabotage, strikes and lockouts, natural disasters, and geological changes and impacts. Each party is obliged to inform the other party immediately after the occurrence of a force majeure, in the form of a detailed message. In addition, the parties have to discuss appropriate measures to be taken.

§14   Secrecy

Both contract parties undertake to use all the data and documents provided solely for the provision of services. Any other use requires prior written consent of the respective contract parties, which states explicitly that the client may dispose of the documentation freely for the entire scope of the contract.

Both parties are obliged to maintain silence relating to the provision of services for the processes that have become known in the operations for the other party. The obligation to silence extends to all employees of the parties. The contractor should pass this obligation on to employees through appropriate measures. Both contract parties must act in accordance with the relevant provisions of the Data Protection Act. Both contract parties will undertake to destroy or return the data disclosed to them after completion of the project, except where the information is needed to guide a legal dispute with the other party.

§15 Severability clause
Should individual provisions of this contract prove null and void, the authenticity of the remaining provisions will not be affected. In place of the void, a valid provision should be entered that is feasible and in accordance with the meaning of the contract. The same applies during contract execution if one party was to show that certain provisions were not feasible.

§16 Place of fulfillment, court of jurisdiction, and applicable law
The place of fulfillment and jurisdiction is Munich. It is the right of the Federal Republic of Germany under international private law and the provisions of the United Nations Convention on contracts for the international sale of goods.

New York, on 4/15/2008

Jeff Bridge   Susan Sea
CEO Telekom Atlantis GmbH   COO Software delivery GmbH

Appendix A: Commercial agreement

1. Maximum price
The indicative maximum price in the amount of

$$USD \$1,980,000$$

results from an expert assessment by the contractor and is based on the following elements:

- Effort required for the reference user stories of the epics, which are already described fully in Appendix B
- List of all the epics from the backlog, as described in Appendix B
- The overall project vision with its frame conditions
- Total overhead on the basis of an analogy estimate for all epics
- Uncertainty surcharge in the amount of 10%

The indicative maximum price defined above within the context of an agile fixed price contract is comprehensible for both parties at the time of contract conclusion. According to the complexity points (referred to as story points) associated with the reference user stories specified in Appendix B, it is noted that the following charges apply for all future additional user stories or change requests outside the contractual scope:

$$1 \text{ story point} = \text{USD } \$4000$$

2. *Commercial approach to the project*

(a) **Initial on checkpoint phase.** The parties agree to an initial phase within a scope of 50 story points in order to verify the estimate and quality of cooperation. The aim is to define and implement two sprints. After completion of the initial phase, each party may terminate the contract without giving reasons. For example, the definition of user stories or the respective efficiency of a party may not be in accordance with the expectations of the other party. In case of termination after the checkpoint phase, the supplier will be compensated for only 60% of his or her price per story point (USD $120,000) (in the sense of a riskshare model).

(b) **Agreement on a final maximum price.** If the initial phase is successful from the perspective of both parties, they agree mutually on a final maximum price (in contrast to the indicative maximum price) with additional assumptions, if seen to be necessary by one of the parties. This maximum price is a fixed price insofar as the contractor is obliged to provide additional effort to reduce the cost per story point by 60%. This does not include additional requirements that could not be offset by the free exchange approach. Additional expenses are determined either by mutual agreement or by the escalation process defined in §7 of the contract.

(c) **Pricing during the implementation for individual sprints within the maximum price.** With regard to effort in the approach, both parties agree to ensure close cooperation and transparency according to the following principles:

- At the beginning of each sprint, the work expressed in the analogy estimate is verified and agreed to in writing for this sprint, based on the final user stories presented previously.
- Should the effort of a sprint not correspond to the initial analogy estimate, the parties will attempt to find a solution within the maximum price, according to the following procedure:
  ○ *Option 1.* The product owner of the contractor decides that the cost variance is within the security surcharge agree to. In this case, the client's project manager will be informed via e-mail about the changes in expenditures. This must be stipulated and accepted in writing by both project managers in a centralized document.
  ○ *Option 2.* The product owner of the contractor informs the client's project manager in writing that the work involved in this sprint is

considerably higher than that stated in the expectations. In this case, a meeting is arranged to agree ex ante, as far as possible, to reduce the complexity for this specific sprint or for future specifically known user stories. This will guarantee the maximum price (including the safety margin).

(d) **Escalation process.** If the project manager is not able to achieve consensus on the actual effort of a sprint, the scope steering board will be convened to make a decision. Further escalation process work by the expert is defined in §7 of the contract.

If it is not possible for the project manager and product owner to secure the maximum price through a justifiable reduction in the complexity of the user stories, the additional effort that lies above the maximum price is divided. The impact on scheduling as well as additional costs must be borne by the client. However, for the purposes of this model and as part of a fixed price, the contractor is obligated to deliver the expenses for the remaining story points that are above the total price at a 60% reduced hourly rate for each story point. The client's right to terminate the project with the contractor at any time remains unaffected.

(e) **Efficiency bonus on completion of a project.** In the case of successful completion of a project within the planned scope, the parties agree under the maximum price that 40% of the remaining budget will be paid to the contractor as an efficiency bonus, without further delivery obligations.

3. *Payment milestones*

A total expenditure of 495 story points is agreed to for the maximum price defined, including a 10% security surcharge. This is based on the complexity of the reference user stories. The contractor is entitled to present an invoice in the amount of 80% of the total compensation for these sprints, each in accordance with the partial acceptance of two sprints, with a scope of supply for the approval of two user stories. The last 20% of the compensation is linked to the final acceptance and, only then, invoiced accordingly.

4. *Project termination*

Both parties agree that this contract defines a cooperation model based on a partnership. The nature of this cooperation is that no party binds the other to itself forcibly. Therefore, each party may declare the project finished and terminate the contract with a lead time of two sprints, thereby releasing themselves from their obligation to perform.

On the one hand, after every sprint, the contractor supplies the client with usable software functionality implemented according to the plan up to that point. On the other hand, in each case the contractor pays for the services of sprints and accomplishes no massive economies of scale or preliminary work for future functionality. This approach is therefore beneficial for both parties and represents one of the foundations for the cooperation model. With project termination, the contractor may claim the remaining 20% of sprints already performed in a final invoice to the client.

Appendix B: Technical scope and process

1. Requirements: Project vision

The goal of this project is to newly implement the existing list of interfaces in their current form and to ensure that the results of the new system correspond to those of the current system. However, the frame condition is that the specification is according to the behavior of the current system and that just slight discrepancies will occur. The complexity is to be kept within the agreed-upon framework and the main objective is to provide any detailed features for the go-live date of the individual countries. The project teams are encouraged to work on the solution cooperatively, because the project will be successful only if the essential functionality is implemented within the time agreed upon, achieving at least twice the performance of the current system (assuming the hardware set out in the contractor's proposal).

The entire scope of the contract is defined by the backlog shown in Table 10.1. It is important to note that the L1-1.x.x reference user stories apply and

TABLE 10.1

No.	Priority	Backlog Item	Type	Story points
L1-1.1.1		interface X1	User story	8
L1-1.1.2		interface X2	User story	5
L1-1.1.3		interface X3	User story	3
L1-1.1.4		interface X4	User story	21
L1-1.1.5		interface X5	User story	13
L1-1.1		interfaces for country L1	Epic	50
L1-1.2.1		Operation monitor—display	User story	21
L1-1.2.2		Operation monitor—export to csv	User story	5
L1-1.2.3		Operation monitor— automatic alarms	User story	7
L1-1.2		Operation monitor	Epic	33
L1-1.3.1		Create roles	User story	5
L1-1.3.2		Create user	User story	5
L1-1.3.3		Assign user roles	User story	3
L1-1.3.4		Delete user	User story	3
L1-1.3		User rights	Epic	16
L1-1		Implementation for country L1	Topic	99
L2-1		Implementation for country L2	Topic	
L2-1.1		Interfaces for country L2	Epic	
L2-1.1.1		interface X1	User story	Twice as complex as Z1
L2-1.1.2		interface X2	User story	As complex as Z2

represent the source agreed to for the pricing and analogy estimation. The details of each backlog item can be found in the table.

2. Process for development and approval

The project managers agree in writing on the functionality to be implemented for each sprint. This agreement takes place, at the latest, one week before the start of the sprint, and is in the form of sufficiently detailed user stories with corresponding good and bad cases. These cases represent the test cases agree to for the acceptance test procedure.

Should the client not have specified enough requirements in the form of user stories one week before the sprint, the efforts of the already planned teams are nevertheless charged at an agreed-to flat rate amount of 10,000. The scope and executive steering committee is informed immediately about this critical situation as well as the extra costs. Should the client, upon written agreement of a user story demand changes, this may result in additional effort. To continue to achieve the total price agreed upon, refer to Section 3.1.

The contractor carries out the development with comprehensive testing and at the end of each sprint hands over a piece of executable software, including documentation and the test protocol, to the client according to the quality criteria of Appendix D. For the purposes of user stories that may potentially affect the overall architecture, the project manager and product owner may agree in writing for the first two sprints that a working software increment will not be delivered until after the second sprint. The client undertakes to report discrepancies to the contractor or inspect and approve the sprint delivered, including documentation, within five business days.

3. Changes to the scope of the contract

Process of managing the scope.   The process of controlling the scope is initiated for each user story, where the predicted cost exceeds that which was estimated originally on the basis of an analogous estimate (as described in Appendix A). The process of scope substitution includes the following steps:

1. Both parties work together to simplify other user stories; or the parties define the user stories for epics that are not yet defined in user stories but where the potential to simplify and reduce complexity is recognized, and thereby try to reduce the complexity; or the parties eliminate nonessential user stories from the product backlog.
2. If these options are not acceptable to both parties, either party may appeal to the steering board to make a decision. The parties then agree that this cost is higher than estimated originally. This cannot be put down to overly aggressive estimating of the reference user stories, but, rather, to a simple case of "hidden" complexity.

In summary, scope substitution means reduction in the complexity of system requirements or elimination from the contractual scope of some other not as important system requirements that have not yet began to be implemented, such that the overall agreed-to fixed-price compensation, effort, and time line remain the same (free exchange).

(i)   If a detailed definition of a user story unveils a discrepancy of the initial scope and the scope that is now requested, or if a request is made to add a new requirement to the scope of the agreement, the project manager and product owner verify the scope change and try to avoid additional costs by scope substitution.

(ii)   If the project manager and product owner can agree on such scope substitution, they proceed with subparagraph (viii) below.

(iii)   If the project manager and product owner cannot agree on such scope substitution, they must prepare a joint statement with respect to this new or changed system requirement explaining why this is necessary to achieve the purpose of the agreement. In addition, the project managers must prepare a joint comprehensive report to illustrate why also all other elements of the backlog in the scope are also essential ("must haves") to fulfill the purpose of this agreement.

(iv)   If the project manager and product owner are not able to agree on a joint proposal regarding a revised fixed-price compensation and/or time line with respect to this changed or new requirement, the project managers uses the reference user stories to prepare a joint report for decision by the scope governance group.

(v)   The project manager and product owner present this joint report at the next scheduled scope governance meeting, and the scope governance group must decide how to handle that scope change (either by exchange, reduction of other complexity, additional compensation to be paid to the contractor, and/or time line change).

(vi)   If the scope governance group makes a joint decision, the scope governance group proceeds with subparagraph (viii) below.

(vii)   If the scope governance group cannot make a joint decision the issue is passed on to the executive steering group, which makes a decision and proceeds with subparagraph (viii) below or agrees on alternative further steps.

(viii) A change request form is filled out and signed by both parties to show agreement on this change of scope. The form has to be accepted by representatives of the scope steering group.

Exchange for free.   In each case, before fixing the sprint backlog for each sprint, the client has the opportunity to exchange new requirements with the same effort (as defined by Section 2 of this Appendix) against existing requirements in the product backlog. If the existing requirement is not eliminated from the product backlog, however, it is agreed that these additional requirements are not included in the agreed-upon maximum price but are clearly incurred as additional expenses (change requests). This exchange will be documented and has to be approved by the scope steering group.

4. Deliverables and services

The following services provided by the contractor which lead to the deliverables noted below:

- The backlog, maintained for communication, reporting, and discussion of the requirements with the client
- Biweekly status reports
- Maintenance of an impediment list
- Implementation of the user stories
- Cost estimates for the budget framework for implementation of the above (the sprint) include:
  ○ Participation by the steering board
  ○ Weekly reports
  ○ Weekly project manager meetings

The following deliverables are provided by the contractor in the scope of this agreement:

- Software based on the specification of user stories that comply with the quality parameters listed in Appendix C.
- Tests and/or test protocols for:
  ○ Automated unit testing
  ○ End-to-end testing
  ○ Integration testing
  ○ High-level architecture documents delivered as a PDF and MS Word file
- Additional project management and project office support required in the field of business analysis, rollout, and support for client-side testing are offered, in addition, based on time and materials and invoiced according to expenditure.

5. Mechanism for calculating the effort for future user stories

According to the agile process, a comprehensive mechanism which collectively determines the effort that will be needed for future requirements or changes in the requirements should be agreed upon. The contractor's goal is not to bind the client to him or her in the first project and capitalize on future dependence.

The process for each user story is specified as follows:

- The client delivers the detailed specifications to the contractor.
- The contractor creates a corresponding user story with the requirements. Any parts missing in the detailed specifications are delivered by the client.
- There is coordination and approval of the scope of the user story.
- The contractor creates a cost estimate and delivery date for the user story.
- The client examines the cost estimate and the delivery date. If both are found to be comprehensible and acceptable, item 8 from this process follows. If the effort is not comprehensible and therefore not acceptable, item 6 follows. If the effort is acceptable but the delivery date is not, item 7 follows.
- The technical contacts on both sides agree with respect to the effort and try to create an understanding on the technical level. If successful, the resulting effort will be discussed with the project managers and the agreed-upon value applied. If not, the project manager will coordinate the effort with the technical contacts, taking into account the reference user stories (from the past). The last stage of escalation is preparation for the decision and submission to the steering committee.
- The effort is fixed, and the delivery date is discussed and determined jointly in a consultation between the project managers of both parties. The last stage of escalation is a preparation for the decision and for sub-mission to the steering committee.
- The work required and delivery date are confirmed and released by a contact person designated by the client. This will be retrieved within an existing order (budget) or it will be triggered on the basis of the contract framework of a corresponding order.

The preliminary calculation based on story points (for the purpose of abstraction and the resulting benefits) is up to each party. At the client's request, estimation of the work required takes place based on person-days and appropriate job levels. Appendices C and D are similar to the example provided in Chapter 4.

10.2   EXAMPLE 2: CREATING A SOFTWARE PRODUCT

Next, we want to consider developing a new software product based on an agile fixed-price contract. Parts of this example are taken from a real project. We have, however, simplified some facts considerably to present this example in a comprehensible manner in as few pages as possible. Some of the assumptions within this example are also influenced by our experience in the development of software products in the context of traditional fixed-price and time and materials contracts.

In contrast to Example 1, we did not have the unique situation here that the same project was implemented twice, once based on a traditional contract and once based on an agile fixed-price contract. We use this example, however, to compare all three contract methodologies presented in this book applied to the same example scenario. Additionally, in the first example the traditional fixed-price contract was linked to the waterfall principle in the implementation, whereas now we assume that regardless of the type of contract, the implementation always takes place according to Scrum. With this setup, problems at the interface between implementation and the various types of contract materialize more clearly.

10.2.1 Initial Situation

As with most product development projects, one thing is evident from the beginning: The market provides certain requirements that are not yet covered sufficiently by well-known software products. Developing new software means creating an innovation. During this development process you must keep an eye on the market and react to its variability. Only then will you create a product that reflects the needs of the market at the time of launch: high quality and innovation. In this specific case the developers were under a huge amount of time pressure. Analysis of similar products on the market have shown that the competition is also working on this issue and is expected to bring a first version of the product onto the market in 10 months. So the clear guideline could only be: A product development is meaningful only if the product launch is managed after nine months at a major trade show with live demonstrations.

What could be established and described at the time of signing a contract was nothing more than a vision with some key features. It was not clear at the start exactly what these functions should do and even less clear what they should "look like." In other areas, where there was more clarity, there was not enough time to spend months dealing with a detailed specification.

10.2.2 Contract and Procedure for a Traditional Fixed-Price Contract

We first evaluate and discuss a situation in which a project was set up according to a traditional fixed-price contract. In this way we can take a closer look at problems that have a high probability of being encountered by clients and/ or suppliers when using this form of contract. As mentioned, this setup is partly a constructed example, but we discuss it as if we would analyze everything as facts that happened not really making a distinction if some parts are filled out with experiences from other projects.

10.2.2.1 Tender stage

The client had to find a way to substantiate the requirements in a very short time so that a sufficiently detailed tender could be sent. In this specific case, the client had to invest at least a month in the specifications. All functions that had not yet been described accurately at this time were supplemented through assumptions by the client. The client was already experienced enough to know that vague assumptions were included by the supplier for areas where he had no idea of the objective of the product.

The plan was as follows:

(A) Weeks 1–4: Create the detailed specifications and requirements.
(B) Weeks 1–4: Create the commercial-legal framework for the tender.
(C) Week 5: Review the tender and send it to potential suppliers.
(D) Weeks 6–7: This is the time period for the tender response.
(E) Week 8: Review offers and create a short list.
(F) Week 9: Lead a workshops, with the first two suppliers on the short list.
(G) Week 10: Obtain, supplementary offer.
(H) Week 11: Negotiate with the first two suppliers and make a decision.
(I) Week 12: Negotiate the final contract and conclude the contract.

The schedule was quite spotty but certainly represented the minimum necessary for a reasonable tender following the traditional fixed-price method. This meant, however, that the implementation that the nine available months would be reduced to six months.

In step (A), six people worked on the specifications of the product for four weeks, resulting in a total effort of 120 days. This meant investing money into activities with uncertain outcomes. Even here the client described something that was going to be subject to change, and in many ways the client had no idea of what it should look like. In many companies it was noticeable how the motivation of the unfortunate people who wanted to solve this impossible task dropped significantly even before the project began. Often, nobody could identify himself or herself with the solution described (knowing that this was not covering all details required), and this caused a negative mood to run through the entire project.

We can normally quite easily determine whether the scope of a contract is surrounded by "not knowing": You bring the requirement specifics from different departments to the team. These are often people who we do not know very well, but they represent a larger group. Then one or two people in this group will be asked to take on the task of being responsible for the detailed specifications. A person from this group will report very quickly if this would be a highly standardized IT project such as a standard ERP system. On the contrary, if you ask the same question for a complex IT project with many unknowns, you will receive silence or evasiveness. For project sponsors this is a good indicator that something is wrong (assuming, of course, that the project sponsor is interested in such information and the experience to know what that means). We do not want to give the impression that standardized IT projects are particularly easy. It is only the type of contract and also the transfer of responsibility that make the difference, because at least you know where the journey is heading.

Referring back to the example, the situation here may also have been presented such that the mood at the start of the project was subdued on the client side. Certainly, the client is making an investment whose benefits are questionable and whose decline in value is increasing permanently.

The invitation to tender contained these essential standard components:

1. Specification of requirements
2. Specification of a time frame
3. To make the required development method clear, a specification of Scrum, to verify the initial results at an early stage

The suppliers created their offers according to the following criteria:

1. **Scope.** The specification was accepted as a client requested, and its implementation was estimated accordingly. Nevertheless, the underlying agile approach in the development offers a possibility to reformulate the specification. Through a reformulation of the specifications when putting them into the user stories, a presentation of "what the client wants" thus occurred. The disadvantage is that on the basis of a fixed-price contract, this unfortunately resulted in modifying the scope of the contract, which meant a mostly negative-prone change request.
2. **Delimitations.** The essential parts of the offer assumed the original specification of the client from the tender stage being quite complete. There was, however, a delimitation by many assumptions and thus a narrowing of the scope for interpretation. This is not negative per se, but this delimitation in the offer is often not sufficiently analyzed and possibly is misinterpreted by the client.
3. **Agile process.** The supplier responded to the agile approach and confirmed that the project would be implemented in this way. However, since a rigid fixed-price contract formed the foundation, the offer in no way stated how the supplier could share the benefits of the agile approach with the client. Scope changes and subsequent detailing of the specification would not comply with the contract.

The remaining parts of the offer were standard content that was delivered by suppliers or provided by clients for such offers according to the traditional fixed-price contract.

10.2.2.2 *Negotiation*

Based on the offer, the client held workshops with each of the two highest-ranked (ranking based on a predefined "rucksack" evaluation matrix) suppliers.

The client wanted to synchronize the details and assumptions in the offer in order to easily perform comparisons. With intensive and professional preparation of the commercial negotiation, the assumptions were at least partially aligned. However, they were usually scattered across dozens of pages in the proposal, and therefore the alignment was not fully successful. The tight schedule in this example did not leave much room, and the commercial negotiations had to take place within one calendar week. In this negotiation, the fixed price was optimized by putting massive commercial pressure on the two highest-ranked suppliers. As we know by now, and as also assumed in this example, the supplier ensured a reduced fixed price in the negotiation through the applied assumptions and delimitations. Perhaps even worse, what if they hadn't carried out these delimitations properly? Because of the delimitation, the scope is at least somewhat contained and anchored in the contract, although to the detriment of the clients. If this fixture point were missing, you would have no basis at all for subsequent discussions.

After week 12 a traditional fixed-price contract was negotiated and finalized based on:

1. A detailed description of the scope of the project, which to the best of the client's knowledge and belief also partly described content that was not yet known
2. A detailed description of the scope of the project in which certain details were not yet worked out, due to a lack of time
3. A detailed description of the scope of the project, which was expected to change significantly due to the degree of innovation in the new product.

With knowledge of the inadequate description of the detailed scope, the client's tender team had already withdrawn to a defensive position in the knowledge of the contractual inadequacy. The client knew that this situation usually led to cost overruns and change requests and set the project budget to 20% above the contractually guaranteed fixed price. In this example, the entire process was based on a ranking (price and backpack) that included technical compliance to the offer, supplier references, and costs (i.e., the fixed price and possible daily rates for any subsequent amendments). The following really crucial question remained completely open: "What does it cost me as a client to get software that enables my vision?" The assumed 20% was pure speculation and was certainly an underestimate. Why so low? Didn't the client have experienced IT staff who could provide a reasonable estimate? He certainly had such personnel, but you could not simply estimate the detailed quantity, and the project sponsor would probably seriously question the project if the client's experts use their experience openly and admit that they would rather guess an overrun of 50 to 100%. If the project sponsor (a member of the client's management team) has not yet read this or a similar book, he or she would probably be greatly surprised. But even in those rare situations where the debate has reached this point, a pragmatic approach is found to explain away the 100%. Why would you employ a traditional fixed-price contract if the fixed price specified does not allow any real prediction about the final cost of the project?

10.2.2.3 *The traditional fixed-price contract*
For this example the traditional fixed-price contract also included the following relevant components:

- **Scope of the project.** This is described clearly and completely because there are no indications in the contract that certain topics are not developed until during the project. Because of that, how to deal with such a situation is not included. The order of the relevant contract documents is as follows:
  - ○ Negotiation protocol
  - ○ Contract
  - ○ Supplier's offer
    In this example we introduce the not uncommon case in which the supplier has prevented the invitation to tender from being referenced and thus made part of a valid contract. The reasoning is logical, since the supplier delivers only that which he or she describes in the offer, not the more general parts of the original RFP. The implications are clear: The client still believes that he or she gets what was originally requested in the tender, but in the project, the client recognized that what the supplier offered was severely limited. This led to further discussions, change requests, delays—and hence costs.
- **Assumptions and delimitations.** The more ambiguously the requirements of an IT project are defined, the greater the risk of losing the overall view through a set of complex assumptions. With this project, as with most, the supplier noted that there were uncertainties within the client's RFP, and secured his offer with perfectly formalized assumptions.
- **Effort.** The work was expressed in US dollars and illustrated by the number of person-days and the respective professional levels used, including their daily rates. An appropriate margin of safety was not omitted in this example. What was omitted, however, was a clear illustration of the reason for this safety margin. Its source was buried under common clichés and hidden assumptions. The question of what should be jointly adopted to minimize the margin of safety was not asked and is generally asked all too seldom!
- **Obligation to cooperate.** Although the software that still had to be developed had its roots in the client's vision, the duty of the client to cooperate was not clear. The client saw his or her interpretation of the project vision in his or her mind's eye and tried hard to convey it. Even with this fixed-price contract, a regular feedback loop could be agreed upon contractually

within the client's obligations, to ensure that parts of the "agile advantage" were actually delivered. But this first step in the direction of an agile fixed-price contract was not specified in detail within these obligations and was simply added as an ineffective add-on in the contract.

- **Project or milestone plan.** At this point in the contract, the go-live date was specified after six months. For the two months before, the handover of software for acceptance testing and going-live was agreed to RFA. The confidence of both parties was frightening, although it was sometimes just an act: An IT project in which you do not know exactly what to really require in detail immediately gets a fixed completion date, without outlining how this deadline will be achieved when obstacles are in the way. The underlying agile development methodology, which could have been incorporated in the contract to handle exactly this situation (which is the case for the agile fixed-price contract, which we therefore also call an evolution of the traditional fixed-price contract), was therefore simply ignored.

- **Payment plan.** A payment plan was provided with payment milestones, as in Example 1. Although the project was developed based on agile methodology in the background, the fixed-price contract was still designed in such a way that milestones from the classic waterfall method, such as approval of the design, were enshrined in the contract.
  - ○ 20% at project start
  - ○ 20% upon approval of the design (which is in contradiction with the agile methodology)
  - ○ 30% upon completion of the implementation (i.e., at RFA)
  - ○ 30% upon acceptance

Side remark: We have recently seen a fortunate tendency in various contracts for IT projects that even if they are not based on an agile fixed-price project, they align their payment milestones to the story points delivered and not to some obscure design document which, per se, brings no business value.

1. A provision was included in the contract which stated that changes in the scope were accordingly dealt within *change requests* which caused additional charges. Although the client was clear that some details would emerge only in the coming months, the contract provided no way to operate more flexibly.
2. From the perspective of the supplier, *delays* (in relation to the agreed project plan) were handled with the formulation that a delay caused mainly by the client entitled the supplier to recover these additional expenses in the form of change requests and would lead to a delay of the final delivery. Through contractual penalties in the amount of 2% of the overall price per week, the client was ensured that the supplier was motivated enough to meet the time frame.

3. Change requests were regulated as expensive *directing*, according to a standard governance process.

4. *Project team.* The supplier offered a project team in which the individual employees were recognized according to their qualifications. The offer of this team of possible experts was doubtful, however, as the contract noted that this was a provisionally planned project team.

5. *Acceptance.* At this point the agile development process was taken into account. The contract formulated that monthly drops be delivered and presented to the client. Since the drops were contractually difficult to weave into a fixed-price contract, they remained reviews and not part of the binding partial acceptance. Alternatively, it would have been possible to bind the drops to payment milestones and include an obligation for partial acceptance. To this end, however, any statement as to the delivered scope of these milestones would have to be included in the traditional fixed-price contract. Very often the initiative to take certain (agile) aspects into the contract separately does not work because this might lead to misunderstandings or cause contradictions within a standard fixed price contract. There was great risk with this type of contract that the advantage of product increments developed and deliverable using the agile method would not come to fruition.

The remaining components complied with the standards of such traditional fixed-price contracts and thus are not discussed further at this point.

10.2.2.4 *Project progress, the teams, and critical situations*

To master the challenges of working in cooperation, let us look next at what opportunities a traditional fixed-price contract offered in the context of this example.

Project progress

In keeping with a traditional fixed-price contract, the project proceeded classically. Based on high-level information, it was announced in the big kickoff meeting that everything was prepared perfectly, so that not much could go wrong. After six weeks, the design document had to be finalized and handed over to the client. The client then had a week to approve the document.

Due to the fact that agile development based on Scrum was carried out in the background, the high-level architecture based on a defined user story was created in the first sprint. In the pure agile approach, where no adjustments have to take place due to an inappropriate contract basis, you would simply add more detail to this basic concept with every sprint. With this procedure, the detailed design document would be created iteratively, and as it would really reflect what is implemented, it would additionally have the characteristics of a document.

But to do justice to the fixed-price contract, a separate task was initiated after the first sprint, which read: "Write the requirements of the design in a design document as you believe it should be implemented by the developers." One of the advantages of the agile approach is that when the user story is processed in detail, many of the best minds work together and suggest individual design decisions. Here, however, an employee had to find solutions on his or her own, which unfortunately often later often proved to be inappropriate. This may have been for one of the following reasons:

- The employee had not described the optimal solution.
- With the knowledge gained from previously implemented user stories, the solution suddenly looked different.
- The requirements had changed, due to details or modifications, and the solution therefore had to be adapted.

The client approved the design and thereby confirmed with the supplier that exactly this design was to be implemented, despite the fact that it was confirmed from many sides that software could not be derived in all facets of a design. Additionally, the review process for the approval of this design document was a difficult task for the client.

The implementation started after this approval (we can assume that there were already delays and discussions in the acceptance). However, since agile development was carried out, implementation was already ongoing during these six weeks of design work and review. So another disadvantage has been introduced by this fixed price contract: that the work of the first three sprints (assuming two-week sprints) must be changed once again to the user stories already implemented, due to possible design changes requested by the client. This danger was at least averted after approval of the design, and indeed a new challenge was already visible on the horizon: A good development team would find the optimal solution directly in the sprint during development. Now the supplier found himself in a dilemma between design and perhaps a new, better, or more efficient implementation solution. The first time, the client may perhaps have been persuaded to accept a change request for the design. The second time, discussion with the client was more difficult, as the client had accepted a design and the supplier now said, within the traditional fixed price contract, that it could have been done differently and more efficiently. The client might not be interested in that or request "money back" as things seem to be simpler now. So this can lead to a critical deadlock situation.

Due to the implementation according to Scrum, the corresponding implementation phase ran predictably in this example project. Due to its tight deadlines and innovative character, the client was surprised to be shown the first drop after eight weeks:

1. Although having approved the design, the client was surprised how certain requirements looked in the actual implementation.

2. When seeing these first features, client personnel acknowledged that they fulfilled the requirements, but also realized that they should have described certain remaining requirements differently to obtain what was wanted (first Deming-Cycle iteration where the client receives the result of the interpretation of the requirements).

3. In the last few months the client had found a new functionality as to the high priority required to perform a successful launch of the software: that is, more important than currently recorded functionalities in the project scope. The client now wanted to accommodate these in the project, definitely before the go-live date.

As usual in traditional fixed-price contracts, only in combination with additional costs could the design for those functionalities that were being implemented from then on in the project be changed. This was so because, among other things, the supplier had already counted on it in his aggressive fixed-price offer. Due to the fact that the transmitter–receiver problem had been calibrated by then according to the Deming cycle, a more precise specification of the requirements could have been provided. However, it was not provided during the project, as there was no formulation in the contract that would have motivated such a procedure, and thus this traditional fixed-price contract could not ensure that the effort would be spent on the features most important for the client.

As for point 3, this contract obviously did not specify the "exchange for free" method. (***Note:*** *The agile fixed-price contract always involves changing something in the same scope or otherwise replacing overhead with less important parts in the implementation.*)

It was a problem in this phase of the project that discussions on cooperation were stifled because the client constantly wanted to make more modifications. The client sometimes attempted this by claiming that he or she did even not have to pay for such modifications. However, sometimes the client was willing to pay. On the other hand, the fixed completion date (in such occasions we sometimes hear: "Yes, there are changes, but you have to still reach this deadline or the software/project is dead," which is also quite suitable to the market condition for the product developed in this example) was fast approaching and the supplier could not arbitrarily scale a project team into a project that was only running for another two months.

The acceptance tests were not as big a surprise as they were in the waterfall model, as some monthly drops had already been seen. However, the client still had to contend with the fact that several months had already passed before the functions specified at the time were tested in detail. Additionally an overhead was created because the inevitable decay of knowledge had to be compensated on both sides and people who had reviewed the design several months ago now had to verifiy of the software. Unfortunately, the reviews of the drops were not anchored as partial acceptances in the contract and therefore were not taken seriously by the client.

Project progress was littered with additional costs, delays, and dissatisfaction. The probability that the due date (with the functionalities that were truly necessary and, where possible, functionalities that differed from those listed in the original scope) could be maintained was very low, despite the significant increase in costs. Following the discussion in Chapter 2, the statistical probability that this project would be successful was less than 50%, although this statistic was examined in all IT projects. If you assume that highly standardized projects are not so severely affected, you would undoubtedly have to assume a probability far below 50%.

The teams

From the perspective of the persons directly involved, the project was extremely laborious. The client had to enforce the requirements of the changes through a reduction in the additional costs from the supplier. Since the client did not find out in detail what he wanted until during the course of the project, the discontent spread within the client team. It was obvious that the supplier really could not help it.

The supplier's side position was that he wanted to cover costs and increase client satisfaction in carrying out the project. The supplier could have been more or less flexible here and there, depending on evaluation of the parameter. Although developed within the Scrum context, the willingness to share the benefits was limited, as the supplier also needed to earn money. The power struggle could be conducted fairly, depending on the size ratio of the client's and supplier's companies. The motivation of the team was extremely low at many points in the project.

We are repeatedly surprised by statements from clients such as: "I prefer to assign a fixed-price project to a larger supplier." The fact that top management used the "good names" of big suppliers to protect their decision is somewhat understandable. It should have be more important to lay the foundation for success with an appropriate contract, together with a supplier who possessed the expertise and agility, and a successful IT project is always the best protection for the decision maker. However, we are not saying that all big players in the software supplier market are unqualified or are not agile. However, it appears that all suppliers are also able to implement successful IT projects only under the right conditions, and sometimes the internal change in mindset takes longer in big supplier organizations.

Critical situations

The following critical situations occurred (or may have occurred) in this project in addition, based on this contract:

- **Failure to meet the obligations to cooperate.** Here, the contract only covered the delay caused by a client due to a failure of the obligation to cooperate. Transgressions with the obligation to cooperate were extremely difficult to quantify (e.g., questions, discussions, or an inadequate review of the design). In this respect, the contract offered neither support for the quantification nor clarity for describing the supplier's obligation to cooperate.

- **Discussion about the interpretation of the requirements.** The interpretation of the requirements often degenerated into out-and-out horse trading on the steering board and caused both parties to dissociate from the facts. Due to a climate of mistrust, there was no way to seek advice from a third party without it being viewed as a declaration of war. The contract said that the requirements had to be implemented. It said very little, however, about which path to take when there were differences in interpretation.
- **Delay.** How to deal with delays is illustrated by the following two examples:
  - If the design had been delivered late, the client could have demanded a contractual penalty. Thus, the design was delivered on time to prevent this penalty, at the expense of quality. When the time for the review of the design is too short, the client team often makes statements about this review being too difficult, and the real functionality could only be understood in the final test. So there is a heated discussion as to whether or not the design is now really approved. We believe it is not possible and suitable; however, the contract includes the client's obligation to perform this unpleasant task.
  - When the project would in fact reach a milestone at which the entire development should have been completed and delays still had to be declared, the penalty for the supplier (if the delay was caused by the supplier) was governed by the contract. This tool is seldom used, however, because it destroys the last spark of willingness to cooperate, and the client rarely wants to risk this. On these grounds, the monetary claims of the supplier through delays by the client are usually only theoretical.
- **Change in scope.** The client wanted to record three new functionalities in the scope during implementation. This was possible only through change requests being approved, and resulted in additional costs and time shifts. The possibility of exchanging nonimplemented functions was unfortunately still associated with certain additional costs. The supplier quite often uses this chance to compensate for self-induced delays.
- **Quality of development.** The quality of development was secured at least superficially in the drop reviews. If serious discrepancies begin to surface, however, the supplier cannot resolve these in the next sprint, but instead, up until the acceptance test (because these were only drop reviews and not partial acceptances). Accordingly, these reviews also have a degree of uncertainty. If the discrepancies are so severe that confidence in the delivery performance is lost, there is no contractual assurance that the

client would have the right to look over the shoulder of the supplier (no transparency contractually agreed). Even getting out of the project would be difficult for the client, as there is a contract, and if the supplier does not commit any major breach, the project continues.

10.2.2.5 Project completion

The project was (probably) completed with delays and additional costs. The functions of the software were not likely to coincide with the functions that the client identified as the optimal feature set but rather a trade-off of possible changes, time lines, and additional costs. The teams were frustrated because they had once again gone through a serious schooling from a wrong contract without seeing real improvements on the contractual side. On the part of the supplier's developer there was always loud criticism as to why the key account managers corrupted a good development method with incorrect contractual constructs.

The procurement representatives, with outdated and locally optimal objectives, were no longer actually involved in any phase of the project implementation. Their bonuses were not affected by delays in the process of implementation nor in the overrun of the budget. Of course, this project could also have become a "black swan." That would have meant that project completion could have been delayed for years and achieved only through massive additional expenditures. The damage would have been ruinous, as other software products would already have covered the market. The probability was perhaps low for this project because highly risky issues, such as rollouts in different countries, were not involved, and we are not referring to a year-long project with tens of thousands of person-days. Basically, it true that with an increasing degree of complexity and a growing project size, the traditional fixed-price contract becomes more and more unsuitable. This is in contrast to the widespread opinion that the new type of contract and development method are more relevant for smaller projects. Even medium-scale projects such as this example may result in a commercial nightmare when, for example, the deadline would have been missed and the competition brought the product to market earlier. The sunk costs, costs of delay, and lost profits should have sufficient weight for a change in mindset!

Summary

This outline of software product development has shown how the interface between agile development and the underlying traditional fixed-price contract inhibits the benefits of agile development and brings a loss of efficiency to both sides. The following disadvantages arise, among others, from that unsuitable interface:

1. Late changes in requirements cannot easily be incorporated into the agile development process.

2. The obligation to cooperate would be easier to plan if it were already contractually adapted to the development cycles.

3. New findings (new knowledge) on the client side about the scope of the contract cannot easily be incorporated into the development process.

Further disadvantages and risks of a fixed-price contract, such as delays and additional costs, obviously remain. Specifically, within the scope of its delays, this project could have been a fully stranded investment!

10.2.3   Contract and Procedure for a Time and Materials Contract

Setting this example project up according to time and materials also has certain aspects that bring disadvantages to clients and also partially to suppliers (for the details, see in Chapter 8). In this chapter we look at the development of this exemplary innovative software product provided with the assumption that the project is conducted based on a time and materials contract. Again we treat this example as if everything was really performed in that manner and analyze it so, even though the example is a creation based on our joint experiences.

10.2.3.1   Tender stage

The advantage of tendering this software project according to time and materials was that the scope of the contract did not actually need to be specified before the start of the project. However, the reality is often somewhat different:

- In most cases, the client wants (or the management of the client) to know the planned project costs (budget) in advance. To perform this estimate, the client's internal experts needed a description up to a certain level of detail.

- In a tender based on a time and materials there are also often requests regarding the estimated overall project effort (not purely time and material resources). In this case, the provider needed sufficient information on the scope of the contract.

We assume in this example that not only were the prices of resources requested by the supplier in the tender according to levels of experience, but also an overall estimate of the work required. This request for the total price estimation was clearly identified as an indication (as this is a time and materials and not a fixed-price contract request). When the contract is based on time and materials there is often a discussion as to what happens when the supplier is exceeding the original estimate. Still, if the client expects precision, the scope definition would have to be detailed enough; otherwise, there is no possibility that any supplier would get into such a discussion. However, in this example we did not want to get too close to this area of uncertainty because the discussion would then effectively be moving as in a fixed-price contract.

With respect to the preparation of the scope, the planning of the tender could proceed in a somewhat more relaxed manner. A description at the level of vision, topics, and epics can usually be completed within a week, including one or two alignment workshops and reviews (assuming, of course, that the issue was a high priority for the people involved). Assuming that the cooperation and collaboration were in terms of an agile mindset, the description could also be prepared without a workshop in exceptional cases.

The planning in this example looked like this:

(A) Week 1: Prepare the high-level scope.
(B) Week 1: Create the commercial-legal framework for the tender.
(C) Week 2: Review the tender, release, and ship to potential suppliers.
(D) Weeks 3–4: This is the time period for the tender response.
(E) Week 5: Review the offers and create a short list.
(F) Week 6: Renegotiate with the first two suppliers on the list.
(G) Week 7: Negotiate the final contract and conclude the contract.

What stands out immediately is the fact that the processing time for the proposed tender phase was much less than that for the traditional fixed-price contract (7 weeks vs. 12 weeks, on about 60% of the time). The massive effort in step (A) with a traditional fixed-price contract could be reduced drastically in this example to only a description of the relevant level of scope necessary. This also had a positive effect on the motivation of the tender teams: The members did not feel compelled to take responsibility for something they had no knowledge of and certainly could not describe.

The tender for this time and materials sample project did, however, have to include the following key components:

- **Requirement for the required roles.** Together with the rough specifications of the contract scope, the client delivered information regarding what qualifications were required from his point of view.
- **Technology.** Usually, the clients had already decided on the technologies (e.g., Java J2E, Oracle 11g, Tomcat, Ajax). This leads to specific requirements in the bidding for the desired time and materials resources as to skills in these technologies.
- **Rough estimation by the supplier.** The supplier should, due to his experience, deliver an effort based on the available information (rough specification, technologies, etc.). This effort is indicated as purely informative. The client must be aware that the supplier cannot make a precise estimate here because the final team, the methodology and the procedures were

not controlled by him and the details as to the scope have not yet been described. However, a large part of the variability of the project effort is dependent on these factors, and therefore the indication is just an indication based on similar projects the supplier might have delivered in the past.

- **Proposed project organization.** In this example, the client specified the proposed project organization in order to give suppliers the opportunity to take the overall situation into consideration as regards the resources offered.

- **Purchase orders.** The client specified how the order cycles were planned in the tender. In this example we assumed that quarterly orders for resources were planned.

- **Quality assurance.** The client suggested which quality assurance mechanisms the supplier had to operate. In this case, within the context of Scrum, test-driven development within a continuous integration platform was highlighted in the tender as a development method. According to this, it was stated in the tender that the resource personnel understood and committed to writing appropriate automated tests for each functionality (unit tests) and knew about continuous integration.

- **Reporting obligations of the supplier.** The supplier had to hand over the employees time sheets for countersigning by the client. (Which employee has worked on this project on what day and for how long?) This should have been done no later than the fifth working day of the following month. As performance is not measured—only time—this is the central controlling mechanism.

- **Exchange of resources.** The supplier could exchange the resources in the project only after obtaining approval from the client.

- **Résumés of employees proposed.** The résumés of all employees, had to be attached to the offer, with a list of relevant project experience.

The supplier created the proposal for the invitation to tender according to the following criteria:

- A number of key resource personnel with impressive experience were offered for this project.

- A few "cheap" resource personnel were added to increase the profit margin of the project.

- The indicative overall effort was estimated very low by the supplier, but freed clearly from any liability in the offer. Why should the supplier become unpopular through a realistic estimation or even take himself completely out of the bidding race, when it comes to nonbinding estimations where the essentials required for any serious calculation are missing anyway?

- A positive statement was issued for the remaining aspects (e.g., quality assurance), even though not all the resources offered actually met these requirements.
- The résumés were "optimized" to a certain extent. This has by now become so common that excessive honesty is perceived as almost a competitive disadvantage. Suddenly, people who have worked three weeks on a Java project are developers with Java experience. Although no lies are told, as this is true to a certain extent, it is nevertheless misleading.

The remaining parts of the offer include the standard content of IT service contracts on a time and materials basis and are not discussed further here.

10.2.3.2 Negotiation

Negotiating a time and materials contract often only involves negotiations about volume discounts, and in exceptional cases the exchange of certain employees whose résumés appear to be unsuitable. In the optimal situation, business or IT department staff have spoken in advance with the employees of the first two suppliers lined up, and have forwarded their recommendations to the negotiators (which is incorporated into the backpack described in Chapter 5).

Nevertheless, the purchase volume discounts are a sensitive topic. What the client wants to avoid with a time and materials contract is an almost irreversible binding to the supplier, as is the case with a traditional fixed-price contract (at least for the duration of the project). Therefore, the negotiation over purchase volume discounts can only be based on an intention, not on the assurance of a purchase volume. In our example the client tried to maximize the volume discount in this competitive situation. The supplier tried to achieve a scale of discounts (e.g., 5% discount for the first 1000 person-days, 10% discount for days 1001 to 2000). At the end of this negotiation, the client had a contract that guaranteed certain resources at a certain price. But what was missing was binding information on the final cost of the project. This is usual, as it is dependent on the internal organization and planning of the client and the detailed scope, which is "steered" by the client only.

10.2.3.3 The time and materials contract

The time and materials contract that originated from negotiation of this sample project contained the following parts which are relevant to the discussion in this chapter:

- **Prices in the form of daily rates per experience level.** The price was fixed to the qualifications and not to the employees. But there is seldom a unified scheme that can be defined across different suppliers for these experience levels. Who determines what constitutes a senior developer as opposed to a "normal" develope or a junior developer?

- **Approved employees.** The list of suggested employees and the resources that may have been adapted in the negotiation were included as part of the contract.
- **Exchange of employees.** In addition, it was recorded in the contract that the client had to agree to an exchange of resources. Exceptions to this were fundamental reasons for a supplier to replace an employee. Furthermore, the client could request the supplier to replace a person within four weeks if the person's performance was unsatisfactory.
- **Purchase volumes and discounts.** It regulated the purchase volume and the discount based thereon.
- **Responsibility.** The supplier was obliged to provide the resources. He or she did not assume any responsibility for the project's progress, as the control of the project lay solely in the hands of the client.
- **Invoicing conditions.** The time sheets that were signed by the client formed the basis for the monthly invoicing.

The contract was a classic time and materials contract. The items highlighted above were selected specifically to observe their impact during the project's progress, the team situation, and the handling of critical situations.

10.2.3.4 *Project progress, the teams, and critical situations*

After just seven weeks of the bidding phase, the project began. The client had already nominated an internal project manager for this project, who, in turn, immediately planned a kickoff and, thanks to some experience in development with Scrum, had grouped the teams and informed them of the proceedings. (*Note: Often these challenging positions for project managers are occupied by external personnel from a third party. In this case it is advisable that the client select a third supplier or even a special personnel who the role of "trusted advisor" instead of normal supplier.*)

For the most part, the teams comprise employees of the supplier. In addition, individual employees of the client and a freelancer, contracted directly by the client, were appointed.

The client now faced a challenge: He wanted to develop based on Scrum together with the resources of the supplier. This required that the client provide the general conditions for agile development. Thus, the client could not drive the project forward under time pressure and escalation, as this is somehow in contradiction to Scrum. If, as we assumed for this example, the client had no real extensive experience with Scrum and agile development, this would have rapidly lead to Scrum being modified to accommodate smaller planning units. The disadvantages that accompany this are dealt with in detail in the literature (Gloger, 2011; Schwaber, 2003).

The supplier's personnel resources carried out their work accordingly in each sprint. However, based on time and materials, they did it so that it was just sufficient. Their motivation was:

- To provide delivery performance
- To invoice as many days as possible and make themselves irreplaceable

The last point has a very negative impact on the work of the Scrum team. The attitude should actually have been characterized by openness, transparency, and mutual support. The individual persons (i.e., the supplier's employees as well as the freelancer) tried to present themselves in a good light. In the background they monopolized the knowhow and only shared it reluctantly, to make themselves irreplaceable.

From our experience in this setup, there are normally increasing quality problems during acceptance at the end of the sprint. Compared to homogeneous teams (i.e., in comparison to an established team of suppliers), commitments are often not kept.

The following critical situations in the project carried a certain potential for escalation.

- **Time sheets were completed only very superficially.** Time sheets were considered by the client to be a control of the time with some predicted link to performance. Very often there were problems with them, at least in the eyes of some of the personnel. The time sheets were not completed very accurately, so the project manager found it difficult to estimate exactly what had been developed and whether it corresponded to the performance desired. Combined with the next point, the critical question regarding time and materials contract is simply: How do you measure performance within this contract?

- **Time sheets were incomprehensible.** Time sheets citing many hours were delivered, and the project leader found them difficult to allocate. The underlying agile development methodology at least created some transparency scripted because of the fact that the team controlled themselves. In addition, the cycles in which the output of the teams were verified were also of manageable length. Teams that consisted exclusively or predominantly of employees of the supplier were always in danger of concealing something in the actual performance, in the sense of "information hiding." The situation was much more critical when working according to the waterfall principle. Contractually, it was difficult to find a solution.

- **Exchange of resources from the supplier's perspective.** Although the contract clearly defined this point, the supplier would probably want to exchange a couple of personnel resources in this example. These are mostly resources that were either needed for other matters because of their expertise in other subjects or were plain and simply too expensive. The personnel costs and the other agreed-upon costs therefore got in each other as way at this level. For this reason, these employees were replaced by others who were able to increase the profit margin of the supplier. Although the client could refuse consent, the supplier usually proceeded "skillfully" and announced, for example, that a certain person, could not, for personal reasons, be in the project. The clients possibilities were then very limited. The supplier also optimized his profits in this sample project, thereby risking deadlines and quality criteria.

- **Information and documentation.** There was an escalation in the project because the supplier's employees had not provided proper documentation and there was therefore a risk that a third party would not be able to take over the supplier's role (after the project or during the project, if required). The specific cases were reported to the steering board in an escalation and resolved by the supplier. After some time, the supplier's employees once again began to create just sufficient documentation and transparency in the source code. A new escalation was difficult. The information and documentation were so incomplete that a third party could not take over the tasks without enormous effort. A time and materials contract supports the project manager for such an issue only if the documentation rules were clearly defined. However, definition of a required degree of documentation in clear rules is quite difficult.

- **Exchange of resources from the client's perspective.** The client wished to exchange a resource because in his or her opinion the performance was not sufficient. This was very well regulated in the contract, but in practice there were still discussions. Even if the client did not want to deal with a resource due purely to antipathy or for reasons of team spirit, this person had to be replaced by the supplier within a reasonable period of time.

- **Exchange of supplier.** Basically, time and materials contracts allow the client to change the supplier for the current project without too much trouble. This is not often enough articulated clearly or even included in the contract, although it would lead to a constant competitive situation for the supplier, thereby increasing efficiency and motivation. The situation in this example is very common: The exchange could not be performed because the documentation was not sufficient to ramp-up a new supplier quickly. In addition, many project details were already "hidden" in the employees' minds, and the risk of losing this knowledge in the ongoing project was high. In this example, the situation could only have been avoided through strict guidelines in the agile iterations and their partial deliveries. Unfortunately, with time and materials contracts it often seems that "definition of done" for a delivery after each sprint is not considered as strictly as in agile fixed-price contracts (where the "definition of done" is contractually binding).

- **Quality problems.** The client complained that the supplier's resources were providing inferior-quality code during the course of the project. The supplier explained by return mail that the control criteria and quality assurance were the client's responsibility. He as a supplier could only ensure that the qualified resources were ready for the task, which the client transfers to him. Thus, in principle, only the client could be responsible for quality issues. Here again a serious problem of a time and materials contract comes to light: The client buys time, not qualitative performance, and the supplier is interested to sell more time not to be most efficient.

- **Delay.** Even with this type of contract, there will probably be delays in a project that was very tightly scheduled, such as the one in this example with an implementation period of only seven months for a new software product. However, the delays were rather profitable for the supplier, and the entire responsibility lay with the client. Seen from this angle, a time and materials contract offered no guidance to prevent or reduce additional costs.

- **Change in scope.** Due to the fact that the underlying development using Scrum was working properly, the scope could be adapted at any time by the client before each sprint. It was up to the client how he or she managed to keep the project within budget limits. One possibility would have been an internal process that was similar to that of an agile fixed-price contract! The client needed to develop a way of motivation in the project, as the client educated the supplier to come up with the most *efficient* solutions rather than only generating the most revenue by using up more and more time.

10.2.3.5 Project completion

The sample project based on a time and materials contract would probably have proceeded efficiently under the coordination of an effective project manager. The project goal, which changed during the course of the project, would also probably have been achieved. The changes were acceptable and not associated with high costs. The internal effort for the client in managing the team, and especially for controlling the supplier, would have been massive, however, and that is the major drawback of this type of contract. Walter Jaburek made a remark regarding this in our interview in March 2012: *"Time and materials is the best form of contract if there is absolute honesty on both sides."*

Summary

From a supplier's perspective, a time and materials contract fits very well with agile development. The break in methodology is also not too big for the client; however, the client must have someone available who has expertise in agile development. We assume that the expertise from the supplier is higher and that the client thus resorts to a suboptimal state. The client is alone with regard to ensuring the delivery performance, quality, and all project risks, and the supplier withdraws to area of pure provisioning of resources. And what about the experience levels, which indicate the price of the time of the provided resources? Who actually determines whether an employee who has been offered is referred to as a senior consultant, an analyst, a consultant, as whatever? The employee's résumés offers a rough idea, but the client must be careful that the résumés are not polished too much in favor of the supplier.

A time and materials contract in comparison to an agile fixed-price contract is a valid alternative for product development. The decision depends greatly on the expertise of the client. However, once the first doubts regarding agile fixed-price contract have been cleared up, the question arises as to why one does not eliminate the negative aspects of time and materials contracts on the client side through this type of contract. Why not a fixed fee of 50% and the remaining 50% when the quality and documentation are suitable? This would facilitate the control, but is rarely employed.

10.2.4 Contract and Procedure for an Agile Fixed-Price Contract

In this section we describe how the development of the new software product is prepared, tendered, and implemented based on an agile fixed-price contract. Again, we present some of the topics in a simplified form. The example illustrates how the tender process up to project completion is supported by the correct contract, and in this way a project can be realized with cooperation instead of distrust. The software product was really implemented accordingly to an agile fixed-price type of agreement, so most of the facts presented below are taken directly from this simple project experience, which we used when setting up this example.

10.2.4.1 Tender stage
As with a time and materials contract, the advantage that the contract can be concluded on the basis of a broadly defined scope also arises in an agile fixed-price contract. Thus, no massive effort must be put into the specification of something unclear and uncertain.

The tendering process can therefore be time-scheduled very strictly:

(A) Weeks 1–2: Create the high-level scope.
(B) Weeks 1–2: Create the commercial-legal framework for the tender.
(C) Week 3: Review the tender, release, and ship to potential suppliers.
(D) Weeks 4–5: This is the time period for the tender response.
(E) Week 7: Review the offers and create a short list.
(F) Week 8: Lead a workshop with the first two suppliers on the list.
(G) Week 9: Renegotiate.
(H) Week 10: Negotiate the final contract and conclude the contract.

The turnaround time for the planned tender phase is lower than in the traditional fixed-price contract (10 weeks vs. 12 weeks); although it is noted repeatedly in discussions by clients and industry representatives that this tender process is more complicated in an agile approach. Perhaps by this it is meant that top management and procurement are integrated in the project longer, which is a hassle but certainly not a disadvantage. Or it might be based on the fact that a change in the already well-known procedures contains some efforts to be invested, which is true but necessary.

In the sample project, the effort in point (A) is reduced to the essentials, and they built an easily to understood overview of the content of the project, based on a vision. The detail specifications of reference user stories can be prepared by the two employees responsible for this in the estimated two weeks without special pressure, and thus also is an appealing quality.

In the tender preparation, the following parts of the agile fixed-price contract framework were easily adapted and transferred within the RFP to the supplier:

1. Description of general action summarized briefly:
   (a) Estimate of the reference user stories
   (b) Workshop on the common estimation and common definition through assumptions about epics and topics as well as reasoning over possible uncertainties in the requirements
   (c) Projection of an indicative fixed-price range
   (d) Willingness for a checkpoint phase and query of the riskshare the supplier is willing to commit
   (e) Update of the fixed-price range after the checkpoint phase
2. Description of the processes for setting the effort of not yet exactly specified requirements (see Chapter 4).
3. Willingness of both parties for an additional governance authority in the person of a third-party expert.
4. Willingness to cooperate; the ability to terminate the contract early is acknowledged as a standard process.
5. Request of a riskshare for additional hidden complexity that cannot be compensated through the agreed process and that is not a new functionality.
6. Interrogation of the technologies that are used to ensure the daily quality assurance and regular delivery.
7. Request the delivery of Scrum with the appeal for descriptions and references, as well as naming the employees trained in this methodology.

In addition to these key elements from an agile fixed-price contract, a contract template was attached for validation. In this case, the supplier created the offer based on this invitation to tender, inter alia, according to the following criteria:

1. The supplier places his experience with Scrum in the foreground (so that the client can easily filter out those suppliers who do not have sufficient competence).
2. The supplier estimates the reference user stories realistically, because it will have a massive impact, if he miscalculates by multiplying the analogy estimate. Loud complaints would not be possible at a later stage, because:
   (a) The client simply changes the supplier or the project terminates.
   (b) The client can use the checkpoint phase for verification, so in the case of project termination by the client, only a certain percentage of the efforts of suppliers is paid (namely, not the remaining 20% that was subject for the final acceptance).

3. The supplier knows that the workshop calls for transparency in the implementation of the reference user stories. Therefore, accountability is already respected in the estimate.
4. The supplier tries to optimize the personnel resources and teams as well as the mix of experience levels so that the effort is realistic and the price is attractive.
5. The supplier specifies a riskshare that he or she is ready to commit according to the complexity of the requirements and his experience.

Compared to previous contract considerations, you can see that the considerations of the supplier through the requirements were (had to be) much more "honest" in an agile fixed-price contract. According to the motto "structure creates behavior," you are already encouraging the right mindset in the tender for the project.

10.2.4.2 *Negotiation*
In addition to the tender process, negotiating an agile fixed-price contract was a big change for the negotiating team (see Chapter 5). Instead of only optimizing the prices, the buyer was also interested in the implementation process and its clear rules, due to bonuses on the actual costs. Finally, the buyer was also commercially responsible after contract completion.

The negotiation was realized in two stages. First, the process view was treated and finalized. In contrast to other IT contracts, the process was no longer just an issue of the business department. The parameters were then negotiated (this, of course, also included those existing in the agile fixed-price contract). The parameters were:

- The rate for functionality of a certain degree of complexity
- The riskshare in the checkpoint phase
- The riskshare for the maximum price range
- The warranty
- The percentage rate, which was kept until final approval and not paid at every sprint

The overall complexity and the complexity for the reference user stories were not negotiated here. These had already been verified by the department in the workshop, together with the suppliers. The task here was to coordinate the realistic values, choose the supplier who managed to substantiate them best, and explain them in the most trustworthy manner (along with other parameters, such as competence and references).

10.2.4.3 *The agile fixed-price contract*
The final agile fixed-price contract contained the following components in this project:

- **Scope of the contract (backlog).** We will not go into any detail here for this point. (An example of backlog can be found in Chapter 4 or 9.)

- **Transparency and "open books."** The contractor was obliged to document the project, and therefore the source code, during implementation of the project at all times, so that the client could continue developing or using the project at any time on her own or with a third party. This documentation was generated by describing the features in user story format. In addition, a total overview and rough architecture was passed as a PDF at every sprint (and enhanced incrementally with every additional sprint). The source code was built according to the coding guidelines of the supplier, which was previously accepted by the client's department. This level of documentation was described in the contract. However, the real advantage was that this could be verified at the acceptance of each sprint deliverable.

- **Reports.** The contractor had to send a detailed report to the client every 14 days. This report included the efforts already incurred, the project progress as opposed to the plan, as well as a forecast for the overall cost and the duration of the project. This report contained a number of finished and unfinished user stories; in other words, it represented reality and not percentage estimates, as the agile methodology allows a binary measurement (done or not done) on the user story level..

- **Client involvement.** The client was entitled to take part at any time in the development process and in on-site meetings with the contractor, to obtain a picture of the project effort and work methods of the contractor. This was even encouraged as part of the agreed procedure.

- **Interim acceptances.** The interim approvals had to take place by appointment with the client, every second week on Tuesdays, in a one-day workshop between the project leaders (and any persons involved). Test cases defined per user story were performed during the intermediate acceptance. The client approved the user story in a report at the end of this workshop, subject to the discrepancies noted.

- **Cooperation in the project development.** The process was described and the dates were set for the entire (!) project:
  - When the detailed specification of user stories to be implemented in the next sprint must be available
  - On which days the scope governance workshops will take place with the client (these workshops are used to prioritize the user stories for the next sprint and to confirm on both sides that these are fully specified) (e.g., every other Wednesday, 2 to 5 pm)
  - When the interim acceptances will take place with the client (e.g., every second Thursday)
  - That the client may also look "behind the scenes" of the development team, and is even encouraged to do so.

- **Technical tools.** Noted here was which tools were used to perform the automated tests (e.g., Silenium) and what tool was used to support the agile process (e.g., in this case, Confluence, JIRA, and the Taskboard).
- **Escalation to the steering boards and the experts.** An additional instance was introduced, which could provide rapid agreement, if necessary. The schedule was set for the scope and executive steering board meetings.
- **Indicative maximum price.** The indicative maximum price range was mentioned in the contract, pointing out that it could be adapted after the checkpointphase by written consent of both parties.
- **Checkpoint Phase and corresponding riskshare.** In the event of termination, it was agreed that the supplier received payment for only 60% of the expenses in a checkpoint phase lasting six weeks (three sprints).
- **Expense control during the project.** This process was taken from the template and can be found in Chapter 4.
- **Efficiency bonus.** Within two months after project completion, the supplier would be commissioned with all the effort (meaning with the remaining story points) that was not exploited up until the end of the project, in the context of extensions of this software or other projects.
- **Project termination.** In accordance with the regulations in the contract template, it was possible to phase out the project with a lead time of four weeks without indication of a reason. For the benefit of the client, it was determined in the negotiation that the supplier could indeed cancel the project, but as a result did not receive the last 20% for the final approval.
- **Exchange for free** This clause was adopted in accordance with the contract template.
- **Warranty.** The warranty could be regulated in various ways. In this case, due to the brevity of the project (seven months) and the unique production rollout, it was distributed not on the individual sprints or drops, but rather was agreed to for six months from the final approval.

The remaining parts of the contract were established according to the template in Chapter 4 and are not discussed further here.

10.2.4.4 *Project progress, the teams, and critical situations*

The project team could already put forward the fixed and final project plans at kickoff, which surprised most participants. That this was possible was due to the use of agile methods: There were no major releases planned with specific details about their content but, rather, a process in which the content would be "purely prioritized." This advantage of knowing what was to be done on what day (over the entire project period without permanent shifts) was known at project launch and very helpful in increasing the commitment of all people participating on the client side. Figure 10.2 shows this process (a plan for an agile project) with the key steps where you can select which days each project step should reserve.

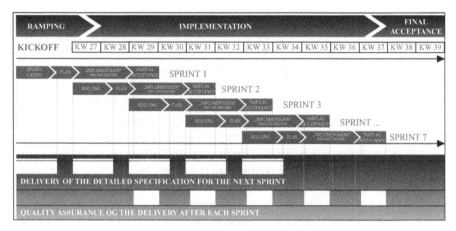

Figure 10.2 *Plan for an agile project.*

Since the supplier had experience with Scrum in a professional IT environment, implementation of the first user stories could begin without further delay. The project was supported intensively and steered in the right direction by highly experienced IT architects during the first sprints. In conjunction with colleagues from the architectural body, the supplier delivered maximum competence across all projects.

After the first sprint, the client got to see a snippet of the functionality and provide feedback. The feedback concerned some discrepancies and there was also feedback on those parts of the functionality implemented correctly. The client's comments were used immediately in the next sprint for a better understanding of the requirements.

A workshop was planned toward the end of the third sprint, just before the conclusion of the checkpoint phase. In this workshop, both parties delivered feedback on the experiences of the last few weeks and provided their assessment of the initial indicative maximum price range. In this case, additional assumptions were still formulated for some epics. During the discussion on a special epic ("Reporting"), many more requirements were discovered, transparent to the client, which increased the effort (without the supplier being able to know this previously, as these were clearly new requirements). The supplier proposed to omit the automatic loading of some auxiliary tables on the surface for the first releases of the product, thereby reducing the agreed-upon scope by approximately the same amount. The auxiliary tables were loaded only once a year but in the meantime could also be done manually by the operating staff. The client accepted and the checkpoint phase was concluded with a "go" and the "exchange" cost nothing to carry out. The project was driven further during the iterations by a few shifts in the scope and many positive discussions.

The following list illustrates how the project was handled in specific critical situations and how the agile fixed-price contract helped to overcome these situations in a solution-oriented manner.

- **Quality problems.** After the fourth sprint, during acceptance by the product owner, the team already realized that the internal and automated testing of the functionality implemented did not consider the benefits required by the user story. Thus, two of the four user stories implemented could not pass the quality assurance gate. However, the product owner had time to obtain background information and analyze the reason. The reason was primarily sloppy work due to lack of time.

  For the next sprint, the product owner organized an additional staff member to help cleaning up the sprint. This was done early in the project to avoid having to live with low quality due to the pressure of a deadline. The client also experienced these problems at the partial acceptance. For this purpose, she got a detailed explanation of why this happened and what countermeasures had been taken. Since the client spent one day with the development team every two weeks, he or she also had no concerns that it could be just empty words. After two weeks, they could verify the countermeasures effect. Due to the interim approvals and the assured transparency regulated in this contract, the problem was resolved quickly.

- **Delays and scope changes.** Due to the problems set out above, a delay in the project was evident, of course. Two weeks of work was only half completed, which already posed a risk of delay in the range of one week. The advantage, however, was that in the smaller iterations, any delays could be compensated in a timely manner, and the effectiveness of the measures taken to do so could also easily be controlled. In principle, the contract stipulated that in case of a delay, the resulting additional costs were subject to riskshare on the supplier side. But the financial implications could go even further. At the very least, these were the additional efforts on the client side. In this example, there was even a risk that the entire product investment would have to be written off if a competitor entered the market faster. The delay in this development project could be recovered quickly, however, using the set of rules provided for quick action.

  Delays also arose due to possible additional features, which were delivered as change requests in traditional project contracts. Just the same, the client could cause a delay through unsuccessful internal reconciliations for the specification of user stories. In this example, it was the first case. Since there was a specific deadline, the solution looked as follows: Any functions that were not essential for the go-live decision were removed from the first release (for which the contract was concluded), which allowed new and more important functionality to still go into the first release of the product.

- **Disagreement about the real scope after reviewing the detail specification.** In discussions with various persons from both parties, and also among the writers, the following was always one of the issues that raised the most questions: How can you ensure that nobody pulls a fast one by claiming that he or she "had anyway meant that this or that was included in the epic"? It's simple: If this happens, it is noticed sooner or later, and the cooperative effort can then be terminated. In this example, efforts were often discussed from this perspective, after a user story had been formulated in detail in the course of the project. However, in the spirit of cooperation, a solution was always found and not forwarded to the steering board until a certain point in time. Neither party was interested in commissioning the experts, because this was also an expense, so pragmatic solutions were usually found.

The experts helped one of the parties from the other projects to realize that the opposite side had not estimated correctly from his point of view. As a result, the opposing party could either change his or her behavior, or if the suspicion remained, could have led to a termination of the project. But everything remained within a regulated framework.

10.2.4.5 Project completion

The software product was completed within the time period agreed to and could be brought to market on time. Approximately 25% of the original scope was exchanged during the course of the project (seven months). Some of the client's representatives were astonished that the product launch was also possible without the features omitted. However, the client was prepared for discussions during the entire project, and therefore the room for maneuver offered by an agile fixed-price contract could also be exploited.

Summary

In terms of the requirements defined in Chapter 2, the project was successful, despite the fact that although a new, complex product was implemented, much had changed in the course of time. The agile fixed-price contract was also used for the implementation of release 2 of this product and due to the good cooperation of course with the same supplier. In this way, the client could use the knowledge that the supplier had built up. In contrast, in a time and materials approach the client would have little control over the actual performance that resulted from his or her investment.

10.2.5 Conclusions

In this example you can clearly see what problems can arise due to dependence on implementation and contract type. The development methodology was Scrum independent of the underlying contract type. Despite some positive arguments for traditional types of contracts, the uncertainties and the break in the paradigm at the interface to the agile development teams were clearly visible.

The agile model offers the possibility of starting a project quickly on a basis that was nevertheless secure instead of endless evaluation and preparation phases. Simply consider major decisions in your personal environment. When you, for example, want to buy a car or a house: After careful consideration of the pros and cons, don't you also feel better if you can simply try it without any particular risks? Take advantage of the significant benefits you request in other "industries" and start a project with a riskshare of 30% for the client in a checkpoint phase. The real challenges are not visible until the project has started.

The following are some of the essential points of difference between the individual types of contracts that were considered in this example:

- In a time and materials contract, the *scope* does not have to be specified in advance. However, if you first need to announce the budget for a project internally, it is still worthwhile, as with the agile model, to describe the scope of the project, at least at a high level of vision, topics, and epics.
- The *effort* for the tender process is highest with the traditional fixed-price contract. The agile fixed-price contract ranks in the middle, and in this example, the time and materials contract ranks lowest. From our experience this can also be transferred to other IT projects.
- Within the framework of time and materials contracts, you can probably select the *resources* that are regarded as the best qualified. However, the resource personnel do not necessarily remain for the entire project period. Does it not make more sense for you to secure a delivery performance for a certain cost, instead of insisting on people who will perhaps be exchanged anyway (or can get ill or leave a company)?
- A *change of supplier* is quite possible with time and materials contracts. However, the supplier often creates artificial dependencies that make them difficult to replace. Also, partial acceptances are usually not treated so strictly within the framework of time and materials projects as opposed to an agile fixed-price contract, where partial acceptances are an essential aspect of the entire contractually agreed processes.

We are of the opinion that certain parts of an IT project that stay static in the course of the project can be processed just as well with a fixed price. Once a project is developed according to agile methods, the agile fixed-price contract nevertheless offers the best solutions, because in this type of contract, detailed descriptions and flexibility go hand in hand with having the same advantages as with a traditional fixed-price contract.

Appendix

Questions and Answers

Sometimes a book is quite long to read or you read it late at night in bed on your iPad, and at the end you still have not gained what you were looking for. For those cases we have collected some questions raised by people who read the book, participated in a training session on this topic, or were consulted by one of us to enable such a model in their organization.

Q: Does the agile fixed-price contract mean that there is no clear picture of what the overall result of a project will be?

A: That is one of the concerns raised most often by decision makers. The answer is *no.* There is a high-level scope that is detailed enough to depict the system in such a manner as to ensure the business value that you want to generate with this project. It is even an advantage to describe the scope that is linked to the business value instead of getting lost in many details, which will be partially deprecated over the duration of the project anyway.

Q: Is the effort required to understand a new contractual framework and to set it up for a project is essential?

A: To understand a new approach and to spread this knowledge among the people in your organization does require some effort of course. However, such effort is required in any situation when you want to do something

Agile Contracts: Creating and Managing Successful Projects with Scrum, First Edition.
Andreas Opelt, Boris Gloger, Wolfgang Pfarl, and Ralf Mittermayr.
© 2013 John Wiley & Sons, Inc. Published 2013 by John Wiley & Sons, Inc.

new, which hopefully you do from time to time. We show in the book that the effort spent in the initial setup and requirement specification in a traditional fixed-price contract is just as high as the effort spent over the course of a project for iterative requirement specification in the agile fixed-price method. So the short answer is *no*, not more effort if you have managed over the first burden to introduce something new.

Q: How can one ensure that the complexity will not increase dramatically over the course of a project when a high-level scope is worked out in detailed user stories?

A: This is a valid concern if people are not aware of what they are doing and what a "project vision" means or how important it is to put assumptions on the high-level scope and frame conditions to the project vision such that the scope governance can really handle the scope. It is a crucial element, however, and if there is an "old style" project manager on one side who tries to push details into the traditional fixed-price setup whatever possible, the project will fail. So if one party is leaving the collaborative path, replace the person or make use of that exit points agreed upon contractually.

Q: Why do you report story points as currency for complexity and not effort? At the end aren't we all interested in the person-days and price?

A: This is a massively discussed topic in the agile community. If you imagine that you should judge whether one functionality is requiring more effort than another functionality, it would be useful if you have already performed the task of implementing this functionality. In IT projects this is rather a rare case, so it is obvious that the people are talking about the business use of a functionality and highlighting how much more complex one functionality of a feature is than another (not really caring how many person-days this takes to implement; this should be the problem of a very experienced supplier and there it strongly depends on which software engineers you have). Still we will not refer to the battle going on over this topic and just take sides here.

Q: How can you be sure that tendering based on such a process really works?

A: Because we have tried it—not often (as this is a quite new topic) in the very optimal setup described here, but several times. Apart from that, we have managed many situations where the procurement personnel looked at a final agile fixed-price type of contract and were asking why they steered the process into the wrong (i.e., the traditional fixed-price heading) discussion.

Q: Do we really need biweekly delivery within the project? My suppliers are also agile, but they can still cope with traditional contract forms. They note that they need a couple of months anyway before they can show the first part of working software.

A: Do not believe that. Any supplier who will not be able to show at least the first results after 30 days is not working in an agile manner or has an unfinished product he or she wants to sell you. So make the agile fixed-price contract method a central principle. If something cannot be developed and shown in a decent amount of time, there is something wrong. Whether the problem lays with the solution, with your supplier, with your requirements, or with whatever else does not matter: what matters is that you see that there is something wrong and that you are able to analyze the situation and react.

Q: *How can legal and IT procurement personnel really participate in scoping workshops given that they do not understand the technical details?*

A: The business purpose of software is very often quite simple, and as the scope is discussed on a high level (not how this will be implemented), it should definitely be understandable by every one involved. Additionally, the scope estimates are done in terms of the complexity of the functionality, which is also an opportunity to get a understanding for business people. Finally, how should people who should participate in a steering group be able to judge if they do not understand what the solution is about and where the complexity is located? We do not know, but go into a steering board of an IT project and in one out of two projects you will have a real-world example of what happens there.

Q: *Do you really believe that there can be a discussion on reducing complexity within a project. Is it not, rather, that the business departments want even more complexity each time you talk to them?*

A: As long as the parties agree contractually on a certain setup, such as an agile fixed-price contract, scope reduction is in the interest of every party involved, and scope creep simply takes everybody farther away from the common aim. Our experience is that this works as soon as the mindset has been set correctly and the right people are selected for the scope steering group (namely, ones that make decisions). However, if it does not work if you just take what is delivered and then walk away from the project.

Q: *What is an example of scope reduction taking place for the sake of another functionality coming in (exchange for free)?*

A: We recently delivered a project that was based only partially on an agile fixed-price contract (we do not always manage to make people understand what the best contract would be). In this project, however, the free exchange philosophy was settled. At a certain point it turned out that the scope creep had increased the effort dramatically. When looking at the items on the backlog we found user stories where a certain functionality was required to be automated. In the discussion it turned out that this functionality was used four times a year and thus—in relation to the project vision—could be eliminated and replaced (exchanged) by a new feature that was really relevant but had been forgotten in the first set of requirements.

Q: Are you realistic or simply drawing a picture of a perfect world?

A: The book does, of course, try to show the perfect setup in every possible situation, and we understand that your circumstances will probably differ. However, we have proven that this is a realistic and very fruitful way to carry out successful IT projects.

References

Alvarez, Cindy (2011). It's Valuable Because I Said So. Nov. 3. http://bit.ly/sUPW9c. Accessed May 9, 2012.

Ambler, Scott W. (2005). Agile Outsourcing. http://www.drdobbs.com/architecture-and-design/agile-outsourcing/184415344. Accessed Nov. 10, 2012.

Assure Consulting (2007). *Current Trends in Project Management*. Assure Consulting GmbH, Wehnheim, Germany.

Belz, Ch.; Zupancic, W.; Bußmann, F. (2005) *Best Practice in Key Account Management: Successful Processing of Key Customers by the St. Gallen KAM Concept*. Modern Industry, St. Gallen, Switzerland.

Boehm, Barry (1981). *Software Engineering Economics*. Prentice-Hall, Englewood Cliffs, NJ.

Braun, Gerold (2008). *Verhandeln in Einkauf und Vertrieb: Mit System zu besseren Konditionen und mehr Profit*. Gabler Publishing, Wiesbaden, Germany.

Brooks, Frederick (1975). *The Mythical Man-Month*. Addison-Wesley, Reading, MA.

Cobb, Charles G. (2011). *Making Sense of Agile Project Management: Balancing Control and Agility*. Wiley, Hoboken, NJ.

Cockburn, Alistar (2012). Agile Contracts. http://alistair.cockburn.us/Agile+contracts. Accessed Nov. 10, 2012.

Cohn, Mike (2004). *User Stories Applied*. For Agile Software Development. Addison-Wesley, Reading, MA.

Cohn, Mike (2005). *Agile Estimation and Planning*. Prentice Hall, Upper Saddle River, NJ.

Darwin, Charles (1860). *The Origin of the Species*, 2nd ed.

DeMarco, Tom, et al. (2008). *Adrenaline Junkies and Template Zombies: Understanding Patterns of Project Behavior*. Dorset House, New York.

Deming, W. E. (1982). *Out of the Crisis*. MIT Press, Cambridge.

Emergn (2012). *Sourcing for Agile: How Does the Procurement of IT Development Services Change in an Agile Environment?* Emergn, Ltd., London.

Fewell, Jesse (2012). http://www.leadingagile.com/2012/11/calculate-budgets-agile-team/ ?mkt=tok=3RkMMJWWfF9wsRohua7AZKXonjHpfsXw4uQlX6eg38431UFwdcj KPmjr1YQGTsV0dvycMRAVFZl5nRpdCPOcc45P9PA=. Accessed Nov. 27, 2012.

Feynman, Richard; Leighton, Ralph (contributor); Hutchings, Edward (editor) (1985). *Surely You're Joking, Mr. Feynman! Adventures of a Curious Character.* W.W. Norton, New York.

Flyvbjerg, Bent; Budzier, Alexander (2011). Why your project may be riskier than you think. *Harvard Business Review*, Sept.

Forrester Report (2005). *Corporate Software Development Fails to Satisfy on Speed or Quality*. Apr. 11. Forester, Cambridge, MA.

Gloger, Boris (2011). *Scrum: Developing Products Quickly and Reliably*, 3rd ed., Canl Hanser Verlag, Munich.

Goodpasture, John C. (2010). *Project Management the Agile Way: Making It Work in the Enterprise*. J. Ross Publishing, New York.

Hören, Thomas (2007). *IT-Vertragsrecht*, Cologne, Germany.

Jaburek, Walter (2000, 2003). *Handbuch der EDV, Verträge 3*, Vol. 2, Medien und Recht Verlags GmbH, Vienna, Austria.

Kelly, Allan (2008). *Changing Software Development: Learning to Become Agile*. Wiley, Hoboken, NJ.

Kelly, Allan (2012). Agile Contracts. http://www.infoq.com/articles/agile-contracts. Accessed Nov. 10, 2012.

Kleusberg, Peter (2009). *E-Collaboration and E-Reverse Auctions*. VDM Verlag, Saarbrücken, Germany.

Klinger, Paul; Burnett, Rachel (2012). *Drafting and Negotiating IT Contracts*. Bloomsbury Professional, New York.

Landy-Gene K.; Mastrobattista, Amy J. (2008). *The IT/ Digital Legal Companion*. Syngress, Waltham, MA.

Larman, Craig; Vodde, Bas (2010). *Practices for Scaling Lean and Agile Development: Large, Multisite, and Offshore Product Development with Large-Scale Scrum*. Addison-Wesley, Reading, MA.

Lewicki, Roy J.; Saunders, David M.; Barry, Bruce (2009) *Negotiation*. McGraw-Hill Higher Education.

Marly, Jochen (2009). *Praxishandbuch Softwarerecht*, 5th ed. Verlag C.H. Beek, Munich.

Mnookin, Robert H.; Neubauer, Jürgen (2011). *Verhandeln mit dem Teufel. Das Harvard-Konzept für die fiesen Fälle*. Campus Verlag, Frankfurt/M, Germany.

Overly, Michael, et al. (2004). *Software Agreements Line by Line: A Detailed Look at Software Contracts and Licenses and How to Change Them to Fit Your Needs*. Aspatore Books, Boston.

Pfarl, Wolfgang (Hrsg.) (2007). *IT-Verträge*, Vienna, Austria.

Pichler, Roman (2012). *Agile Product Management with Scrum*. Addison-Wesley, Reading, MA.

Poppendiek, Mary; Poppendiek, Tom (2011). *Lean Software Development: An Agile Toolkit*. Addison-Wesley, Reading, MA.

Pries, Kim H.; Quigley, Jon M. (2011). *Scrum Project Management*. CRC Press, Boca Raton, FL.

Reed, Angel (2007). *Computer Law*. Oxford University Press, New York.

Reinertsen, Don (2009). *The Principles of Product Development Flow: Second Generation Lean Product Development*. Celeritas Publishing, New York.

Roland Berger Strategy Consultants (2008). *Keeping Projects on the Right Track with Launch Management: Why Large-Scale IT Projects Often Fail, and Successful Projects Are Not a Coincidence*. Roland Berger, Munich.

Royce, Winston (1970). Managing the Development of Large Software Systems. *Proceedings of IEEE WESCON 26*, Aug., pp. 1–9.

Schneider, Jochen; v. Westphalen, Friedrich (2006). *Software-Erstellungsverträge*, Dr. Otto Schmidt Verlag, Cologne, Germany.

Schranner, Matthias (2009). *Teure Fehler: Die sieben größten Irrtümer in schwierigen Verhandlungen*. Econ Publishing, Munich.

Schwaber, Ken (2003). *Agile Project Management with Scrum*. Microsoft Press, Redmond, WA.

Schwaber, Ken (2007). *The Enterprise and Scrum*. Microsoft Press, Redmond, WA.

Schwaber, Ken; Sutherland, Jeff (2012). *Software in 30 Days: How Agile Managers Beat the Odds, Delight Their Customers, and Leave Competitors in the Dust*. Wiley, Hoboken, NJ.

The Standish Group (2009). *Chaos Report, 2002–2009*. Standish, Boston, MA.

Stepanek, George (2005). *Software Projects Secrets: Why Software Projects Fail*. Apress, New Zealand.

Takeuchi, Hirotaka; Nonaka, Ikujiro (1986). The new new product development game. *Harvard Business Review*, Jan.

VersionOne (2011). State of Agile Development Survey Results. http://www.versionone.com/state_of_agile_development_survey/10/. Accessed May 8, 2012.

VersionOne (2012). Must-Haves for Agile Contracts. http://blogs.versionone.com/agile_management/2012/08/31/must-haves-for-agile-contracts/. Accessed Oct. 1, 2012.

Wildemann, Horst (2006). *Studie zum IT Management*, Feb.

Wolf, Henning; van Solingen, Rini; Rustenberg, Eelco (2010). *Die Kraft von Scrum*. Addison-Wesley, Reading, MA.

Zeitler, Nicolas (2011). Die Scrum-Erfahrungen bei Immobilien-Scout. http://www.cio.de/scrum/2265436/. Accessed May 8, 2012.

Index

Agile Contracts: Creating and Managing Successful Projects with Scrum, First Edition.
Andreas Opelt, Boris Gloger, Wolfgang Pfarl, and Ralf Mittermayr.
© 2013 John Wiley & Sons, Inc. Published 2013 by John Wiley & Sons, Inc.

YACOV Y. HAIMES
Risk Modeling, Assessment, and Management, Third Edition

DENNIS M. BUEDE
The Engineering Design of Systems: Models and Methods, Second Edition

ANDREW P. SAGE and JAMES E. ARMSTRONG, Jr.
Introduction to Systems Engineering

WILLIAM B. ROUSE
Essential Challenges of Strategic Management

YEFIM FASSER and DONALD BRETTNER
Management for Quality in High-Technology Enterprises

THOMAS B. SHERIDAN
Humans and Automation: System Design and Research Issues

ALEXANDER KOSSIAKOFF and WILLIAM N. SWEET
Systems Engineering Principles and Practice

HAROLD R. BOOHER
Handbook of Human Systems Integration

JEFFREY T. POLLOCK and RALPH HODGSON
Adaptive Information: Improving Business Through Semantic Interoperability, Grid Computing, and Enterprise Integration

ALAN L. PORTER and SCOTT W. CUNNINGHAM
Tech Mining: Exploiting New Technologies for Competitive Advantage

REX BROWN
Rational Choice and Judgment: Decision Analysis for the Decider

WILLIAM B. ROUSE and KENNETH R. BOFF (editors)
Organizational Simulation

HOWARD EISNER
Managing Complex Systems: Thinking Outside the Box

STEVE BELL
Lean Enterprise Systems: Using IT for Continuous Improvement

J. JERRY KAUFMAN and ROY WOODHEAD
Stimulating Innovation in Products and Services: With Function Analysis and Mapping

WILLIAM B. ROUSE
Enterprise Tranformation: Understanding and Enabling Fundamental Change

JOHN E. GIBSON, WILLIAM T. SCHERER, and WILLAM F. GIBSON
How to Do Systems Analysis

WILLIAM F. CHRISTOPHER
Holistic Management: Managing What Matters for Company Success

WILLIAM B. ROUSE
People and Organizations: Explorations of Human-Centered Design

MO JAMSHIDI
System of Systems Engineering: Innovations for the Twenty-First Century

ANDREW P. SAGE and WILLIAM B. ROUSE
Handbook of Systems Engineering and Management, Second Edition

JOHN R. CLYMER
Simulation-Based Engineering of Complex Systems, Second Edition

KRAG BROTBY
Information Security Governance: A Practical Development and Implementation Approach

JULIAN TALBOT and MILES JAKEMAN
Security Risk Management Body of Knowledge

SCOTT JACKSON
Architecting Resilient Systems: Accident Avoidance and Survival and Recovery from Disruptions

JAMES A. GEORGE and JAMES A. RODGER
Smart Data: Enterprise Performance Optimization Strategy

YORAM KOREN
The Global Manufacturing Revolution: Product-Process-Business Integration and Reconfigurable Systems

AVNER ENGEL
Verification, Validation, and Testing of Engineered Systems

WILLIAM B. ROUSE (editor)
The Economics of Human Systems Integration: Valuation of Investments in People's Training and Education, Safety and Health, and Work Productivity

ALEXANDER KOSSIAKOFF, WILLIAM N. SWEET, SAM SEYMOUR, and STEVEN M. BIEMER
Systems Engineering Principles and Practice, Second Edition

GREGORY S. PARNELL, PATRICK J. DRISCOLL, and DALE L. HENDERSON (editors)
Decision Making in Systems Engineering and Management, Second Edition

ANDREW P. SAGE and WILLIAM B. ROUSE
Economic Systems Analysis and Assessment: Intensive Systems, Organizations, and Enterprises

Printed and bound by CPI Group (UK) Ltd, Croydon, CR0 4YY

27/10/2024

14580337-0002